SPIRITS OF THE AIR

Also by Kurt Diemberger

Summits and Secrets
The Endless Knot: K2, Mountain of Dreams and Destiny

SPIRITS
OF THE AIR

Kurt Diemberger

Translated from the German by Audrey Salkeld

THE
MOUNTAINEERS

ISBN 0-89886-408-9

First published in Great Britain by
Hodder and Stoughton
a division of Hodder Headline PLC
338 Euston Road, London NW1 3BH

Published in the United States of America by
The Mountaineers, 1011 SW. Klickitat Way, Seattle WA 98134
Published simultaneously in Canada by Douglas & McIntyre Ltd.,
1615 Venables St., Vancouver B.C. V5L 2H1

Typeset by Hewer Text Composition Services, Edinburgh
Printed and bound in Great Britain by
Mackays of Chatham plc, Chatham, Kent

To my father

Only the Spirits of the Air know
What awaits me behind the mountains
But still I go on with my dogs,
Onwards and on . . .

This old Eskimo proverb defines my existence – and not
only when I am in Greenland. I have been called 'the
Nomad of the Great Heights' – certainly ever since I
clambered to my first summit as a crystal-hunting boy,
since I set out on my grandfather's bicycle with two friends
to reach and climb the legendary Matterhorn, I have felt
urged beyond the horizon in search of the unknown.

And that haven of peace behind the last mountain? Does
such a thing exist? There is always a new enigma springing
up to meet you. Some new secret. That never changes.
However far you travel . . .

Only the Spirits of the Air know what lies in store for you,
says the Eskimo on his dog sledge.

That is Life.

K.D.
1994

Contents

PART FOUR

PART FIVE

PART SIX

Credits and Thanks

Unless otherwise specified the illustrations are from the Kurt Diemberger archive: for collaboration in some cases I want to thank my companions named in the book. Professor Karl Weiken's historical pictures of the Alfred Wegener expedition were a great help and a notable contribution. Other photographs came from: Robert Kreuzinger (Alfred Wegener memorial plate), Sadamasa Takahashi (Kurt with guitar in the Hindu Kush), Doug Scott (spirits of the air in the Western Cwm), Hermann Warth (climbing above 8000 metres in the spindrift on Makalu).

Credits for the sketch maps are given, but I want to thank my son Igor and my daughter Karen for helping in their adaptation for *Spirits of the Air*.

Most of my photographs were taken with Leica R3 and SL2.

A special thanks goes to my father for historical work in the Greenland chapter and to Professor Karl Weiken for checking my text and lending expedition reports. I am also very grateful to Axel Thorer for the permission to print his humorous story describing the atmosphere in a hotel bar in Kathmandu which appeared in May 1980 in the German edition of *Penthouse*.

Last but not least, Audrey Salkeld has again shown her great sensibility and patience in the translation of this book into English and Maggie Body was the personification of a gentle but accurate spirit keeping an eye on everything.

KURT DIEMBERGER

PART ONE

I can never give up the mountains

We are climbing up Nanga Parbat, my daughter Hildegard and I, entering the Great Couloir of the Diamir Face. Behind us rear the wild summits of the Mazeno Ridge, a fiercely serrated wing of blue ice and steep rock jutting from high on the main body of the mighty mountain. Way below, glints the green of the Diamir valley.

Here, all is steepness and shadow. We keep plunging our axes into the snow, and of course, we are wearing our crampons. Hildegard – blonde, twenty-five years old – is a confident climber, even if, as an ethnologist, her deeper interest lies with the people of the mountains. She has come with me this time to the peak that was Hermann Buhl's dream – and, who knows, the two of us may reach as far as 6000 metres. Perhaps, in a few days, I might even go to 7000 metres, but I am not pinning my hopes any higher. I have no idea how my K2 frostbite will bear up at altitude. It was only just before Christmas that I had the amputations to my right hand – and with my damaged toes I cannot entertain any hopes of the summit. Yet neither can I accept the prospect of staying down. There is no way I can give up climbing mountains.

Below us, on the slope, Benoît has just come into view, the young French speedclimber attached to our expedition . . . tack, tack, tack, tack . . . his movements are like clockwork, as is the rhythmic throb of his front-points and his axe in the steep ice of the couloir. He wants to climb the 8125 metres of Nanga Parbat in a single day. But not today – today he is only practising.

Quickly he draws nearer.

'Who goes slowly, goes well – who goes well, goes far . . .'

Whatever became of that old proverb? The wisdom of the old mountain guides, it seems, is now out of date. Tack, tack – tack, tack, tack, tack – tack, tack . . . Benoît is a nice guy and has remained refreshingly modest, despite his prodigious skills; he is small, fine-boned, gentle. I like him, even if some of his opinions send shivers down my spine. Others I have reluctantly to accept (not wanting to start any arguments up here! But what is the point in all this *running*? What good are records up here?) It must make some sort of sense to him.

Here he is! Benoît Chamoux. The speed artist, the phenomenon! He pants a little, greets us, laughing, and we exchange news; then I fish in my rucksack for the 16 mm camera. My job is filming, but it's my pleasure, too. Showing other people what the world is like up here . . . that is part of what mountaineering means for me. Not this alone, of course . . .

Still, I want to bring down truth, not fiction! And if, for some bright spark, happiness is running up mountains – then he, too, is part of this world of Nanga Parbat. (My daughter, I must say, has thought so for quite some while – perhaps that's an ethnological observation?)

I film the young sprinter: well, it looks fantastic, I think, eye to the viewfinder, the way that guy comes up! So I have him do it three times more, up and back again – the way film-makers do, and he is in training, after all.

Before I can dream up further variations, big clouds start rolling in. A change in the weather? Nothing unusual for Nanga Parbat. We descend.

Base Camp, down where it's green . . .

Only the Spirits of the Air know – how this will turn out for me. I contemplate my discoloured toes – all red and blue – as I swish them round in a bowl of water. Our cook, the good Ali, has tipped at least half a kilo of salt into the water, anxious to do what is best for me. How long will it take till I am fit again? Months, or years?

This is not the first time I have felt all is nearly over, that I am stretching life thinly: coming down from Chogolisa after Hermann's death, or during the emergency landing I made with Charlie – what I call our 'second birthday'. But this time? This time it is different.

Do I still enjoy climbing? It can never be as it was before.

And I will never come to terms with what happened on K2. Up on our dream mountain I lost Julie, lost my climbing companion of so many years, sharer of storms and tempests, joys and hopes on the highest mountains of the world. How often did we count the stars together, or look for faces in the clouds?

And then, suddenly . . .

So many people died on K2 that summer. Julie and I had been in such fine form, we were perfectly acclimatised – we ought not to have lost a single day! But I've no wish to set off that spinning wheel of thoughts again . . . It's over. Nothing can be changed. The dream summit was ours – and then came the end.

Life, somehow, goes on. The mountains, like dear friends, have always helped me before. Whenever it was possible. Where is the way forward now?

Agostino da Polenza, our expedition leader on K2, was here at Base Camp until a few days ago. Then he dashed off to get another project under way, one on which I am again to be cameraman: remeasuring Everest and K2 for the Italian Consortium of Research (CNR) – or, more accurately, for Ardito Desio, the remarkable ninety-year-old professor who, as long ago as 1929, pushed into the secret valley of the Shaksgam beyond the 8000-metre Karakoram peaks till he was stopped by the myriad ice towers of the Kyagar Glacier. Yes, it's true, the secrets are not only to be found on the summits . . .

They wait also behind the mountains. And I think of years that have long past, adventures in the jungle, in Greenland, but in more 'developed' areas, too, places like Canada; or the Grand Canyon with its rocky scenery – where time is turned into stone. I remember Death Valley. And expeditions to the Hindu Kush . . . that first glimpse into hidden corners of the glacier . . . the first circuit of Tirich Mir.

There was an eighteen-year gap between my second 8000-metre peak and my third. But I have no regrets about that: it was time well spent. Many chapters of this book bear witness to that.

*

'*Guarda lassù* – there they are!' Hildegard turns her head excitedly from the camera tripod, swinging her long blonde hair, 'Look!' She points up at Nanga Parbat, which even from this distance fills the sky above the treetops. 'They're almost up!' Her eyes are shining. We are in a small summer village in the Diamir valley, surrounded by cattle-sheds, herdsmen, women, many children . . . and goats, goats and more goats: two or three hundred of them! You can scarcely hear yourself speak over the sound of bleating. There are millions of flies, too, but they do not seem to bother Hildegard. I flick them irritably from my forehead and press my left eye to the viewfinder to peer through the 1200 mm lens: yes, I see them! Three tiny dots, and a fourth one, lower down, right in the middle of the steep summit trapezium. They are going to make it!

We are beside ourselves with joy. Those lucky sods – lucky mushrooms, as we say in Austria – just the right day they've picked for it! And I feel a twinge of sadness not to be up there with them. But not for long: as we watch our companions inch higher, happiness suffuses every other feeling. But one dot is missing up there. It worries us at first, then we tell ourselves it must be Benoît. He will not have left Base until the others reached their High Camp.

He is bound to catch up with them before long!

Then the clouds swallow everything.

We scoop up our belongings and hurry away, anxious to get to Base Camp before the others come down; we want to prepare a welcome-home party, a summit feast.

Two days later: they are all down. Soro, Gianni and Tullio all made it to the summit – shortly after the clouds cut them from our view. Only Giovanna, the lowest dot, turned back before then. And Benoît? He had a real epic up there . . .

At first all went well. He reached the summit as planned in a single day from Base Camp. (Normally – if you can speak of normality in terms of Nanga Parbat – it takes at least three days for an ascent.) But then began a chain of misfortune: during the descent, Benoît was overtaken by darkness and lost his way in the giant Bazhin basin. All night long he wandered backwards and forwards up there at around 7000 metres because, with his lightweight equipment, he dared not sit down for a bivouac. He did not discover his companions' final camp until morning . . .

Benoît looked thin and drawn, almost transparent, as he staggered finally into Base . . . but an incredible willpower still burned in his eyes. We flung our arms round him, so happy to have him back.

*

The sun is shining, its light reflecting off the small stream which runs across the sloping meadow on which our Base Camp stands. A good place: protected by a moraine bank from the air blast of the many enormous avalanches which thunder down from the upper slopes and teetering ice balconies of Nanga Parbat and the Mazeno peaks. Here, at 4500 metres, frost binds our little brook every night, covering it with an embroidery of wonderful ice crystals. But in the morning, when the sun appears behind the inky blue bulk of the mountain, it flashes and sparkles everywhere and, as the crystals and plates of ice crackle and split, gradually the murmur of the little stream starts up again between the tents. Gianni and Tullio, inseparable as ever, stroll across the grass and kneel on its bank, dipping their hands in the icy water and splashing it over their faces . . . they chatter and laugh; Soro and Giovanna stretch out in the sunshine; Hildegard, lost in thought, wanders over the moraine, and Benoît sleeps, and sleeps, and sleeps. He has earned it. The good Ali prepares breakfast, and Shah Jehan, our liaison officer, squints lazily into the sun above his enormous beard and tells again of all the ibex he has bagged in the Karakoram. This is the man we know could never hurt a fly. In the summer of 1982, on my first expedition here, I climbed with him to 6500 metres on the Diamir Face. Next time – 1985 – he was unfortunately not with us. That was when Julie and I went to 7600 metres: only another 500 metres or so would have seen us on top, but when we came to make our final attempt the weather turned against us . . .

I am looking up at the dark blue trapezium, in shadow now: some day I'd love to go up there. It will have to wait till I'm better, and that could be years yet. But look, there it is, the summit that Julie and I were so close to.

Will I get another crack at it?

Will I ever stand on the top?

And, if I do, will I come down again – or stay up there for ever?

Even if I never make it up there, I have to have the experience again, this moving up between the clouds . . .

Once you have started that . . .

'I climb mountains for such moments,' Julie had said, 'not just to reach the top – that is a bonus!'

I *will* go up again.

Then my thoughts turn to Makalu.

Many years ago that was, when I faced the question of whether or not to make one last try – knowing that, on whatever I should choose, would depend my whole future.

Spirits of the air

Strange eddies of cloud spill over the summit of Mount Everest, twisting veils, transparent fans, mysterious phantoms. Catching the light, they shimmer in all the colours of the rainbow – deep purple, radiant green, yellow, orange – a swiftly changing kaleidoscope.

Does it herald a storm?

As I watch, some of the clouds take on a mother-of-pearl lustre, others drain of all colour. It is a strange cavalry, galloping, multiplying, gradually filling the whole sky. The red granite summit of Makalu, just over 3000 metres above me, wears a wide-brimmed hat, like a gleaming fish. I have often seen such clouds in the Alps, on Mont Blanc, and again I'm prompted to wonder if a storm is on the way. Down here in Base Camp the air remains very still, with only an occasional limp flutter from Ang Chappal's prayer flags. He hung up two strings of them when we first arrived to keep favour with the mountain gods and spirits. I look beyond them and out over the stone cairn on its little hill to the side of camp: what should I do? Should I attempt Makalu? What hope have I got of reaching the summit? It is eighteen years since I last climbed an eight-thousander.

The prayer flags stir weakly, while high above, the wild clouds charge in every direction. The rainbow colours have disappeared, but light and shadow animate the spectacle. The sun – one minute a fiery ball, the next a pale disc – sinks slowly towards the ridge of Baruntse, the great seven-thousander on the far side of the valley. Down here it is still warm, even though we are above 5400 metres.

So what's it to be? Shall I give it a try, make a start?

Not today, certainly. But soon I have to come to a decision; we have already ordered porters for our return march. On the other side of the

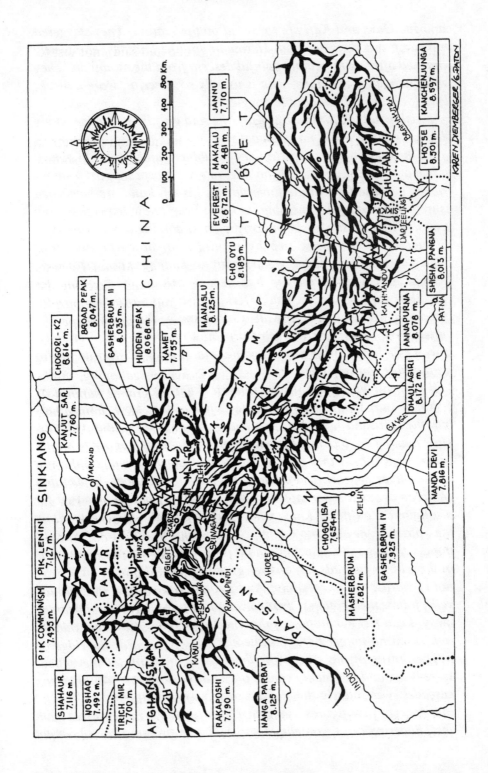

SHAHAUR 7.116 m.

NOSHAQ 7.492 m.

TIRICH MIR 7.700 m.

RAKAPOSHI 7.790 m.

NANGA PARBAT 8.125 m.

PIK COMMUNISM 7.495 m.

PIK LENIN 7.127 m.

KANJUT SAR 7.760 m.

CHOGORI – K2 8.616 m.

BROAD PEAK 8.047 m.

GASHERBRUM II 8.035 m.

HIDDEN PEAK 8.068 m.

KAMET 7.755 m.

MANASLU 8.125 m.

CHO OYU 8.185 m.

EVEREST 8.872 m.

MAKALU 8.481 m.

JANNU 7.710 m.

KANCHENJUNGA 8.597 m.

LHOTSE 8.501 m.

SHISHA PANGNA 8.013 m.

ANNAPURNA 8.078 m.

DHAULAGIRI 8.172 m.

NANDA DEVI 7.816 m.

CHOGOLISA 7.654 m.

MASHERBRUM 7.821 m.

GASHERBRUM IV 7.925 m.

KAREN DIEMBERGER / G. PATON

AFGHANISTAN

PAMIR

SINKIANG

CHINA

TIBET

HIMALAYA

TRANSHIMALAYA

KARAKORUM

HINDU-KUSH

KASHMIR

NEPAL

BHUTAN

SIKKIM

PAKISTAN

INDIA

KABUL
PESHAWAR
RAWALPINDI
GILGIT
HUNZA
SKARDU
LEH
SRINAGAR
LAHORE
DELHI
YARKAND
KATHMANDU
DARJEELING
PATNA

INDUS
GANGES
BRAHMAPUTRA

0 100 200 300 400 500 Km.

campsite Hans and Karl are sprawled on the ground. They staggered into camp two days ago with Hermann and the Sherpas, completely whacked after an incredibly painful descent from the mountain. They were changed men. Hans, who is usually so cheerful, wore a bleak, dead look behind his double goggles.

'I wish you luck for the top, Kurt,' he said gruffly, in a voice barely above a whisper, 'but no bivouac!'

All the toes on one of his feet are frostbitten, and Karl is in almost as bad a way. He can scarcely hobble, or even accept support from his friends because four of the fingertips on his left hand are blackened as well. He muttered something, too, but I can't now remember what it was. Those must have been horrific days, coming down from their bivouac at 8250 metres, step by painful step, down through four High Camps. Later, helping Karli with his bandages and medicines, I asked him whether the top had been worth all the anguish. He was silent for a while, then said, 'Oh, yes, it was worth it . . .' and, indicating his swollen foot with a bitter smile, the old Karli-smile, added, 'We've got this under control now, haven't we?' Certainly, it won't be long till the porters come, but Hans and Karl are in for a miserable journey back.

If I do still want to go for the summit, I dare not delay any longer. I should start tomorrow, or the day after at the latest. I sink back into the soft sand near our tents and gaze up at the chasing clouds. How many men, like me, have wondered what their tomorrow would bring, and known that on the decision of the moment, all the rest of their lives depended? Perhaps they have known that the decision could be avoided – perhaps they did sidestep it, but what is that for a solution? You never know what you'll encounter tomorrow. Only the Spirits of the Air know that . . . So what's to do? Looking up, I ponder that age-old question, and it is as if, while I am losing myself in the whirling clouds, an answer gradually reveals itself: an answer not in words, but in certainty. And I continue gazing at the weaving veils, follow their courses, their variations, while all questions dissolve away. I can feel the motion of the wheeling shapes, and if I surrender to it, I am no longer here, but there . . .

The Spirits of the Air: with what power they rise from nothing, secretively, and as quickly vanish once more. Rolling mists, tumbling cascades, weightlessly dancing on their way, multiplying as they go into strange new figures that reach out to embrace each other with their fluttering arms, sometimes succeeding in bringing an evanescent new creature into existence, but mostly melting away before they can touch. Spirits of the Air? Can they really know what tomorrow will bring? Where do they hide when the air is cold and clear, and when in the icy stillness mountains stand like blue crystal in the morning sun, when a pale full moon floats in the daylight sky until, sapped of all strength, it sinks to a mountain ridge and you imagine it rolling, like a barrel, down the hill.

Are they behind the mountains then? Somewhere they must be continuing their ballade. Where is certainty? The secrets are on the summit and beyond. 'Only the Spirits of the Air know what awaits me behind the mountains.' So runs the old Eskimo proverb. 'But I go on with my dogs, onward and on.' Some days ago, when I was lying sick, down below in the rainforest, I fully believed there was no future for me on big mountains, that my fate lay away from them, somewhere behind.

But now I know: it is up there, on the summit of Makalu. If I don't try this climb, I have no future. And if nobody wants to come with me, then I shall have to go alone. Sometimes there is no way forward for a man if he does not find the answer to his question.

The Spirits of the Air told me: Go up!

The second birthday

Whatever happens to me now is a bonus. By any normal standards my life should have ended several years ago . . . it all came about innocently enough.

'Charlie's bought an aeroplane!' – the news went round like wildfire.

How come so fast?

Never imagine climbers to be strong, silent types, not given to chatter! Nothing could be further from the truth. The discussion over the placing of a single piton can rage for hours. And if, in putting up some great new route, a climber strays beyond the iron disciplines of the purists (let alone, he may not have done it at all) then the talk spreads faster than bush telegraph. Usually the sole topic is mountains but this news about Charlie was something extraordinary. It was common knowledge that he had started out as a modest ski instructor, then for some years shuttled between America, Australia and Europe before opening a small sports shop in Innsbruck. Nothing extraordinary. But now, all of a sudden, Charlie has surprised everyone.

'Hey, guys, heard the latest? Charlie's got himself wings!' Brandler tells Raditschnig, Nairz passes the word to Messner, Stitzinger phones up Sturm . . . Where did he get that kind of money? Does he know how to fly the thing? How long before he breaks his neck? These were the questions doing the rounds. But sooner or later almost everyone looked forward to a joyride. Only the more cautious of us preferred to wait and see. As one of Charlie's oldest friends, I knew some of the facts: one, that the machine was a single-engined Cessna 150; also that Charlie was not his real name. He had been born Karl Schönthaler, and cannot abide his nickname; nevertheless, 'Charlie from Innsbruck' is how everyone knows him, and if I refer to him differently, nobody will know who I'm talking about. Aeroplanes are easier: they have an identification number, and all those with the same number are similar. Charlie's, however, must have been something of a one-off, but I don't want to anticipate . . . He was delighted with it. At first.

'Fancy seeing you!' Charlie greets me on the fateful day, his blue eyes crinkled with pleasure. 'Hey, remember our Piz Roseg climb?'

he says, 'I went and took a look at it the other day.' Easy for him, I think. Just a hop, here, there, wherever he wants . . .

'Come on, let's go there now, why don't we?' He pushes back his ski cap rakishly, and throws me a challenging look. The old devil doesn't change! Should I take up his offer? I am cautious by nature, but he has been flying for a year now, and I have always had complete faith in him as a mountaineer. I convince myself I trust him just as implicitly as a pilot . . . and that is how I come to be standing on Innsbruck airfield shortly afterwards, while Charlie squints up at a clear, blue sky. 'Okay,' He smiles, content. 'Let's go! Let's spin over to the Bernina and say hello to that route of ours.'* Seeing your old first ascents again is fun, especially from the air; you can congratulate yourself on how great you used to be. (Mountaineers are no less vain than anyone else – and certainly, we two are no exceptions.) Again, he says it, this time more solemnly: 'Come on then, back to the scene of our triumph,' and slipping on his gloves, he caresses the shining aircraft, at the same time casting me a stern glance. 'Flying is a serious business, Kurt,' he warns. 'You are not to make me nervous. No taking photographs the whole time and, *Kruiztuifl*! above all, don't bother me with a string of questions . . .'

Charlie comes from the South Tirol. He has this habit of lapsing into dialect at moments of great importance or stress. 'It's all right,' I try to calm him. 'I'll only take pictures from my side of the plane,' and I hug my two cameras to my chest. (The reader should know that many pilots have this obsessive fear of photographers getting in the way of the controls, besides wanting to know the name of every last garden shed on the ground. A flying doctor friend in Italy would grow very nervous when I used to persuade him to open the door for a better view of the fields and villages.) But if Charlie is worrying that I might block his view, at least he's keeping his eyes open, I think, not pinning all his hopes on his instruments.

That turns out to be true. As we take off, my friend continues his lecture: 'It's more important for me to catch a glimpse of the mountain, than that you get it in your viewfinder . . .' Okay, Charlie. I take the point.

---

* It was the direct North-East Face of the Piz Roseg that Karl Schönthaler and I climbed in 1958, at that time the hardest route in the Bernina group. It still belongs in that category. The first direct exit from the Klucker route over the ice bulge of the North Summit also fell to us.

We are already passing the crags of the Innsbrucker Nordkette – on my side, luckily. Charlie is whistling cheerfully, and seems utterly at peace with the world (with me, too). As he gently runs his snow-white gloves over the gleaming fittings of his beloved plane, I think how well he has done for himself. How good to have such friends! Who work so hard. Ski instructor to aeroplane proprietor – whoever would have thought it? But Charlie has always been one of those silent, unexpected geniuses.

I aim my tele-lens down into the Inn valley to capture a neat village – or small town – for my picture archive. 'Where's that, Charlie?' I ask, since a photograph isn't much good without a caption (publishers don't take kindly to invention . . .)

'There you go – at it already,' he answers with irritation. 'I don't know what it is. Isn't it enough that we're airborne, who cares what the village is called?' And he snorts, 'It's not a village, anyway – that's a town. Telfs, probably. Yes, it's Telfs!'

Don't ask a pilot about geography, I think to myself. (It comes as a surprise to learn that pilots don't always know exactly where they are. My Italian doctor friend once circled with me above the small town of 'Stradella'. Wasn't it curious, I ventured, how similar the big golden Madonna on the church tower was to the one in Tortona – which, as it turned out, was where we were. Clearly, my friend didn't open the door often enough!) It seems to me pilots are so busy taking care not to bump into another aircraft – that they are happy to just watch the ground go by, knowing only vaguely where they are.

Now, on Charlie's side, a wild valley appears, hemmed in by high peaks – even today, I am not sure if it was the Kaunertal or the Ötztal, everything looks so different from the air; Charlie will not commit himself beyond saying it is the Ötztal Alps. Not to worry, I tell myself, we should soon see the Wildspitze – and then we'll know where we are. The distinctive three-thousander is the highest mountain for miles around. Charlie confirms the Wildspitze will be coming up shortly, and I cannot resist a mock-polite cough. He glowers in my direction, remarking huffily that the main thing is not to bump into the mountain! (Motto for all Innsbruck pilots, that!) Then, after a pause, 'There was a bad incident recently, with a photographer . . . To be fair, he had more camera equipment than you . . .' This latter he says more kindly, and I am glad I have only brought two Leicas along. 'The guy insisted on flying to the end of a valley – the very end – and just when the pilot said "Enough!" and tried to pull the plane round, he found he couldn't because the telephoto-lens was caught under the joy-stick! They had to make an emergency landing, and it's nothing short of a miracle they didn't turn the thing over! That's another rule of flying, by the way, always keep your eyes skinned for emergency landing places.' My friend is in lecture-mode again. He casts an exaggerated glance out of the window, then nods back at me, satisfied. Meanwhile I hurriedly scoop all the lenses on to my lap. He seems perfectly calm now. Slowly and steadily we gain height.

'Three thousand six hundred metres,' he advises cheerfully. 'Any minute now for the Wildspitze . . .'

From my window I can see right into a high valley filled with hay-barns, a beautiful green valley running parallel to the Inn River, which by now has almost vanished into the distance. Such parallel valleys high in the mountains have an ancient, perhaps Celtic, name – 'Tschy'. (That this was the Pfundser Tschy I did not know at the time, any more than did Charlie. Nor were we aware that the farmers would be haymaking there, scything the grass and spreading it to dry across this wide green valley at 1500 metres, a valley hardly ever visited – perhaps no more than a couple of tourists go there in a summer . . . But, back to our flight!)

Impressive silhouettes of mountains and dark rocks float by on Charlie's side, just as if they had been cut out with scissors. This must be part of the Kaunergrat, and I cannot resist leaning over for a moment – just this once – for a closer look. Charlie growls, banks the plane to a steeper angle and, yes, there it is, the Wildspitze! Over there!

How fantastic, the glacier world of the Ötztal! The engine labours with what seems to me a slight change in tone, but Charlie gives no sign of alarm and I continue gazing out of the window: the Ötztal peaks! It is twenty years since I was last here, as a young lad. Soon, I will spot all the old places! Thanks to Charlie and his kite. The plane shows little enthusiasm for the shining Wildspitze – the motor definitely sounds different now, more hollow. Is it anything? Surely, Charlie would tell me if something was amiss? He sits silent, just a bit hunched, and not sparing a glance for the Wildspitze. I take a photo of it, and another into the depths where suddenly a small emerald-coloured lake has appeared, set in a rocky cirque and surrounded by weird, eroded ridges, thrusting upwards.

What an abyss! It makes you dizzy to look at it. Hey, that engine noise is really most peculiar now – although I know nothing about such things – and I see Charlie fiddling with various buttons, turning them this way and that. No wonder he has lost interest in the landscape! I feel the blood rising, hot to my head: something is wrong! Is it serious? Charlie confirms my anxieties. 'Get the bloody cameras out of the way,' he bursts out. 'The engine's in trouble!'

It's true, then. I swallow. Try to stay calm. 'I thought there was something,' I say. 'It sounds just like an old car before it claps out.'

'Don't talk nonsense,' my friend snaps. 'It's practically brand new – it can't clap out. I've probably just got to change the mixture.' He pulls another handle. (The reader, flying with us, must excuse the lack of technical precision: a cipher I am, merely, when it comes to things mechanical, having no idea how to fly a plane. You must rely on Charlie for that: after all he has been a pilot for a whole year. By now, even the most ignorant landlubber will have recognised we were in dire straits, with our stuttering *huppada-huppada – hupp*! Alarming, when that is all that holds you in the air.)

Charlie radios Innsbruck: 'Charlie-Mac-Alpha, Charlie-Mac-Alpha – engine trouble, we have engine trouble.' He has to speak English – all pilots do. Some practical advice obviously follows, which he tries out right away, and for a moment he succeeds in bringing the motor to a *huppuppupp-uppup* . . . but our hopes are soon dashed: we are hardly moving forward at all, even though we stopped trying to climb ages ago. The aircraft rocks from side to side, like a boat on Lake Como in a light swell. (Would we were on any lake, rather than up here.)

'Charlie,' I hear myself saying, 'let's turn round and try to get down to the Inn valley.'

'That's our only hope,' he retorts. 'Don't bother me now.' And he calls up Innsbruck again.

This is a moment I know will live with me for ever – the swaying aircraft, the motor on its last gasp, those sharp ridges below and, at my side, Charlie clinging to the microphone as if it holds the key to our salvation. My thumping heart feels as if it is shrinking. Are we going to fall out of the sky? Yet, even terror has its tragi-comic moments. Charlie, gabbling into his walkie-talkie, forgets the rules

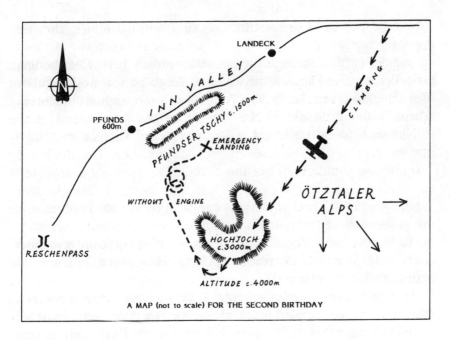

LANDECK

INN VALLEY

CLIMBING

PFUNDS
600m

PFUNDSER TSCHY c.1500m

EMERGENCY
LANDING

WITHOUT ENGINE

ÖTZTALER
ALPS

HOCHJOCH
c.3000m

)(
RESCHENPASS

ALTITUDE c.4000m

A MAP (not to scale) FOR THE SECOND BIRTHDAY

and breaks into Tyrolean. There must be a different controller at the other end, unaware of how critical our position is. 'Why don't you speak English, Charlie-Mac-Alpha?' the man says.

It is the last straw. 'Stuff your English!' yells a furious Charlie, as the propeller makes its last half-hearted revolutions – one, two . . . oone, twoo . . . o-n-e, t-w-w-o-o – then, quietly, as if it were the most natural thing in the world, coming to an oblique halt. 'The bloody crate has died on me!'

He roars into the mike in his broadest Tyrolean, and suddenly no one gives a fig about the rules. The propeller has given up the ghost: no time for niceties. The aeroplane is still rocking gently like a little boat, but it hasn't flipped over. Not yet. That means you won't be falling out of the sky right away, a small, rational voice announces from some uninvolved centre of my brain, bringing transitory relief. But then, how long before you do fall once your engine cuts out? How many minutes have we got? Charlie is silent, hanging on to the steering with an abstracted expression. The plane continues its swaying. Seven hundred and fifty kilos it weighs, the same as a Volkswagen Beetle. A glance down reveals barren mountains, cirques, peaks rising from deep valleys, and over there, the Ötztal glaciers, shining, white . . .

No, the two of us are not in a rocking barque on any lake: we are 4000 metres up in the sky, in a Beetle-heavy plane without an engine, cutting through the air with a steady hiss. The slanting propeller, outlined against the white of the glaciers, slides gradually over the grey-green depths . . . A chaos of rocks appears below us, a basin with a little lake.

'Nowhere for an emergency landing there,' Charlie says in a low voice.

If only we could get out of this thing.

How simple to break down in a car: with its last momentum, the driver can roll to the road side, then call out the rescue services. Seven hundred and fifty kilos would require a pretty strong guardian angel to hoist us out of trouble up here. How much longer now, before we hit the ground?

As if in answer to my thoughts, I hear Charlie say, 'If we can maintain enough forward momentum, we can glide down.' Glide? With this weight? Glide like a cockchafer, I think. But so far it seems to be working. Hoarsely, Charlie radios our position to Innsbruck – in English. 'I'm trying to reach the Inn valley,' he tells them, then turns to me. 'Kurtl,' he says, 'I have practised this several times over the airfield. It's going to be all right . . . If we find somewhere to land . . . If we don't get caught in any turbulence . . . and if . . .'

The thought of 'coasting' this box of tricks down imbues me with new hope. 'The most important thing, Charlie,' I tell him, 'is to stay calm . . .' He is all for calling Innsbruck again, but I tell him that it is no use. We are on our own. Nobody on earth can help us. Our only hope now is to keep our heads, just as we did on Piz Roseg all those years ago, when eighty-metre séracs were poised above us, ready to break off!

Silence. Utter, utter silence . . . apart from the hiss of air around the wings. Charlie, my friend, stay calm . . . and I lay my hand briefly on his shoulder. We have everything to gain, everything to lose. I may not know how to fly this box of tricks, but I can help him not to panic.

What a strange coincidence that we should have bumped into each other today, that Charlie and I are together again, now, so many years after our big climb, linked once more as surely as by a rope, for better or worse.

What a stupid coincidence! Another voice intrudes in my mind:

you would never have dreamt this morning that such a thing could happen. How come, after a year of flying, it should be today of all days that Charlie's plane breaks down, and on our first spin together? A couple more minutes and it could be all over . . . for good . . . Never mind the thousands of dangers we have survived in the mountains! What irony! I can just imagine what the newspapers will make of it: MOUNTAIN AIRCRASH, CLIMBERS DIE FIFTEEN YEARS AFTER FIRST ASCENT. There will be gruesome pictures of scattered wreckage alongside our portraits. Bloody hell, that's no way to be thinking! I have more important things to do . . .

'Charlie, you'll make it,' I shout through the hissing air. He nods, grimly, clinging tightly to the controls and peering towards the Inn valley, from which we are still separated by a high mountain ridge. The expression on his face suggests he is calculating our chances of 'leapfrogging' over it. Luckily, we had climbed to over 4000 metres earlier – now we are 'living' on that. The wings slice the air, we sink lower . . .

'Everyone makes it down!' That is a macabre piece of pilots' lore. But down where? We are still over a rocky amphitheatre, though there is more and more green ahead now.

Deeper and deeper we sink.

I seriously doubt we will clear this ridge which guards the deep furrow of the Inn valley. But shouldn't there be that high valley pasture first, the one I noticed this morning? I look down, trembling with fear and anticipation. Never have I wanted anything so much as to be down there on firm ground, treading the sweet grass. Never have I been further from all that the earth means; only my thoughts touch it now: they want to melt into the ground, the rocks, the forests – all of which are coming closer by the moment. Yet though I long for this fusion, the moment of contact will almost certainly whisk me to infinity, into a world without space, beyond all that lies so far away, down there. My children . . .? I think only how glad I am they have no idea what is happening to me. Perhaps they are just enjoying a fine day, somewhere down in the green.

It makes me so happy merely that they exist.

'Charlie, I don't think we'll make it over that ridge!'

'Depends on the air currents. It's our only hope.'

No, no! Ahead of us, a bright green patch approaches, deep

down, coming up now, rising above the jagged line of trees. It's getting bigger, down in that wide trough, just before the barrier of hills. The high valley! It's the Tschy! Look, look! Glinting up like a promise! I can make out wooden barns, see them quite clearly, sprinkled like tiny dice in the bottom of the valley. 'Charlie, we can land down there! We don't have to go over the ridge. It's not that we know what's the other side anyway. Let's put down here!'

My friend hesitates for no more than a second. 'Right, here we go!' And already we are banking almost vertically, the air rushing and swishing around the plane, our downward wing pointing directly into the bottom of the Tschy. 'I'm going to spiral down now,' yells Charlie through the noise, leaving me lost for words at this sudden change. Then begins a slalom to play havoc with the senses. It's like being suspended inside a moving spiral staircase . . . a chaos of sight and sound as we descend into the green cirque of the valley. Charlie has suddenly become a wondrous ski-ace, launching himself into the unknown in quest of 'gold'. The 'game', increasingly difficult the lower we get, is played for life or death, countless spur-of-the-moment decisions where no error is permitted, swooping down a spiral staircase whose end is hidden from us – and where we need nothing short of the 'gold' to survive. From Charlie it demanded the utmost in ability and instinct, an almost overwhelming demand after only a single year's experience.

Tighter and tighter grow the spirals as we etch whistling circles between the mountain flanks. Ours is an oblique world, the wings of the plane continuously above and below us. Charlie's concentration remains absolute, his eyes staring fixedly ahead, his brow deeply wrinkled. Once I yell, 'Watch out! Mind we don't flip over!' and he snaps back at me to shut up, saying, 'You don't know a thing about aerodynamics. Of course we're not going to flip over.' Our weird spiral gouges on into the depths, into this gigantic green funnel. I cling to the seat as the forest rotates 500 metres below; watching the wheeling treetops, I am still unconvinced we will not end up nose-first. Charlie wears a frozen smile, or is it a grimace of effort? He has the joy-stick in an iron grip. 'You're doing fine,' I tell him. 'Keep it going!' And, however uncomfortable my position, it's a fact, we haven't dropped from the sky yet. We are still flying: increasingly it looks as if we might see this thing through. The earth appears much nearer now, and my longing for it has grown out of all bounds – as has my fear.

'I'm going to turn the plane on its head – see if the motor will restart,' Charlie announces suddenly. Every muscle in his face is tense.

'No, no, don't!' I yell. 'It'll never work!' Having come to terms with the spiral, I am reluctant to face another manoeuvre. But when Charlie is convinced of a thing, he does it: already we have gone into the headstand. Three hundred metres below are the roofs of the hay-barns, and small dots on the meadows – people – moving . . . the rush around the wings has risen to a roar as they slice the air, the roofs grow closer, the people bigger – they are running. God, I wish I was with them! Charlie tries the ignition, but the propeller makes only a couple of feeble turns . . . 'It's not going to work!' he curses. And down there, suddenly, the roofs disappear from view and the mountainside arcs steeply upwards in front of us, as we are pressed into our seats with full force. Blue sky? Clouds? Whatever is happening now? Panting, Charlie holds – no, leans with all his strength – against the steering. We've had it, then, I whisper to myself, just another couple of seconds . . . I want to say something to Charlie, but my throat narrows and nothing will come. I am suddenly overwhelmed by a sense of weightlessness, and at the same time, of helplessness . . .

'Charlie . . .' A glance across shows his face distorted, his eyes mere slits. That was it then, Charlie, was it? Suddenly the weightlessness vanishes and in its place an immense pressure seizes me: my arms are lead, my body is lead. The seat, the elbow-rests thrust up at me with great force, countering gravity. But we must be falling . . . aren't we?

For a moment I do not know what's happening.

Charlie draws a deep breath. 'That was hairy,' he says. No, we aren't falling any longer, we are hanging once more sideways in the air. 'We must choose somewhere to put it down,' says my Charlie, 'there's not much time left.' He is maintaining the curve. I feel life has just been given back to me, I am thankful for every extra moment. But now, God, another decision! Those meadows, which looked so smooth from above, we see are full of bumps. And the valley is dotted with hay-sheds, fatal wooden cubes: we don't want to smash into them. There is a ditch, too, beside a narrow dust road.

'Go higher up the valley,' I call instinctively. 'Charlie, over there!' And I point ahead.

'Yes, that'll do,' he yells back and is flying now straight towards a meadow immediately above the dust road, which looks more promising. It is racing towards us – oh, hell! It is just as bumpy! 'Can't do anything about it now,' Charlie mumbles, 'I'm lowering the flaps.' A second later, I hear the rush of air. A couple more seconds, and all will be decided, one way or the other. It is almost a relief. The earth is close. I am full of hope.

The road! There's a farmer, running; he throws himself into the ditch, but already we have swooped over him. Again I hear Charlie. 'When we're down, try to get out right away. If that's possible.' His voice sounds urgent. Roofs skim past . . . a big grassy dome approaches – there? No, not there! That's it, no more choices . . . no time . . . The road! The road with the ditch – here too! We're still moving at a hundred kilometres per hour, we'll just get over it . . .

'Tuck in your legs! Any minute now . . .' Charlie roars over the noise. Fractions of seconds, fragments of time: the green dome, again . . . there are humps behind it, too! In between . . .

CRAAAAAASH! Then a wild kick, and we are flying again, thrown up with enormous force. We flop over the hill, an enormous jump of at least forty metres! CRAAAAAASH! I hug my legs, bent, hanging in the harness. And we're airborne again, like a football. Will it never end? CRAACK! That was very hard, that one! Another jump – into the air – PRANGGGGGG! At last we seem to have come to rest. GET OUT! QUICK, OUT, OUT! In a fraction of a second I am free of the harness, hurl open the door, and I am outside!

The world does not move any more.

The meadow. The grass. The flat, still ground.

My feet are planted back on earth. I feel it coming up through every fibre of my body, from the surface – life. It is a miracle.

'Kurtl!' Charlie laughs crazily, 'We're alive!' And I see him pulling at his hair and running round and round in the meadow, like a lunatic. And I'm running through the grass too, deliriously shouting and screaming. And we fall on each other's necks, hug one another and gallop round again. We are totally beside ourselves – over the edge with joy. Here we are, here we are . . . we are alive!

'Kurtl,' Charlie yells suddenly. 'You might not know how to fly, but you're the very best companion for a crash! Without you, I'd have been really nervous!'

'Charlie . . .' I say. But I cannot say anything: all of sudden I have no more words. Charlie, I think, without *you* . . .

To Charlie, I owe my life, my second life – that's why he is here, at the beginning of my book – even if his real name is Karl Schönthaler and not Charlie at all. Forgive me, Karl . . .

What else remains to be told?
A lot: we had been incredibly lucky. The aeroplane didn't catch fire, we didn't nosedive, or turn it over, we didn't even break any bones – nothing at all! Charlie walks round his plane in sheer disbelief: 'The only damage is to one of the struts. And at the back, there's a little bit torn away. That's all! And we are alive!'

Beside ourselves with happiness, we are standing in our flower-decked 'birthday meadow', 1500 metres above the sea, in this beautiful Pfundser Tschy, as the first farmers, men, women, boys and girls come flocking round. They look at us as if we had risen from the dead and shake our hands. Some shake their heads as well. A farmer's wife remarks with feeling that you would never catch her sitting in one of these contraptions . . .

Straightforward country people, who do not waste a lot of words; we are happy they came; we are happy about everything. Happy beyond measure, beyond words. Real birthday kids! And into this 'contraption' which Charlie has just coaxed safely out of the sky, this box with which he struck 'gold' for us – our lives – I, too, will never venture inside. Never again.

Everyone living in the high valley had to come and visit this meadow, of course. At first glance you would never know the plane had made an emergency landing, even if it was standing a little cock-eyed. Only closer inspection revealed the cracked strut and damaged rudder. By chance, in the afternoon, two German tourists dropped by – and they had heard nothing of our drama. One of them, a well-fed man with a shaving-brush of chamois hair on his (new) hat, remarked to his wife, 'Did you realise, Wilhelmine, that these Austrian farmers are now *flying* in to harvest their hay?'

I guarded the plane next day, in case it became an irresistible 'toy' to the children of the valley, and there were even more visitors. I had to explain over and again what happened. But I didn't mind, I could have stayed for days in this meadow. Charlie

had gone down to the Inn valley to find a mechanic and some heavy
vehicle that could tow us. The whole plane would need dismantling
screw by screw to load it on to a transporter and get it down to
Innsbruck.

. . . Later, I have to say, Charlie preferred to buy a new plane.

Double solo on Zebru

Zebru looks like the raised fin of a giant fish. Sunlight, catching
its north-east face obliquely, reveals a fine design like radiating
bones. These are snow and ice ribs, varying in number according
to the prevailing conditions on the face. Up to the right, the
piscine image is fortified by an overall pattern of dark speckles
– islands of rock penetrating the thin skin of snow and ice. The
top edge of the fin runs more or less horizontally, though it
carries a summit-point on either end. The face below the one to
the right – the northern – was unclimbed from this side, although
a route had been pushed to the South Summit, up a completely
white flank which lies almost always in shadow, being inclined
towards the north. There is a plinth of outcropping rock at the
base of the fin, surmounted by a small hanging glacier – except
that nothing is really 'small' here. The height of the face itself is
some 700 metres. My two-fold climb of this giant fin took a full
day, giving many adventurous hours: a first ascent to the North
Summit, followed by a first descent from the Southern Summit,
both solo.
   In some way it was another birthday.

I was climbing on my own because my friend Albert Morokutti's
leave had run out before I felt ready to go home. I don't really consider myself a soloist; I far prefer sharing an adventure with someone
else. That is not to imply anything against solo mountaineering: it is
just a different kind of experience, often more dangerous, sometimes
more intense, and one which takes you to the limits of existence – no
other human can help you find the answers, only the mountain . . .
and yourself.

*

In a storm on the Aiguille Blanche, surrounded by the spirits of the air.

My double solo route on Zebru in the South Tyrol. *Inset*, a 'second birthday' hug for Charlie on the meadow after our emergency landing.

With hammer and chisel on Mont Blanc, where I found so many crystals.
My son, Ceci, smiles secretly.

My wife, Teresa – 'the judge' who knows I am a case beyond solution. 'I also belong to Mont Blanc,' said the small fly that landed on my finger as the sun caught a piece of quartz.

Thinking about this climb, I sat alone in the hayfields of the Pfundser Tschy, waiting for Charlie to organise recovery of the damaged plane.

What brought it into my mind? During my solo on Zebru all those years ago, just as in the crippled aeroplane, there had been moments when I longed for some good flat earth beneath my feet. And it had been just as far away.

*

A thirty-metre hemp rope over my shoulder, some pitons in my rucksack and an ice axe in my hand: that's how lightly I set out for Zebru. The hut warden had thoughtfully provided a couple of sandwiches, but these weighed scarcely anything, and my rope was quite thin – sufficient only for a self-belay on some of the more difficult passages, or for abseiling if it became necessary to retreat – you never know.

It was still only half light as I approached the face. The pale bulk of the Ortler rose to my right with its snow patches and the rock bastions of the Hinter Grat; and to the left, the Königspitze soared into the sky. Only a few days ago I had climbed that great face with Albert; true, the Giant Meringue still beckoned, the impressive summit cornice which no one had yet managed to overcome, but as a soloist, without the possibility of help or belay, I saw no chance of doing that for the time being.

Thus, everything was uncertain, as so often in life, even today. But casting light into uncertainty, transforming it by degrees to clarity, is the adventure of the mountaineer, an adventure for life. I will never be able to do without it!

The first rays of sun come up as I put on my crampons, but the spectacle affects me less than usual: I am tense with anticipation. What lies in store for me on this Zebru North-East Face; and how will I cope with it, just on my own?

I feel in great shape. It is autumn now, and a whole summer of climbing lies behind me. Across the gently sloping glacier, I approach the steep face where it sweeps down from the North Summit. The snow surface sparkles all around, scattered with crystals from the overnight frost – but I keep my attention on all the troughs and hollows, which could indicate a hidden crevasse. Falling into one of these is a great danger of soloing, when you have no lifeline, no companion with a rope to haul you back to the surface. Usually, nobody even knows where you are. You might manage to extricate yourself if uninjured, but the odds remain against you. A big transverse crevasse bars the way. I had already noticed it from below, had even discovered a snow bridge – but now, close up, I don't fancy it at all. It is frozen bone-hard, but very flimsy. I probe around with my axe, but in the end I can see no other possibility and rush across it with momentum, catching a second's-long glimpse into the frigid blue depths. Otherwise, the glacier holds no problems, simply becomes increasingly steep. On all fours, I crawl up the white flank, plunging in the pick of the ice axe with every step. (I call it an axe, but it also has a hammer head.) The front points of my crampons, too, I thrust into the white surface, and I clutch a pointed ice piton in my left hand to make the fourth point of contact. I take great care always to have at least three points in contact with the mountain before making a movement: either two hands and one foot, or two feet and one hand . . .

To an outsider, this juggling of holds might sound a complicated and risky procedure, but when you have been climbing for years, it has long passed into your flesh and blood and you don't think about it. The precision demanded by each step becomes second nature. On a mountain, imprecision takes bitter revenge, sooner or later!

At last I reach a vertical barrier of grey rock. Friable limestone, very similar to that on the Ortler, or over there on the Königspitze. For a while, I pause to study the possibilities . . . Then, I inch my way carefully higher, testing every hold. No one has ever held this rock in his hand before! I am right to be cautious: a handhold crumbles away . . . Frozen with horror, I watch the jumping pieces disappear into the depths. If more than one hold comes away at a time, so much for my good shape!

With infinite care I retreat back to the foot of the rock barrier, find a fissure in sound rock, and hammer in a piton. Then, belaying myself to this with the rope, I start climbing again. Careful only to trust my weight to holds by pressure – pushing down, not pulling on them – I sneak up the wall, stopping just once on a small ledge to extend my rope belay. That's the way to secure myself with no partner gradually paying out the rope. At last, the rock band! There is a good crack. Bang! Bang! Bang! In goes another piton . . . give it a vigorous wiggle . . . it's solid. Then, descending the rope, I hammer out the first piton. With a rope from above and easier now in my mind, I clamber back across this unfriendly fragile wall. True, it is a long-winded technique, but perfectly secure if the pitons are well placed. Taking out the upper one, I reflect that, alone like this, somehow these pegs become companions. (I could not know then that many years later a sort of belaying device would be given the name 'Friend'.)

Coiling the rope, I take another look down the barrier . . . That was some circus act, and no mistake, only without an audience. I feel totally calm, in balance, not bothered at all by being on my own. My gaze sweeps over the mountains: how blue they are, on this silent autumn morning. And then it occurs to me that perhaps there is a spectator after all: Fritz Dangl, the warden of the Hinter Grat hut, the only person to whom I confided my intention, maybe he is watching through his telescope? It feels fine to be alone with the mountain – but it is good, too, to know that another soul shares your secret – even if only from outside.

But soon, climbing onwards, I forget all about Fritz and am conscious only, in this direct relationship with the face, of the overwhelming pleasure in discovering something new, a sense which increases by the minute. No, I don't feel lonely at all! The face and I. Then, having been on the go for perhaps three hours, I find myself among the rock islands which stud the upper part of the giant fin, below the North Summit. Every so often I can escape from the steep white snow to catch my breath in one of the faintly defined niches below the rocky islands. I am already high on the face, and totally content. The wall is surely mine! Yes, full of boyish presumption, I look across at the North Face of the Southern Summit: perhaps I could climb down that way instead of the normal route? Pig-steep, it looks, no interruption, no niche, no place to rest. Still . . . *Ma gia che si balla, balliamo davvero*! . . . since we are dancing, let's do it properly! I'll give it another look from above, from the top – without obligation. Mmm . . . but it would be very tempting to descend that way, clinging like a louse on a polished shovel, with everything around tilting away and plunging into the depths! Perhaps that's not such a good metaphor after all: a louse has the benefit of six legs, which must make everything safer . . . my goodness, imagine! Five points of contact . . .

A cool breeze! Does it mean the summit is close? A breath of wind that plays around the last rocks in this white world? The Ortler – over there – still rises above us, above me and my mountain. So it is higher, the Ortler, so what? What do height and size really matter? This is my mountain, my discovery – my route for all time.

Well, for a moment only.

Nothing lasts longer . . .

An edge, the sky above me – and I've arrived. The summit! I scramble up the last steps, happiness storming through me – here it is, my summit!

I stand on it.

Yes, I have reached you – and by a path which no one's eye had so closely beheld before; what streams through me may well be the joy of an explorer. What else? Contentedness, certainly, that the venture succeeded. And satisfaction, too, that I did possess the ability to move up here, to overcome the difficulties; in knowing for me mountaineering was not just a gamble. What else? A feeling of being part of nature. It surrounds you here, this nature, silently, with its greatest creations – the mountains.

Squatting on the summit, I look over at the Königspitze, soaring against the light – it is not yet noon, so it has taken me four and a half hours to climb the face. What a powerful cornice that Königspitze has! Will I ever succeed in climbing that? Not by myself, I won't.*
But the big snow roll continues to bewitch me as I skip along the airy waves of the connecting ridge between Zebru's North and South Summits, a bridge of no sighs or problems, wonderful with plunging views on both sides and distant panoramas. Where does the normal route go down? I have completely forgotten to take any interest in that. Probably, the face absorbed me so much that I thought: you will find out when you are up there. A mistake. In the meantime, this is the South Summit! The whipped cream roll looks quite close from here. I lie down for a while to ponder it. When I rouse myself, it is time to start thinking about how to get down! What about the North Face of this Southern Summit? Coming up, didn't I flirt with its white steepness? From where I am now I cannot look into it. Towards its top, the face curves like a belly, and one would need to descend a bit before getting a good view down it. Gingerly, I step lower, turning in to face the mountain as it gets steeper, and continuing backwards on all fours, similar to the usual way of coming up on snow and firn. So

* See the chapter 'The Giant Meringue' in my *Summits and Secrets*.

far, so good. Finally, below my crooked arm, I catch a glimpse down
. . . Heavens! It shoots off into nowhere! About 600 metres below,
I recognise the small glacier where I started out this morning. Of
course exposure is a feature of steep ice walls like this – you certainly
do feel as if you're hanging on them, and no better than a louse on
a steep polished shovel standing against the wall. I'll have another
think about it – slowly I scramble back to the summit.

Whatever you do, you ought to have a rest first, my inner voice
tells me. And so I lie down and it doesn't take long till I fall asleep,
stroked by the light breeze which plays around the summit, warmed
by the mild autumn sun . . . It is about an hour later when I wake
up. Hop-la, time to go! If it takes as long to get down here as to
come up the other face – this is going to turn into a very full day!
There must be no more hanging around!

With no real relish, I set off down, into the abyss – it was so
pleasant lying dreaming there on the summit. Yes, I definitely have
to rediscipline myself to being on such steep ground again, to pay
attention to every step and not make any mistakes. Sometimes, I
glance through the gap between my arm and the wall, and the drop
immediately concentrates my mind!

Zack! Zack! I ram the front points of my crampons into the steep
and rather hard white surface. At the same time, I take my weight on
my axe, the pick of which I press into the firn. With the other hand,
I thrust in the long pointed ice piton, though it will not penetrate
very far, so that I have to shorten my grip by putting a karabiner
in the ring of the piton. I am wearing my hard hat, of course, since
a small piece of ice or even a little stone could be fatal for a solo
climber!

Zack, Zack . . .

Zack, Zack . . .

Zack, Zack . . . the way down is endless.

After about an hour of this, I peer to see if there's anywhere to
rest. In vain. There is nothing. Everywhere, above and below me,
is steepness.

So, go on. Zack, Zack . . .

Zack, Zack . . .

Finally, I hack a stance out of the wall, and take a breather.

*

How long I spend, leaning there, I don't know. At first, I don't look
further than the snow in front of my nose. Then I try to estimate how
far there is still to go. But it's hard to say. Several hundred metres
below me the small hanging glacier projects like a ski jump, and
then, further down I see the valley floor, and out in the distance
the Hinter Grat hut. Once down on the hanging glacier, I should
have almost made it. It should be possible from there to traverse to
the bottom. Looking down, far beyond the points of my crampons,
I notice some rock islands which appear to be just above the small
hanging glacier. Could I rest there? But they are still a long, long
way down. I sigh, and start off again with increasingly painful calf
muscles. How different this descent is from my sunny climb this
morning.

Zack, Zack . . . another two steps . . .

I am in shadow, here, and it's cold – and gloomy. And the depth
doesn't want to come to an end.

Zack, Zack . . .

Can you ever get used to such monotony?

Is this how you lose attention . . . grow careless, don't give
a damn?

It must be like that – all of a sudden one of my crampons slips
and I am left hanging on the ice axe and the point of the ice piton.
Blood is hammering in my temples! I go rigid.

This face has been storing up even more suprises for me, I realise
now – black ice below me! Hell! That makes a difference.

Already on a steep ice face, it is even harder to go down than up.
Especially when it's smooth and sheer like this. And on black ice?
You need to have tried it to know what I mean – and not just for
a short section . . .

I prefer to chip handholds here, and even several small notches
for the front points of my crampons: that is not easy because the
axe only has a short handle, so that I have to bend right down to
fashion the notch for the next step. At the same time I am hanging
with my fingers to another nick in the wall – a handhold which needs
to be carefully chiselled out!

It is a lonely and acrobatic art, preparing this handhold, and the
next, and the next, making them bombproof, so they don't come
off under my weight when I'm hanging on them to carve the
next foothold below. I say lonely because, despite knowing that
the warden of the Hinter Grat hut is almost certainly watching

now, I have for the first time the sensation of being really alone. Nothing else in the world counts, except how to get down. Out of minutes, grow hours . . . I have slowed right down, I'm very slow. But the hanging glacier down below, that white El Dorado, which even looks flat from up here, has inched a little bit closer! Its surface, down there, is, for me, the earth to which I return. I am looking down more often now, estimating more often how much is left to do. Fatigue, tense muscles, the continuous need for acute concentration . . . all this suffering will fly away like a bird once I'm sitting down there in the snow! I keep thinking of this moment with anticipated pleasure.

Don't rush it, take time, be precise! The message keeps flashing in my brain. Yet the temptation to hurry grows with every minute. Suddenly, something catches my eye: forty metres below me a black rock projects from the wall, like a pulpit, like an upholstered chair! A resting place, a gift from nature, by good heaven!

It was my greatest discovery on this face – the 'easy chair' on the North Wall of the southern Zebru. A crazy invention, a cosmic joke: somewhere to sit in this relentless steepness, the only place to draw breath on the whole face.

I take advantage of its hospitality for, I guess, half an hour; sitting and looking, stretching my overtired muscles and relaxing completely – in the end I like it so much here that I feel it to be the most beautiful place in the whole world; and its only disadvantage is that I have to leave it. Still, the very presence of this heavenly pulpit, in the end made the wall seem a wee bit friendly.

Getting going again, after this long break, is a different matter. I am in high spirits, and the hanging glacier comes nearer. Here is the snow roof that leads to the bergschrund, but it's still separated from me by a steep cliff. I manage to climb down a short distance on rock and sheer ice – then the business seems too delicate. I bang in a belay piton. Will the doubled rope reach to the bottom? No! Hopeless. Well, then, how about single? I tie the rope to the piton and descend over ice slabs and broken rock. With a deep sigh of relief, I finally stand in the snow of the roof above the hanging glacier. A couple of chops at the rope with the ice axe – it's cut! I stuff the rest in my rucksack, (It's not normally my habit to be so brutal with ropes, but I'd had enough.)

Down now, down the sloping roof! Whew, I look forward to being able to sit down there in the snow. Still on all fours, I scramble down quickly – it is almost a joy to move here. Now I am at the upper lip of the bergschrund. Boy, that's a drop of all of five metres! But down there it's flat. The snow looks good, no ice. For a moment I hesitate. Then I jump. There's a flurry of powder; it's like landing on a feather bed. I sit and laugh and laugh, I am so happy. I have done it! I have done it!

All that remains now is to scamper down to the valley, and back down to the hut, to Fritz. I have so much to tell him!

For a moment, though, I stop at the bottom of the plinth, and look back up at the giant fin. Two firsts in a day: one up, one down! The summit and the abyss. Like the light and the dark side of the moon. I'll probably never do that again . . . not alone.

*

Even though I have climbed solo from time to time since then, hardly ever have I found myself forced to ask: Where is your place? The soloist experiences the entire might of the mountains, without the outline of someone else between him and his peak. So, he can go beyond limits which the presence of another would impose . . . But, in so doing, doesn't he run the risk of losing the measure of reality? Doesn't he build a surreal world for himself? What do people still mean to him?

Standing there at the foot of the Zebru face, it became clear to me again that my thoughts needed an echo . . . an altered, variegated echo – one which is not reflected just from a wall, but comes from the heart of another. I am no soloist.

*

While I was busy on Zebru, my friend Wolfi was in the Dolomites with his girlfriend – Wolfi Stefan from Vienna, my ropemate on almost all my climbs in the western and eastern Alps. We continued to be an indivisible partnership until our professional activities separated us. Amongst our friends there were some outstanding soloists; the one who most readily springs to mind was Dieter Marchart. We used to meet him often on the Peilstein, the outcrops in the Viennese Woods, and in other places, too. He climbed the Matterhorn North Face solo – in five hours, if I remember rightly. And then, he was hit by a pebble from the ice couloirs of the Eigerwand . . .

Wolfi Stefan and I have remained alive. Of course we have had our full share of luck. But we never envied the soloists their adventures.

I think of the Eiger: how much it meant to both of us to be roped to someone we'd known for years, finding the way together through stonefall, bad weather, and the vertical maze of slate which makes up this forbidding wall. Someone to lessen the hardship of bivouacs, to share a laugh with . . . Seeing plans come to fruition, and the joy of your friend, too, when you are blessed with success . . . All that, the soloist misses out on.

Perhaps some do it only because they have not yet found the right companion . . .

*

Having fallen asleep in the Pfundser Tschy meadows, I am awakened suddenly by two small boys wanting to know how the aeroplane's rudder works. I do my best and, not entirely satisfied, eventually they leave. The rudder, it must have been, which was responsible for that descending spiral we made, that weird spiral staircase ride that brought us to this place.

The sun is pleasurably warm . . . and soon I am dozing off again . . .

Séracs! A spinning icefall! Oh my, everything is going round again – at top speed. But what are all these shining towers? Crystal shapes of ice. What's happening here, Charlie? Oh-oh! that's not Charlie, that's Jay at the controls. He is a Californian who lives in Courmayeur near the foot of Mont Blanc, and he often goes flying. I met him once, guiding: a blond, open-faced lad. He flings the plane into another steep turn, laughing with excitement. The motor roars and the Brenva Face arches over in front of us like a spinnaker before a storm. Now the Aiguille Noire rotates above us, its pointed silhouette an immense dark crystal in the sky. Beyond it, barely moving at all, is Mont Blanc. My Mont Blanc.

Crystals from Mont Blanc

The dream bursts like a soap bubble. I am lying in the meadow, my eyes open now, unable to shake Mont Blanc from my mind. That summit – I did not reach it whenever I wanted; and when I went crystal-hunting there, would frequently return empty-handed – but what matter! I love that big white mountain.

Its beautiful Peuterey Ridge – which I consider the finest route in all the Alps – resembles a sequence of crystals rising from the valley. Eight kilometres of climbing it offers, if you follow the skyline with all its indentations. The first – dark – crystal is the Aiguille Noire with its stunning upwards stab; next, after a clutch of slender needles, comes the white, three-pointed Aiguille Blanche, more than 4000 metres high. Finally, the rhythmical line steepens from the Col de Peuterey to a shimmering crescendo, the dome of Mont Blanc itself, 4810 metres. A magic silhouette.

No, we didn't reach the summit the last time I was there, though we spent five days on that great ridge. In my mind's eye, I am still there.

The Aiguille Noire, steep and black like the prow of a ship, cleaves the storm winds. That's how it seems to me, looking down at the banners of cloud rising sharply from its crest. We are clinging to the ridge, surrounded by the rushing, roaring waves of tempest; tatters of cloud scurry and merge in whirling circles of light at the snow's edge.

Sepp, Walter, Edith. 'Never saw the Peuterey so wild, so powerful,' I shout to them over the wind. 'I hope we'll be able to make the Col today.' We have already endured one bivouac. Conditions up here at 4000 metres on the Aiguille Blanche could hardly be worse: fresh snow everywhere on the rocks and it is so cold – it may be only September, but – heavens! – it's like winter.

I remember Edith's creased face this morning; we had tucked her between us for protection through the long hours of the bivouac, and a chill breeze blew in steadily from the west all night. A crust of frost crept over our shoulders and 'ice flowers' blossomed on the stones all around . . . Soon our faces were numb and our bodies stiff . . . we sat out the night on our stone 'bench' above the swelling clouds.

Lightning flashed above the distant Dauphiné peaks – a firework display lasting for hours. Anxiously, I watched the ocean of fire at just the same height as ourselves, willing it to stay where it was. How far away was that? What was the strength and direction of the wind? Bloody hell, we'd be in deep trouble if we had to move from here, down on to the steep slopes! Luckily, the storm finally blew itself out far behind the Barre des Ecrins . . . and the clouds were swaying again, gently up and down, as if the whole gliding coverlet of light and darkness was breathing under the touch of the moon. And we sat on, stiffly, listening to the low whisper of the air around us, watching the crystals grow, and huddling ever closer to one another.

Hours went by.

Something suddenly shook me from my icy torpor; a nocturnal phenomenon I shall never forget. Behind the palely gleaming Gran Paradiso – right in front of us, really close – a round, puffy tower of cloud emerges from nowhere, slowly, steadily, growing all the time. Menacing and cold in the moonlight . . . like a nuclear mushroom. And then it lights up, illuminated from within by the flickers of lightning . . . and nearby, another mushroom rises, and over there, another . . . a whole colony of strange, expanding figures peers over the Gran Paradiso at us. Panic seized me: if they stepped over the crest, we would be done for. And with all my might, I begged the soft west wind to resist them: Do not desert us now, I pleaded. Fear is far too frail a word to describe how it feels to be crouched among the rocks, waiting for the next lightning strike . . . and then the next . . . and the next, the shock running through your limbs . . . and the next. Each one perhaps your last. You never forget that! Many years ago, down there, on the Noire – just below its black summit – we survived eight thunderstorms, one after the other: that was Tona, Terenzio, Sepp, Walter, Bianca and me. Tona suffered deep burns to her palms and heels; our down jackets were spattered with black spots from the sparks. For two days we counted the seconds in those electric clouds.

The big mushroom grows a hat, elongates, stretches eastwards; it becomes a giant ship, gliding across the Aosta valley, lit up repeatedly by sudden internal flashes. I take a deep breath. And then I think of Tona, who was my wife at the time we were fighting for survival in the firestorm on the Aiguille Noire. She still goes to the mountains, on expeditions too, even though we are not together any more. Perhaps, whenever she looks at the Aiguille Noire, she feels as I do. People who have been through something like that can never really separate. And, besides, there are our two daughters – we love them so much.

The great cloud ship had sailed away. 'How are we doing, troops?' I broke the silence. Walter, and Sepp and his wife, were cowering at my side. 'All right . . . but how about changing places? It's your turn to sit on the side of the wind.' We changed places. 'What about making some tea?' We made tea. They go on for ever, September nights.

No more lightning shimmer. Anywhere. All gone. The fear was spent, the danger over. I had not sat on such a fine granite bench in a long while, with its ringside view over the cloudfields. What we had been through! What a fantastic night!

When daytime came at last, it brought a storm wind. The air was biting. On our way once more, now we were crossing the three heads of the Aiguille Blanche to reach the Col de Peuterey. We were moving at the shining edges of snow, past the curled ribbons of overhanging cornices, muffled in cloud, in an arabesque of light and shade. At times, when you touch the snow, or twist in an ice-screw, when you are waiting and belaying, you wonder how long this storm can last. One minute it gets fiercer, the next brings a lull. Mont Blanc looms ahead – immense. Squalls buffet its rocks. Glistening veils are sucked at fantastic speed up into the blue sky. We are going to have to bivouac on the col! There's no alternative: a snowhole in a bank on the saddle. Sitting on a ledge carved out of snow. We stay there for two whole days . . .

No way up! Even after that. Fresh snow lying waist-high. Higher up, the storm continues its raging. Good old Mont Blanc . . . Though the sky is an intense blue, it is midwinter here. We opt for retreat: abseil down the Gruber rocks. Five hundred metres to the bottom – many hours. We come across the old abseil slings left by Walter Bonatti, Pierre Mazeaud and their companions when they were fleeing from the Frêney Pillar – even find some cut pieces of a harness. Only three of those seven men survived the descent. We abseil down on their slings . . . a long day behind us. We did not make it to the top. It does not matter.

*

A tractor rattles through the Pfundser Tschy, climbing up-valley. It is towing a long trailer. Then I see Charlie, waving. An hour later and our red and white flying machine has been completely dismantled and loaded aboard: we jolt down the mountain valley. Soon the beer mugs are clinking at Innsbruck Airport: Charlie's friends. '*Prosit*! Cheers! To your second birthday!' And this time, Charlie does not have to say it in English. Tired out, we slink off to his house to sleep. Life, that by rights should have ended, goes on. Nothing is predictable. And as I slowly drop off to sleep, I reflect on the phone call I made home to Italy, and the unexpected reception I received. 'What in God's name possessed you to go flying? You're never home – and then you go and nearly get yourself killed!'

Why, I wonder, did I marry again? A person like me, always off somewhere, up to something – heart in the mountains, sworn to adventure – I had no business embarking on it in the first place. That seems to be what most people think.

Maybe they have a point – in principle.

But there is this alleyway – I can still see (and smell) it – with its aroma of fresh bread. A dark passage near the bakery in Via Santo Stefano: the arcades, cars jolting over cobbled streets, students strolling to the university . . . a complete mélange of colour, skittishness, calm and vivacity . . . a spirit, indeed, which permeates the whole town, this town below its pair of silhouetted towers, le Due Torri, pointing obliquely into the sky. As if designed by a drunken architect, they lean towards each other, symbols of Bologna's friendliness.

At the end of the dark passageway lives Teresa. She is a student. Of the many students in Bologna, she is special. She *always* looks at you with such calm and disarming candour, and always says exactly what she thinks. Her eyes are huge and dark, and her features finely drawn. She wants to become a judge. Or a lawyer . . . Shouldn't a man know to beware of a woman with ambitions like that? In principle, yes. But some men choose to live dangerously, or at least find themselves drawn towards exposed situations. I felt drawn towards Teresa, this Teresa who wanted to become a judge.

Those eyes were not on me for more than five minutes before subjecting me to an intense scrutiny; she was like a judge who, having first glanced around the people in the courtroom, tries to put himself into the psyche of the accused. '*Tu sei un po puttano,*' she announced. Those were her first words to me. They cannot be translated literally. To be a bit *puttano* means to be no real upholder of moral values! I was lost for words. '*Le puttane di Bologna*' are famous throughout Italy, those 'easy women' who line the avenues of town – and (occasionally) other roads and squares of importance as well. They are as much part of Bologna as its leaning towers. Well, *puttano* might not be exactly their male equivalent but, certainly, if a woman calls you this, she cannot be thinking you the most upright of fellows! So, I was dumbfounded. And wondered if she could be right . . . It unnerved me that such a judgment should be reached on sight; and then articulated to my face – but it did induce me to look again into those dark big eyes, so calmly regarding me with an expression almost of irony and mockery . . .

Who was this woman who spoke to me in this way?

We married.

Teresa loves nature, the rays of the sun, and the flowers; and she has endless patience. Without it, she would never have been able to put up with me. When I think how little I am at home . . . Teresa is no mountaineer, but sometimes she comes with me – perhaps to hunt for crystals on Mont Blanc.

There is, for instance, a huge boulder, as tall as a house, just above the raspberry patches near the torrent of Dora Baltea. Nobody would imagine you could find crystals there! But there is a good chance you may. Unfortunately, now, a number of people know about it, but on my first visit there, I was amazed to find myself in front of a wall of crystals – beautiful smoky quartz. My daughter Hildegard was with me, and we christened this boulder the Treasure Chamber. It was marvellous, like a shrine. The great pity was, it did not remain a secret . . . From the very start, the evidence of hammer and chisel marks showed that at least one other person knew of its existence. And he must have noticed our presence too, perhaps within days, for the next time we returned, large chunks of the crystal wall had gone. From then on we were like two mice, taking turns to gnaw at the same piece of cheese. And since the spot was so close to the footpath leading to the Dalmazi hut, our activity could not possibly pass unnoticed. There are still many crystals in the Treasure Chamber, even today, but being inside the rock, they require a lot of work to extract. Who knows how many gems are revealed each year on the faces of the big White Mountain? Whenever the cold fractures the rocks.

There are prisms of pure quartz, absolutely transparent – white or rose, or tawny-coloured – tapering to hexagonal pyramids. Hunting for them becomes a real passion, hard to explain. Finding them brings even more excitement and happiness than possessing them; I have given many to my friends. However, it is a pity when such an exceptional boulder as the Treasure Chamber cannot be protected, unscathed. It never really had a chance, with the footpath so close. In the upper basin of a major Mont Blanc glacier, I have found similar rocks, covered in a lawn of crystals – myriads of flashing spikes – and only looked at them. You always know that what you take home are only fragments, that it is better just to move your head and enjoy the thousand-fold sparkle. Nature protects these blocks well up there: ice avalanches threaten the place, and very few people can reach it.

Several even more remote places exist among the wildest faces of Mont Blanc, which hardly anyone knows, and far from any route. No one lets on about them. The two Ollier brothers from Courmayeur, who in the past have brought home smoky quartz crystals of up to half a metre in length, only go out searching for them in the very worst weather, in fog, or at night . . . when nobody can see them. Mario, the cook at the Scoiattolo refuge, where I used to hang out in the light-hearted days when Orazia and Annie ran it, once imagined he had picked up a whiff of their trail. 'Kurt,' he whispered to me, 'yesterday someone spotted the two Olliers on the Dent du Géant, and at the Aiguilles Marbrées – and it occurred to me we ought to take a crawl into the bergschrund there.' Needless to say, Mario is an obsessed crystal hunter. I was not optimistic: plenty of people have attempted to locate secret Ollier-haunts, without success. However, Mario felt sure this was a hot tip . . . It might work, I reasoned, since erosion is always bringing new crystals to the light of day. If the brothers had been seen there, well . . . Soon, we had inflamed each other with dreams of crystal-lined chasms . . .

Full of expectation we approached the place, but wherever we stuck our noses, we found nothing. Finally, above the fabled bergschrund, I noticed an enigmatic hole in the wall. Using ice-screws, crampons and rope, we got ourselves up to it, and I placed a belay piton at the edge of a small cave. Fortunately, it was a solid, nay a very solid piton. Mario was digging like a mole in the hole. Nothing! Still, you are always hearing of people giving up just inches before striking a lucky vein . . . we were not going to let that happen to us! Next it was my turn, then Mario's again . . . each buoyed by our commonly woven crystal fantasies. After two hours, at last we are convinced we must be looking in the wrong place, and give up.

Half crouched at the entrance of the hole, I start belaying Mario's descent. I cannot see him, nor have I any idea how fast he is likely to go. For all I remember now, this may well have been the first time we climbed together. Suddenly, I hear him shout: '*Io vado*! I go!' And the rope snakes through my fingers like a bally trout-fisher's line. My goodness, but these Aostan guys are quick: he must be running down the wall! No, something is wrong! I brace myself . . . and almost immediately comes a gigantic jolt! From way down I hear a plaintive '*Porca miseria*!' and, craning towards the sound, I see Mario hanging in his celebrated bergschrund and wriggling like a frog. He must have slipped the minute he uttered his '*Io vado*'.

To this day, Mario's friends still tease him about his '*Aostan speed*' and his '*Io vado*'. Slowly, we made our way back to Courmayeur – with empty sacks.

Next morning, Alessio Ollier winks at me, 'I hear you had a productive day up there!' I mumble something and we go for a drink. Of course I never stoop to ask him where his secret spot is. He would not give me a straight answer, anyway. But the day will come when I discover for myself where he found his giant black Mont Blanc topaz . . . at night, and in the fog.

*

Fortune can smile on you unexpectedly: this I discover with my wife Teresa on the Triolet Glacier. We are at 2800 metres, skipping happily across little streams and crevasses, when suddenly we are rooted to the spot: in front of us, as if set there by magic, is a pyramid of granite, as tall as a man, and on top of it the most beautiful crystals. Rose-coloured, clear, shining in the sunlight . . . a fairytale splendour! '*Fantastico*,' murmurs Teresa, entranced.

Together we consider the best way to detach the upper part of the pyramid without breaking or chipping the individual crystals, which are several inches long. For two hours I chisel away, with lots of helpful advice from my wife – we even put sticking plaster over each crystal in an attempt to minimise vibrations and stop the tops splintering off.

A yippee of joy! The whole upper crust of the rock comes off without breaking! It is a big block, only just portable . . . but I don't want to tempt fate any more with the hammer. There follows a hard and heavy descent to the valley with a thunderstorm at the end of it. And to cap it all, Teresa sprains her ankle. By the time I get wife and druse down safely, I am exhausted.

Some of the magic comes back whenever we look at the stone.

The next time Teresa and I go there, little Ceci, our son, rides on my back, complete with cradle, up to the Miage Glacier lake . . . and it brings back memories of my father carrying me with him when he went hunting for mushrooms in the steep Austrian forests. Ceci gazed wide-eyed at the mountains, and they looked down on him . . .

Mont Blanc has given me many crystals – and not all of them quartz. There have been those flowers of ice which the wind sometimes fashions on rocks, and the gift of crystal-clear days; there have been thoughts which could never have come to me elsewhere – whether sheer fantasy, or endowed with the clarity of decision. And friendship, happiness and, perhaps, luck.

Will we ever know all that is contained in a crystal?

At the spectrum's other end, during those four storm days on the Peuterey Ridge, when the force of the air had staved in the wall of our bivouac, all of us nursed a secret fear of how it would end. But fear and uncertainty have their place in mountaineering, every bit as much as joy and luck. Life in the mountains is heightened, in all senses: it brings enhanced happiness and pleasure, as well as increased risk and the fear of losing all. It is an extreme way of living, but once you are used to it, you can never give it up.

*

There are a number of very peculiar treasures which came to me from Mont Blanc: Franz Lindner and I, climbing the Peuterey Ridge *intégrale* in autumn 1958, filmed the whole traverse in 16 mm, an ambitious undertaking for two men, which had never succeeded before (nor has since). After five days we sat on top of

Mont Blanc at midnight, with Franz saying, 'What a pity it's over – I've grown quite used to living on the ridge.' The documentary earned my first-ever film award, at the Trento Festival. The lucky streak continued when in 1971 a photo of Aiguille Noire in storm clouds (see endpapers) presented me with a wonderful surprise – and that is a story in itself: at a friend's suggestion, I had entered the picture in a mountain photography competition in Munich – a big event with no fewer than 15,000 entries from around the world. Then I forgot about it and continued roaming around Europe in my old car – a ten-year-old Beetle with a respectable 300,000 kilometres on the clock. When it started letting in the rain, I drilled a hole in the bottom and solved the problem (Austrian vehicle testing has always been more lenient than in Germany). That old car ran and ran, until the day it would run no longer. It was the end, this time, no doubts about it. I rolled it into an Italian orchard, took the numberplate for a souvenir, and rang my father. 'Don't worry, my boy,' he told me. 'You had a letter today . . . you've just won yourself a brand-new BMW 1800! For a picture of Mont Blanc, it said. Must be some sort of competition.' The Grand Prize, it was, no less.

I was speechless as I put the receiver down, and my legs went wobbly. But I soon got over it, and continued my vagabond travels with 'Filippo' (as my daughter Karen christened the new car), and somehow it always remained linked to Mont Blanc in my mind – especially as I would regularly bring the mechanic a crystal whenever I brought it in for its annual MOT. Eventually, I clocked up more than 300,000 kilometres in that jalopy as well.

Filippo's end, when it came, also had a twist in the tail. After many repairs, it was clear that my dear old friend would not get through even an Austrian vehicle check, forcing me to a sad decision. With heavy heart I drove the sorry heap to the scrap merchant's, but it was already late and the yard was closed. Parking Filippo outside, I bade a sentimental farewell and went home. In the middle of the night I was startled awake by the telephone. 'I'm sorry to have to tell you,' an official voice said, 'your car has been run into by a drunk-driver – he's not hurt, fortunately, but the vehicle's a write-off.'

Nothing but a cloud of rust in the road . . . be *assured*, dear reader, that sudden end was the best for Filippo (and for me)! I retrieved a piece of headlight from the ruins and nailed it to my wall. It has the same curve as a horseshoe – a lucky horseshoe from Mont Blanc (you could say that, I think, after so incredible a story!).

*

Many years have passed since my first visit to Mont Blanc on Grandfather's bicycle, when I was twenty. Setting eyes on the white dome in July 1953, I had no idea that later on I would be linked to it professionally . . . The course my life took simply confirmed that I cannot live without the peaks, without feeling their breath close, or at least returning to their shade: after graduation at the University of Commerce in Vienna and five years of teaching at the Academy of International Tourism in Salzburg I turned the rudder through 180 degrees and became a mountain guide! Good old Kuno Rainer, the celebrated Peter Habeler and young Klaus Hoi were my examiners. That was in Austria, of course, but mostly I plied my trade in the Mont Blanc massif. I met with no jealousy from the local guides, since as often as not I turned up with my client from abroad. Sometimes, when an expedition came up suddenly, I would even pass him over to them.

Of my guiding experiences there, I could write a separate book. This kaleidoscope of local and imported characters created a special frame for my mountain, a world of its own . . . There was Don Pino, the 'Don Camillo' with his holiday camp for young people in the Val Ferret, just below the Grandes Jorasses . . . how many toasts did we drink in his favourite blackberry schnapps! Or Dr Bassi – the Courmayeur physician, another daredevil pilot – for whom, after he turned his plane on its nose, the guides created the limerick, 'Sooner or later with Dottor Bassi, you'll find yourself between "quattro assi"' – between four boards! (That is to cast no aspersions on his medical credentials: he is a very fine doctor, and has saved the lives of a number of mountaineers). We have met him before in this book – he is the pilot who dragged his heels at opening the door of his plane to allow me to take pictures of the landscape. Or Wanda, secretary of the local tourist office, who wanted so badly to know what it was like on the pointed tip of the Dent du Géant. She found out (with me) – but there, at 4000 metres above the sea, on a spot no bigger than a table, in the clouds, with a vertical drop of at least 1000 metres all round, was so overwhelmed, she could not stand upright – and on top of everything, suddenly wanted to spend a penny! Thank God, this mountain has two tops, so that I could retreat to the other, after establishing a complicated belay. Last, but not least, of all those many clients from outside Italy – one in particular I should not forget . . . though I have yet to guide him to the top of Mont Blanc. Never mind, Axel, I *shall* . . .

Whatever I say here, I like him enormously. How terrible the world would be if there were no critical journalists – people would simply do what they wanted without regard for others. It can be really bad if somebody big and influential hogs the media. What a good thing that free writers exist, like Axel Thorer. He has an original style, beyond imitation, for puncturing such inflated characters. How much they care depends on whether they have the hide of a hippopotamus or are sensitive mimosa blossoms. Axel himself, who has to be prepared to take as good as he dishes out, is one of the more resilient pachyderms. And not without some anxiety, I fear he will take me at my word one day and want to be guided to the summit of Mont Blanc. Why? He doesn't strike you as someone to lose his balance: he is as stout and upright as the sea-lion in the Salzburg House of Nature, and his handlebar moustache looks strong enough to hang ice axes from at each end – but supposing this mighty Axel should topple . . . All my three-point anchor belays would be as nothing – it would only remain for someone to put two nice 'crystals' on to our tombs in the valley . . . for once Axel is at full velocity nothing and no one can stop him. (We will find that out later in the book.)

*

Mont Blanc is not far from where I actually live, and there have been years when every season would find me on the faces or ridges of this great mountain massif. Even in the Himalaya, I am conscious that Mont Blanc is *the* alpine peak to bear comparison. This mountain, which has never released its hold over me, is the epitome of a great peak to me – in the same way that when I think of a climbing partnership, it is always Wolfi Stefan who springs to mind; with him I made most of my alpine climbs. No less important than the fascinating structure of rock and ice is a good understanding with your companion – such as I enjoyed with Wolfi in the Alps and – many years later, in the Himalaya – with Julie Tullis, the other half of my 'film crew'. In both cases we formed inseparable partnerships, linked by the rope. It is true that to find happiness on a mountain, you need more than simply a fine peak.

There is something else, too, which keeps bringing you back to the mountains, and which is almost impossible to explain: I call it their secrets. That something you feel when you see a tremendous sunset up there, or when you find yourself enveloped in a powerful storm . . . The peak, the companion, and those secrets – their merging into an entity is the real heart of it. That is what makes a person return, time and again.

Strolling through the Val Veni below Mont Blanc, I am aware of the smell of flowers, the rush of the torrent – I pick up a lump of quartz, and the sun shines through it . . . a luminous piece of Mont Blanc! And strangely, as I hold the stone against the light, a small hover-fly lights on my finger, as if to say: Hey! Don't forget me, I'm part of Mont Blanc, too.

*

These are the Mont Blanc crystals: a mosaic of years, people, experiences – which is still evolving. Before I began going to the Himalaya year after year, this place had become my second mountain home. My first? That was the high ranges of the Hohe Tauern near Salzburg. There, the crystal-hunting boy climbed his first summit, and stared with awe at distant peaks and the horizon that bore a question to be answered. But 'Only the Spirits of the Air know what you will meet behind the mountains' – the proverb proved true yet again: on the Brenva Face and the Peuterey Ridge I carried a movie camera, without knowing what my later career would be. It had its roots on Mont Blanc, but then, all of a sudden, I plunged more deeply into the business of filming and it opened up all kinds of adventures, beyond the mountains . . .

PART TWO

The magic carpet

The man sitting opposite me was clearly something of a character. As he spoke I noticed how he emphasised each word with flashes of his dark, somewhat slanting eyes. And, as I listened, I tried to think what it was he reminded me of. He was unusually tall, and extremely thin – and in that overcrowded Italian roadside restaurant he towered over his colourful and noisy surroundings; it was as if an ostrich had dropped in for dinner at a chicken farm. The strong bird-like resemblance was reinforced by a relatively small head. Mario Allegri wore his hair crew cut and an immaculately tailored corduroy suit. His movements were spare and contained, but impressive none the less by virtue of his size. He did not fit my preconception of an 'adventurer' in the least, although friends had told me at one of my Milan lectures how he had been several times to South America with Walter Bonatti. This was after Bonatti, the famous Italian mountaineer, had given up guiding in favour of a life of all-round adventure; he worked now as a features photographer for *Epoca* magazine. Mario Allegri lived, when he was at home, in Milan, but you could tell from his face and those unusual eyes that he was not pure Italian. He told me later that his family tree included a grandmother from the Mato Grosso.

My table companion, it soon transpired, had already organised several filming expeditions of his own. He had little patience, he told me, with large teams, for they would inevitably include someone who found the strain of adventure intolerable.

'Can you work with an Arriflex?' he demanded suddenly, the dark eyes scrutinising me keenly.

Arriflex, eh? The camera of professionals: you have to know

it really well to get good results. My brother-in-law, Herbert Raditschnig, uses one all the time, and I'd seen it of course, but . . . A voice inside was warning, 'Kurt, this is your big chance. Don't blow it!' Mario was clearly looking for a one-man film-crew, who wouldn't be put off by danger or difficulty. And me? I wanted a springboard to the wider, adventurous world, wanted to get to know it not only as a mountaineer. 'Play it very carefully,' my voice whispered, as the question still hung in the air. 'If you want that job, don't give any hint of weakness!'

'Of course,' I replied, hoping I was pitching the right tone of confidence, 'of course I can work with an Arriflex.'

'*Benissimo*. All we have to do, then, is find one.'

'Well, it's true I don't have my own,' I ventured, 'but – given the right advance, of course – I'd be prepared to get one.'

I got the advance. Now I was an adventure cameraman! I could have leapt for joy. The fact that, apart from the camera, I would get nothing out of the enterprise, bothered me not one jot. I had the whole world at my feet, a totally new horizon. This would be the magic carpet to waft us from continent to continent . . .

Every day I practised with my new camera – new to me, that is: it was second-hand, of course, a well-preserved memento from an old Tibet hand.

At last the great moment arrived. The smallest film unit in the world set off from Milan, Mario and I: he the actor, and I the rest. And if we turned out not to be the smallest, certainly we would be the most 'adventurous'. First stop: Scandinavia.

Blind man's buff

Dandelions are blooming in Copenhagen. In Oslo everything is green. A wonderful town, I think, as we touch down. In the waiting room a TV-screen shows us snowploughs shovelling wall-like mounds of snow . . . Funny, I think, to be showing winter films now. Where is that? 'Oh, way up north,' A Norwegian passenger smiles reassuringly. 'A long way from here!' But could it be where we are heading, I wonder? More than likely.

A two-hour flight will take us to Tromsö . . . it is dark as we take off, and we see nothing of the mighty fjords and the many islands, nor the deeply troughed valleys of this ancient ice-fashioned landscape. We will look at it, when our magic carpet will be carrying us on to England and Newfoundland . . .

By and by, as we approach the Arctic Circle, dawn starts breaking . . . in the soft half-light we swoop along the Tromsö airstrip, whipping up sprays of grey ice. Whhoarrr, it's cold here! Midwinter! Soon we are in the air again, on our way to Alta: nothing to see but snow, snow and more snow – it might as well be Christmas! The sweltering heat of Milan, the dandelion meadows of Copenhagen seem surreal now, with this hummocky white landscape beneath us. Only the fjord water remains unfrozen – everything else is buried under deep drifts. No wonder the Scandinavian television was full of it.

We are well kitted out: you have to be prepared for anything on a world tour such as ours. Our boots and high gaiters, for instance, essential in deep snow, will serve as well in the jungle, and might even prove useful at sea – it is purely a matter of style and personal preference. Only in the desert might we find them too hot, despite their obvious protective qualities against cactus spines and rattlesnakes. But that's a long way from this – soon we will be with the reindeer, in the Land of Reindeer. Lapland is full of reindeer, every child knows that. The Lapps centre their lives around reindeer. They eat reindeer meat, make tools and other household objects from reindeer horns, and only keep a few small, rough-haired horses in order to be able to maintain control over their enormous herds of reindeer . . . I can remember the geography lesson clearly. I suppose they don't run around dressed entirely in reindeer fur, but they surely sit on it. And the tents of this nomadic people will consist of birch-pole frames with reindeer-skin canopies pulled over them, and more skins stuffed into the gaps to keep out the draughts.

We eat reindeer schnitzels in Alta's little airport restaurant. Dark meat – very tasty – and surprisingly expensive. There are antlers all over the walls – reindeer, naturally. 'We should be able to wrap up here in two days,' Mario tells me. The publisher who has commissioned the film is not after an in-depth scientific documentary, rather a series of glimpses of different places around the world, all featuring Mario as their (well-paid) hero. (To be fair, he incurs a lot of expenses in the process.) It is to be a publicity film, and, as such, needs to be as colourful and multifaceted as we can make it. I call it the Magic Carpet since – besides taking Mario and me 30,000 kilometres, halfway around the globe – it must be woven in stripes of white, green and red – ice, jungle, and, perhaps, desert. Mario wants it finished as soon as possible . . . whereas I wish it could go on for ever. It seems such a pity to grab everything we need here in only two days. I so much wanted to reach the North Cape, to see more of the country . . . but to picture Mario with a herd of reindeer and a Lapp or two, whether I like it or not, cannot be blown up into a big production. Already, I envisage the first strip of the magic carpet: white, with black polka dots, like a punch card, or a spotted cravat . . . the dots being the reindeer, of course. I cannot resist a sigh at an enterprise more Laputan than Lappish.

Lunch over, Mario asks our host, 'Where are all the reindeer around here?' Instead of the prompt reply he was expecting, the man scratches his head reflectively before announcing at length that we would probably do best to drive to Karasjok. 'You're bound to find some there. It's a Lapp town . . . and all the animals belong to them.' A town? With houses? Well, we shouldn't be surprised: time does not stand still anywhere. We'll just have to find a way of rustling up a few tents from somewhere. Fancy having to drive more than 200 kilometres for the nearest guaranteeable reindeer herd! Mario pulls a sour face, but I am jubilant. Aha! I tell myself. See how it is: an Italian in Norway expecting to see lots of reindeer is no different from the American tourist thinking he'll find everyone wearing chamoix brushes in Austria and Lederhosen in Bavaria. Maybe I'll get to the North Cape yet, who knows? Except, of course, that Karasjok is in the opposite direction, almost on the Finnish border. Our host observes that if only we had landed in Lakselv, we would now need to drive just seventy kilometres. What's the odds? We need a rental car anyway. And soon we find one: an old black Beetle, somewhat rusty. 'You'll find two winter tyres and chains inside,' the car's owner tells us.

'We'll not be wanting those for just 200 kilometres,' Mario remarks under his breath, adding, 'I used to be a test-driver, you know.' And we were off!

Piles of snow everywhere, the road itself is really wintry. Mario drives like an Italian in summer. This must be what you call an occupational hazard, I think to myself and hang on grimly.

But soon I understand: Mario really can drive. Even with summer tyres in winter. I still have a lot to learn about my companion in adventure. So, how do you make small talk with a test-driver? 'I was with Ferrari,' Mario explains laconically, and lets the car glide round another bend. Hills are passing by, cloaked in birch saplings, all sticking out gauntly from the snow, and finally there comes a flat plain. The road is dead straight and Mario steps on the gas. He is a true artist, and I tell myself you should never begrudge an artist. Soon we have covered a hundred kilometres – halfway – and all I hope, as Mario begins telling me chapters of his life's story, is that we don't encounter an icy patch . . . What did I learn about him? Everything has slipped my memory, but for one moment. And that I see and hear as clearly as if it was happening right now: Mario had just remarked that test-driving was only one episode in his professional quest for adventure, 'There was that business with Walter Bonatti . . .' he says, pausing for dramatic effect at the very moment we start a slide towards the edge of the road. Oooop, over we go, plunging down in a cloud of snow. We can see nothing, seem to be swimming . . . I cling to the doorhandle, feel a blow on my knee – and that's it – we have stopped. Silence. A rather exaggerated dramatic pause our storyteller made there, but he appears completely unmoved. 'These things happen,' he continues after the interruption; I, meanwhile, rub my bashed knee. We are stuck in deep snow, some six metres from the road.

I don't answer.

'Won't have done the car any harm,' Mario comments. 'German workmanship.'

'You're sure of that?' I grind my teeth, still hugging my knee, tempted to remark that while the car might be German, it's the bloody Italian stuntman's work that has brought us to this. Better to swallow it. At least we have not turned over. As we eventually scrabble our way out, I enquire wearily whether many of Mario's test runs proved as demanding as this.

'Oh, much harder,' he assures me. 'This was just a minor derailing – come on, put your back in it, push!' That's never going to move, I think, as I strain against the vehicle. And nor does it. The car will not budge an inch. We are stuck.

I am just wondering how we come to be having such bad luck on the very first day of our trip, when I notice the '13' on the car's numberplate. Usually I consider that my lucky number – have done so ever since making the thirteenth ascent of the Eigerwand.

(Even when it later turned out to be the fifteenth!) At least, we can now be sure of an extra two days in Scandinavia! Thoughtfully, I regard the car: everything depends on how you look at it – even the number 13 . . .

Mario hunts for a shovel in the boot and, failing to find one, swears, '*Porca miseria!*' I am still weighing the mysteries of numbers – can any number be luckier or unluckier than others? A superstitious pessimist would have no doubts that was why we came off the road. I am just about to ask Mario whether in Italy test-pilots regard 13 as a good or bad omen when . . . tuck, tuck, tuck . . . across the solitude of this wintry landscape comes the welcome chug of a tractor. It is our lucky day after all! Apart from two snowploughs and five cars, we hadn't seen any other vehicle since we started. We beam delightedly at the tractor-driver as if he were the Redeemer himself . . . Mario jabbers away in Italian and English, I, at the same time, in German – but anyone can see what has befallen us. The man shakes his head, winks, clucks his tongue and mumbles something we, in our turn, cannot understand. Eventually, he clambers from his vehicle and produces a length of rope. I suppose he must be used to this sort of thing. Within minutes, the Beetle gently breasts the surface of the snow – leading its cloven wake like a swan on Lake Constance – and is returned to the road.

Mario drove on with considerably more caution, and in the small town of Lakselv we stopped to put on the winter tyres. Clouds covered the sky, engulfing everything in monochromous grey. We were still surrounded by thousands of birch trees. This was an incredibly lonely landscape, yet one of haunting beauty. I still could not get over how we had stepped from Italy's summer into this deepest of deep winters. Such abrupt transformations throw your feelings into havoc. We were in boisterous spirits, one adventure behind us already, and all the time drawing nearer to the enormous reindeer herds of Karasjok. Every so often I would peer concentratedly into the murk, to see if I could make out any of the animals yet.

Then, all of a sudden, after a bend in the road, the village materialised ahead: small houses, a neat red-roofed church, people. Not a reindeer in sight, anywhere. An old man was sitting on a stool beside a pile of antlers, carving . . . Taking a deep breath, we approached and enquired, with the liberal aid of sign language, where all the animals were. The Lapp smiled, reordering the crinkles on his friendly old face; sometimes nodding at our gesticulations, then he waved expansively towards the open landscape . . .

Not here, did he mean? Not now, or not at all? We pressed him again. The gesture was repeated with more precision. He pointed to the north, saying something that sounded like 'North Cape'. The reindeer were certainly not here: that much was clear. They were either at the cape or on their way there. Mario's face darkened for a moment, while I showed no emotion. Then, shrugging, my friend conceded: 'I guess that means we head for the North Cape. Come on.' Two hundred kilometres, and a ferry ride! Oh, Lapland, Land of Reindeer!

Just then, a small boy, who had been called over by the old man, tugged at my sleeve, pointing up the road . . . Full of expectation we followed him to a courtyard, where there really was a reindeer! The only one in all Karasjok, but here only because it was sick – so we understood from the many signs and words of a kindly Lapp woman in a red bonnet. I was ready with my camera to film Mario, the ailing reindeer and the helpful woman with her round and friendly face. But he would have none of it: 'It's not what we want at all,' he snapped, and his short hair appeared to bristle even more than usual. 'Come on, let's get out of here!'

Karasjok had indeed proved a disappointment – for Mario. Soon, we were racing along again at test-speed. Back towards Lakselv, where we had just come from. For it was clear that we would not reach the North Cape that day.

*

Honningsvog. Colourful houses, red, yellow, green, even blue, overlooked the grey, wide expanse of fjord, surrounded by rounded rocky hills. The mirrored images of the ships danced a weaving pattern of broken lines and colour-splashes on the water's surface. The ferryboat, which had brought us to this island of Mageroy, was tethered to the jetty. A Norwegian we met explained to us that the reindeer were able to swim across this narrow strait separating the island from the mainland. With dismay, we learned that they had done so only a couple of days ago and were now roaming somewhere in the mountains of the island. We might be able to find them, but only with luck on our side. We had simply arrived a few days too late.

So better reconcile ourselves to a longer stay: getting up into the snow-covered mountains with the cameras and all our paraphernalia was not going to be a picnic. And, anyway, where should we go? Where would the reindeer be hiding? Even if we found them, they were not likely to hang around till we got close with our cameras.

A German, I thought wryly to myself, would certainly have come better prepared than my happy-go-lucky Italian friend. A German would surely have contacted the appropriate local authorities beforehand . . . would never have found himself in a predicament like this. But Mario – I understand that now – likes to drop from the sky. He is an adventurer to the root of his soul. Later, I learned to admire him for his art of improvisation. His reaction in this instance was to assert, 'We'll work something out – with the help of these three bottles of cognac I bought in Copenhagen. Not to worry.' It's not that reindeer have a taste for cognac, you understand, but the Lapps might prove a different matter. In Norway, with its strict alcohol regulations, and where almost half the population moonshines, Mario's proposal sounded perfectly plausible. Especially since the Lapps surely wanted to catch their reindeer sooner or later, and knew well enough how to do so – I had no doubts about that. The problem was that so far we had not found any such Lapps.

That was the situation when Mario and I started for a small walk along the coast. We did not take our cameras, we were just stretching our legs, not expecting to find anything. It was night-time and very still, not a person on the road, but – of course – it was not dark. Here we were, just ten kilometres from the northernmost point of Europe, the North Cape, already well inside the Arctic Circle. Some readers will know from experience that when you first visit this area, you hardly shut an eye during the bright nights. The best thing, then, is to get up and do something positive, which is how Mario and I came to be walking along the coast, pondering Item 1 on our agenda, the reindeer problem. After half an hour we turned a corner to discover a small bay. The sloping shore on the other side shimmered in the twilight, a gleaming stripe punctuated with black dots. What's this? The punch-card strip of the magic carpet? It was! Almost exactly as I had imagined it!

'The reindeer!' Mario yelled at the same moment. We hugged one another, then speeded our steps. As expected, there was a

Lapp close by – and we soon arranged with him everything for our filming.

However, the nearer we drew, the more peculiar this herd seemed. Strangely immobile. 'They are never reindeer!' Mario let out a curse, '*Porca miseria*!' And he had a point: the herd turned out to be . . . a graveyard. Nothing but identical dark headstones in the snow, with some coloured plastic flowers between, invisible from a distance. It seemed an inauspicious omen.

'Isn't it time we gave up on this story?' I suggested to Mario.

*

The two brothers were called Jakob and Knut. They lived with their families in a pair of low houses behind a hill above Honningsvog – and where they lived, the mountains began. Not big mountains, archaic stumps, smoothed and rounded by the great glaciers of the Ice Age. Ideal for ski-tourists and, of course, reindeer. Jakob and Knut would be happy to take us to the reindeer, or – if we preferred – the reindeer to us . . . which would take perhaps two days.

The brothers already had an enthusiastic gleam in their eye when I met them; Mario had spoken to them beforehand. 'This time, we really get the animals,' he whispered to me with a knowing nod. There was one bottle less in his box.

Ratta-tat-tat! The skidoo went racing over the slopes, leaving a rippled furrow like a miniature bulldozer track. Not a good comparison, perhaps: a skidoo, which is no bigger than a motorcycle, is no lumbering load-carrier, but swift and highly manoeuvrable. Ratta-tat-tat . . .

Lapps in houses, on skidoos, rather than living in tents and riding small, shaggy horses? Let us not dwell on that: this is no time for nostalgia – which of us, in the Lapps' position, would not seek to improve his lot? Luckily, one of our new friends spoke a smattering of German. Did they still have any horses, I wanted to know. 'Just two,' they told me. I could see how difficult it would be logistically to make a film about the way the Lapps used to be, and it was fortunate that was not our aim. A small 'expedition' was put together: two motor sledges (the skidoos) with crew (the brothers), two long low regular sledges, which would be hitched to the motorised ones, a dog who barked delightedly at the prospect of going into the mountains, and, of course, Mario and me. On to one of the sledges we packed the tripod, one big camera in its metal suitcase, fur skins and other material; the second carried tarpaulins, ropes (which later turned out to be lassos), food, more fur skins and dry birch branches. The power with which those two motor sledges finally pulled all that weight over the slopes was impressive. Mario was in high spirits. He had been watching the younger of the two brothers, Jakob, romping around on his skidoo before hitching the transport sledge to it, and he couldn't wait to try it for himself. I must say, it was spectacular. Jakob at once detached the heavy sledge, apparently honoured at our interest, and proceeded to give an acrobatic display with all manner of tricks. He even jumped the skidoo several times over a snow cornice. Mario, beside himself now, was desperate for a turn, but Jakob would have none of it. Hence, I still cannot tell you, even today, how a Canadian skidoo (for that's where they are made) would stand up to an Italian 'roadtest' . . .

The low sun bathed the slopes in soft light. It was a highly romantic atmosphere. Gold and purple clouds stood high in the sky, while below – in what strange contrast – the young tearaway roared his machine across the wastes.

Several kilometres to the west we could now see a peninsula reaching far out to sea before falling away abruptly in a sheer cliff. That must surely be the North Cape – I remembered it from pictures. Jakob rehitched the transport sledge to the skidoo and we moved higher up the gentle mountainside for a wide view over the sea and surrounding bays. Pulling to a halt on a broad flat patch, the two brothers gave us to understand that this would make a good campsite. They would take a skidoo in turn and go in search of reindeer, while the other waited here with us. Even if it irritated Mario and me to be left out in this way, it was clear that the Lapps would be better able to approach the animals without us. How long was it likely to take? Were we going to bivouac here for a whole day, perhaps? We tried to find out. But Jakob, the brother who could speak some words of German, explained to me that he did not know the answer – but here was Knut to stay with us. Then he leapt on to his skidoo and – ratta-tat-tat – made off at speed until he was nothing more than a tiny dot moving over the next hillock.

Knut now did something which seemed very peculiar to us: he began unloading both of the transport sledges. Why was everything

The smallest film-making team – Mario, the actor, Kurt, the rest – setting off on our magic carpet.

Looking for Mario's unreliable co-star, an Amazon boa constrictor. 'This one's too small, I want her eight metres long,' said my companion. *Below*, the night when we found the reindeer. A Laplander with his skidoo and local version of the Whillans box at the North Cape.

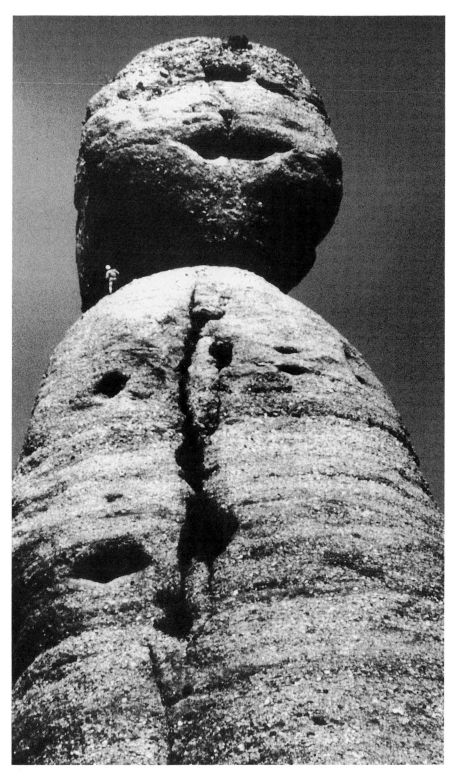

The Bola, one of the giant puppets of Montserrat.

In the Hindu Kush, 2000 metres of fatigue descending to the uninhabited
Gazikistan valley, an exhausting wrestle with hundreds of icy penitentes.
Behind is the sheer North Face of Ghul Lasht Zom (6665 m).

Above, the icy granite fortress of Tirich Mir, with its huge flanks and pillars. A great challenge! From the left, Tirich Mir East (7692 m), Main Summit (7706 m) and the West Peaks I–IV (7487 m, 7450 m, 7400 m, 7338 m) viewed from the north-north-west. Centre, the ice balcony and North Face route of the first ascent of Tirich Mir West IV. The Dirgol Zom (P 6778) beyond right seems a comparative promenade. *Below*, two men and nineteen camps. Didi comes to collect a tent marooned on its perch after strong sunshine had melted the surrounding ice during our twelve days absence.

Climbing Tirich Mir, the King of the Hindu Kush, culminating point in the seven-thousander dance. This time Masaaki Kondo from Japan is my partner. Behind is the West group and the peaks of Afghanistan beyond. *Above*, a last strum at my guitar before leaving for the summit.

The view from the south towards Tirich Mir Main and East Summits as we ascended the Owir An pass on our tour round the mountain. The glacier has retreated considerably since R. Schomberg's photograph from the same spot (see Jill Neate's *High Asia*).

Above, the dream traverse of the future – Shartse, Peak 38, Lhotse Shar, Everest, viewed from Makalu. *Below left*, on the great ridge towards Lhotse Shar (8383 m) during the first ascent of Shartse (7502 m) with Hermann Warth in 1974. *Below right*, Reinhold Messner and I meeting in Kathmandu in 1988.

to come off? We gave him a hand, without knowing what it was in aid of. He took one sledge and, with a single move, upended it in the snow. Then he did the same with the second, tilting it a bit so that the curved front-runners could be locked into a slot on the other. Immediately, we understood and at this point were impressed how simply and efficiently this Laplander was setting up a shelter – a solid wooden 'house' in a couple of easy moves! He adjusted the angle of the first sledge, so that not even a storm could dislodge it. (Was Don Whillans inspired by Lapps, I wondered, when he designed his famous bivouac box?) Already Knut was tugging a tarpaulin over the prepared framework. I had never heard of such a fantastic and simple invention, nor could I be sure even whether all Lapps knew of it.

Knut now clothed the floor of our little 'house' with reindeer skins, arranging them also up into the outer corners so that, in the end, the only snow you could see was a little in the entranceway. Meanwhile the light was fading. It was cold and humid and we were happy to crawl into the welcome warmth and snugness of the furs. The three of us fitted comfortably inside. Knut lit a small fire in front of him with a little bundle of birch twigs, taking care not to singe the furs. Soon its heat and smoke filled the enclosed space. We were lying on the ground, out of the worst of the smoke, which was drifting up through a hole in the roof. This accomplished, Knut yawned and uttered something which sounded like, 'So . . .' He looked first at Mario, and then – with a significant wink – at Mario's rucksack. And Mario, clearly picking up the signal, opened his bag, where I was surprised to see the other two bottles of cognac. Knut either knew this already, or had deduced it from the chinking of glass. For a while the reindeer were forgotten – we left them to Jakob as the first bottle circulated. Knut was taking the most touching care of us – and the spirit. He even prepared hot tea for everyone, laced with cognac. True we could not speak to each other for, unlike his brother, he knew no word of German or English. It did not seem to matter: we smiled at each other warmly, and when the silences became too long, saved ourselves from embarrassment by offering each other another sip from the bottle. The atmosphere became increasingly relaxed, until finally, I fell asleep. In my dreams thundering herds of reindeer flowed by, like seething waves, thousands of animals with immense, nay, truly gigantic antlers . . .

*

Ratta-tat-tat! The brother had returned. Reindeer? Well, he hadn't found them yet, but – and he beamed in at us, passing a handful of eggs through the entrance, beautifully speckled, black and green – he did have a pretty fair idea where they might be. He indicated into the distance before – ratta-tat-tat! – disappearing once more.

Knut smiled pensively. Should we have scrambled eggs with cognac, or make advocaat? Mario was snoring. Before anyone could come to a decision about the eggs, brother Jakob returned – ratta-tat-tat! He'd found the reindeer! Knut sighed. I shook Mario awake. The dog, curled in the snow outside the tent, also came back to life. It was all systems go! We crawled out of the shelter on all fours. I searched for a good place to set up my tripod, somewhere with a good field of vision, then, with a Hey-oop! hoisted the heavy camera on to it. Knut, panting, fished out his lasso, and at Mario's request donned a peculiar three-pointed hat, characteristic headgear of the Laplanders (though not, we were told firmly, when catching reindeer). Then we waited, breathless with tension.

Before long we see them coming! There, along the skyline and the gentle curve of the next hillock. They appear, one by one, so many, then more and more – all these reindeer at last! It is a Fata Morgana, a vision! No, it's real – they are there, the reindeer we have been searching for for days! A fairy tale . . .
I do not have to dream them now! In fact it's imperative that I don't dream at all. I must be wide awake now, make sure to do everything right; even the ground under my feet seems to be heaving (damned cognac!). Already I am picking up the deer in the long lens, am pressing the button . . . Now they are coming into the reach of my zoom. It looks fantastic as they draw closer . . . the midnight sun gilds the slopes all round and every animal casts a long shadow. Some have antlers, others not, some smaller deer – babies, they must be – move in between. It is difficult to describe them: the slowly approaching herd is so much part of this northern landscape. The brown fur of some of the animals echoes the rocks which randomly stud the smooth, snow-covered hills; the mild grey of shadowed snowslopes and the pale hue of the northern twilight are all reproduced in the fur of others; and in their profusion the deer are at one with the constantly recurrent forms of this landscape, with its harmony – it could be a painting . . . Kurt! Concentrate! You are

here to film: action! Now, behind them, Jakob has appeared on his motor sledge, keeping his distance. He glides carefully in low gear closer to the animals, sometimes approaching from the left, then from the right. Close to me, I notice Knut, who has just begun moving towards them, too, with slow careful steps, the dog at his side, lasso in one hand. He keeps stopping and standing perfectly still. Mario stands a short way in front and to the side of me, since he is required to appear in at least one scene. Now the reindeer have stopped. They have apparently recognised Knut, who approaches them now without difficulty. A sudden swift move of his arm and the lasso hisses through the air. Some animals leap backwards, but, incredibly, the swaying figure of Knut has caught a reindeer at his first attempt! I am amazed that the other reindeer are not running away, but maybe they are used to this sort of thing. Meanwhile, I have already run out a lot of film, and I am really only missing a wild 'storming herd' sequence. But will I ever get that? Sooner than I think, as it turns out . . . Mario, all six feet of him and more, now makes his own gentle move towards the animals. But he must appear as some sort of monster to them, for the Lapps, who they are accustomed to, are a small people. Anyway, all of a sudden, there is a stirring in the throng and before we know it, the whole herd begins storming away! Drumming hooves, the sound muffled by snow, bodies streaking, head to head, horn to horn, passing across my lens – a beautiful shot! I keep pressing the button, eyes glued to the viewfinder, following them through the zoom and the tele-lens . . . Photographs? I have none. Not a single picture. How can you film and take pictures together? Impossible, as many readers will know from their own experience.

It was a fine and unexpected end to our game of Blind Man's Buff across the Arctic Circle. And Knut and Jakob kindly set us up a real Laplander's tent later on, nearer to their home. It was made of birch trunks, covered in reindeer skins, and the whole family came and sat inside. The children had a lot of fun – and so, too, did we, even if this was not, by a long chalk, as original as the brothers' traditional 'Whillans box' we had experienced the night before. For a long while the two families waved their goodbyes to the backs of the two strangers, as Mario and I, burdened with reindeer skins as well as our gear, returned to 'downtown' Honningsvog.

On the drive back to Alta, I have to say, three times reindeer jumped across the road! They are everywhere and nowhere . . .

I took home two skins, which I'd purchased from Jakob and Knut – one dark, the other white. Ever since, the house has been filled with wafting hairs – so many, they must outnumber all the reindeer in Scandinavia!

*

The next destination for our magic carpet was Newfoundland, followed by the 1000 kilometres of Labrador's coastline. One day I find myself sitting opposite an Eskimo, staring into a hole in the ice. He has cut it in the frozen sea on which he is standing. The line in his hand moves up and down, up and down as he waits for the next fish. And another, and another . . . Endless patience. Again, I have the feeling of having reached the edge of the world. A different edge . . .

It was a pity we could not stay longer. Soon it was on to South America.

Friendly Margherita

Whether she was really friendly or not is anybody's guess. For Margherita was a giant snake, strong, supple, six metres long, and as thick as a man's thigh. I jumped to the conclusion that she must be warmly disposed towards us simply because she had not crushed Mario in her coils. Admittedly, he was more than one third of her length – but, I mean, to any self-respecting boa constrictor, fresh from the jungle, he should have represented no more than a warm-up routine in her early morning work-out. Don't run away with the idea that I wished Mario any harm – he's a friendly enough character himself – though when I later discovered that my partner in film was getting sixteen million lire from our Italian producer, and I only one, then sometimes I thought . . . (well, maybe it is not necessary to tell all that one thinks) . . . just leave it that now and then fantasies would erupt in my mind, in which the friendly Margherita assisted me in putting the squeeze on Mario . . . I realise I am wandering off the point.

We were in Lima, lying on our beds in the Hotel Crillon, somewhere on the seventeenth floor of that skyscraper. Mario was telling me of his adventures with Walter Bonatti in the rainforests of South America: about the Indians, and an encounter they had had with some harlequin-coloured little frogs, which he only afterwards learned were the ones used for making lethal arrow poison . . . and how Walter Bonatti narrowly escaped being crushed to death by an anaconda.*

'By the way,' continued my companion, 'we will be needing to catch a giant snake of our own – they want us to film with one.' He said this as if it would be as easy a matter as going into the woods for a kilo of mushrooms. I did not answer immediately: this was the way Mario had dropped surprises on me before . . .

'Is it that easy to approach a giant snake?' I enquired at length.

'No problem at all,' Mario assured me. 'The Indios bring them out of the forest all the time. A friend of mine, Pedro, can get us one easily.'

'Where does this Pedro live?'

'In Iquitos, on the Amazon.'

'Send him a cable, then, so that he can reserve a fine specimen for us.'

'No need, Professor,' (that was my nickname from Mario) 'when we get to Pedro's he'll have an eight-metre anaconda for us within half an hour. No tame one, either, one just brought in by the Indios. We'll take it off into the jungle for a couple of days, let it go, then film it being caught again.'

'And who's going to catch this snake?'

'Me,' Mario replied airily.

Cheers, then, mate, I mutter to myself, knowing we're in for some fun and games. Better watch out!

*

* There are known cases of anacondas swallowing fully grown Indians (Grzimek's *Tierleben* (Animal Life). Whilst anacondas can reach a 'guaranteed' length of 8–9 metres, a boa constrictor only grows to $4^1/2$ metres according to all the books. Our 6-metre-long 'Margherita' belonged at any rate to the family of the boa snakes, even if it might have been another kind of anaconda. The animal dealer in Iquitos said it was a boa constrictor.

EQUIPADO CON RADAR it says on all the Peruvian airline planes, making them sound reassuringly modern. Even so, the aircraft are not always as reliable as this device suggests – that is, if one is to believe Mario, who is tightening his seat belt at my side. 'Another one disappeared in the jungle, only recently,' he tells me with relish. What, I wonder, is the radar for, then? These aircraft have to cross the Andes to get to the Amazon from Lima.

Below us, the dark red desert coastline slips away, then come isolated snow peaks, rugged rock faces and deeply cut valleys, a wild mountain area, the highest points of which are all six-thousanders. The further east we go, the more clouds pile up, increasingly filling the airspace above the endless green canopy which shimmers up at us through vaporous cottonwool. Down there, rivers loop like snakes – we catch the glint of water among the greenery, and spot little ox-bow lakes, cut off from the main stream. The clouds through which we are flying – we are reasonably low – are constantly transfigured by marvellous rainbows, half and full circles. 'The Ucayali!' Mario calls suddenly, pointing to the bends of a big river, one of the headwaters that feed the Amazon. 'Soon we'll see the Marañon as well,' he continues. 'Bonatti and I tried to navigate that from its source – but we didn't make it. We took a bath.' A thousand kilometres lay between Lima and Iquitos. Shortly before we get there, the two headwaters join. If you include the length of the Ucayali, the Amazon is 6518 kilometres long. It is the greatest river of South America, the third largest on earth, and having the most extensive catchment area of all the rivers in the world.

We land on the small airfield of Iquitos in a violent cloudburst – within a few minutes we are soaked from head to toe. But, almost immediately, the sun shines again. Mario locates Pedro without any trouble, but he returns with a long face. 'There's been a cock-up with our snake,' he murmurs. 'Pedro says everything went with an animal shipment a few days ago. We have to find our own – I must have one at least eight metres long. It doesn't matter if it's a boa or an anaconda.' Drenched in sweat, we repair first to the hotel.

A full day is spent traipsing around, sometimes wet, sometimes dry – between one cloud and the next, from one animal dealer to another. Iquitos is the main settlement of the Peruvian Amazonas area. Ships keep docking, navigating the giant river without difficulty: it is 1800 metres (over a mile!) wide here.

Besides tourism, rainforest animals are an important source of income. It is incredible how many we see in a day: exotic fish of all kinds, circling in their aquariums, some big, but mainly an infinity of small flashing jewels – as if nature had overturned a treasure-chest, animating all the gems through some magical process. There is the squawking of hundreds of colourful jungle birds. Monkeys swing with grotesque twists of their limbs. A spotted jaguar hisses and jumps furiously against the bars of his crate. Fluttering on the outside of a big cage of birds with red shining head-feathers are others of the same species – trying in vain to get in . . . the sad consequence of human intervention with the freedom of the forest; here at the jungle's edge – because Iquitos is an island of civilisation – all these creatures face deportation. Do they sense that? All of a sudden I seem to feel the invisible shadow outstretched above so much colourful vitality. Our snake – I promise myself – will regain its freedom afterwards!

So far, however, we have no snake, neither boa nor anaconda. 'Too small,' Mario says every time an animal dealer shows us his best wares: pompously striped, patterned with curves, eyes, tangled lines, the markings seem to convey a hint of the immense power of these snakes. However passive they might look, is our two-man team equipped to cope with one of these creatures? Mario – the chief player (and in my thoughts, I already see him wrestling a writhing anaconda!) – and . . . well . . . me? I remember the Saint-Exupéry sketch of a well-satisfied boa, who has just swallowed an elephant, whole: the elastic-sided snake looks like a domed hat, viewed from the side, the brim on one side representing the tail; and that on the other, the snake's head, which is relatively small. It is left to your imagination how so big a meal passed through such narrow jaws: the jungle is full of secrets . . . Would a whole film team fit inside a boa? Or, having swallowed the larger of its two components, would the snake remain sated for the next few weeks and merely sleep? At least, I have never seen an 'Exupéry-hat' with *two* bumps . . .

But the jungle, as I said, is full of secrets.

'Mario,' I ask prudently, 'if I choose the right lens, couldn't we make do with a four-metre snake?'

'No way! She has to be eight metres,' insists the 'dominant half' of our film partnership. I sigh, but then calm down: at any rate my partner, with all his extra height, is going to seem the 'better half', in the snake's eyes also!

Finally, we found her: A BOA CONSTRICTOR. She was asleep, and measured six metres. Her body, at its thickest, you could not encircle with your two hands – but her head was no bigger than a dog's. She had wonderful markings, extending all over her scaly body, and Mario, well content, purchased her. The dealer assured us that she had just eaten a couple of mice. She really looked satisfied and peaceful – and I was about to put Saint Exupéry's 'hat' from my mind, when I remembered the saying, 'One swallow does not a summer make'. Nor do a couple of mice fill a hat! But then, I said to myself, a snake from the Amazon could not possibly know this European proverb.

'Let us call her Margherita,' said Mario. Then we went down to the harbour to Pedro's home.

*

Our boat divides the earth-coloured waters of the giant river. Above the green stripe of jungle on the opposite bank, which passes monotonously by, black thunderclouds build; here, in midstream, the sun strikes the boat with full force, but we do not notice it. We have a shady roof above our heads. Our craft is a primitive houseboat, which we have hired together with its three-man crew – dark-skinned locals, darker by far than the dark, earthy river, and dressed in an assortment of faded, well-worn garments. Pedro, Mario's friend and our manager, is *mestizo*, the colour of his skin considerably lighter than that of the others. He has cultivated a small moustache, of which he is obviously very proud; his sunburnt face with the dark eyes is usually half hidden below a wide-peaked baseball hat – now he has lifted the brim. I can more or less understand his Spanish; he has just told me of a giant fish, very rare now. It looks like a monster and the local hunters kill it with a harpoon. Its name is the Paiche; I had already heard about it from Mario. Hunting this beast has so far never been filmed. The legendary predatory fish is very shy. Nevertheless, you can often find its exquisite scales, which can be as much as five or more centimetres in diameter, and prized here for necklaces . . . usually strung with colourful seeds and snail shells. The bony tongue of the fish was – perhaps still is – used as a file by primitive Indian tribes. But the Indians hunt the Paiche mainly for its meat. It can reach four and a half metres and weigh as much as 180 kilos. To catch it, with just a harpoon, must be a violent and dangerous adventure. Will we ever see that fish? Now, the most important passenger on board is doubtless our Margherita! She is tied in a big jute sack, and unless you knew she was there, you would think we simply had a harmless load of sweet potatoes. It is understood that nobody will sit on that bag . . . So, Margherita, are you still asleep?

All of a sudden, behind the boat grey bodies flash from the water, describe a majestic circle in the air, and disappear into the splashing flood, again and again, playfully. 'Dolphins,' says Pedro. 'You often see them here.' Five thousand kilometres from the mouth of the river where it flows into the Atlantic Ocean, here are tumbling dolphins! At the same time, entire islands of uprooted trees and water plants drift towards the distant ocean. The water plants have bright lilac flowers, which reminded me at first of periwinkle, but they have large bubbly airsacs and can, as I noticed during a rest ashore, continue to grow perfectly well on firm ground. A whole carpet of

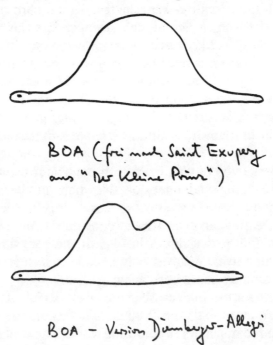

Boa according to St Exupéry and the Diemberger-Allegri version

bladders and blooms cover water and land . . . An amphibious plant, tailor-made for this mighty river, with its ever-changing water levels and extensive floods. Later on, a botanist will tell me that these are water hyacinths and they exist in many places across the world.

We travel well into the dark, through sunshine and pelting rain – most of the boats we encounter have roofs like ours. When we spot the glow of fires on shore, we tie up. Hospitable Indians allow us to pass the night with them. Dog-tired, we spread our mosquito nets above the wooden grille which forms the floor of one of the huts, all of which stand on four poles. As I slide into sleep, I still feel the continuous rocking of the water, and my heart glows at the sensation of shelter under a friendly roof, of people in the forest.

For three days we go upriver, following first the Amazon, then a smaller tributary, the Rio Maniti; our target is not only to film this snake, but as much as possible of its natural surroundings as well. Once here, on the Maniti, we do not meet any more boats and the walls of the forest on either side have crept closer. They have accepted us between them. In the evening we hack out a small space with our machetes, light a fire and sleep in hammocks – inasmuch as one can sleep amidst the multitude of animal sounds. It is like a living curtain descending and enfolding you into itself. Given several more pages, I could perhaps attempt a description, but it really would not help; I could never capture the unification of this flood of nocturnal sound, its *togetherness*, neither its synchronisation, nor the rhythmic, monotonous way it rises and falls in intensity. And this strange sensation of being part of it all.

It takes possession of you, courses through your veins, puts every fibre of your being under tension. Nowhere in the world is life created so abundantly, nor exists so closely together as here in the rainforest. Death is an ever-present constituent, but in the face of this thousandfold prodigality it has lost its horror, simply because here everything lives; death is only a smile, which in the moment of fading is already being born anew.

All my senses are alert because in the forest, so full of dangers, you are never permitted to dream. You need to be able to react quickly, to understand so much; it is a confusing world, one which needs your full consciousness to comprehend it. Even the apparent calmness of the forest people masks their ever-present vigilance. The dreaming, the smiling, the feeling at home in the jungle is a gift, but one which is offered to nobody from today to tomorrow.

A quick brightness invades the sky: the day returns, as suddenly as it went. In between lay eternity.

In the morning Pedro tells me that Margherita woke up, but a couple of mice had quickly pacified her. Our silent companion in the big jute sack would seem to be of phlegmatic disposition – so I think – but Pedro assures us the boa will become lively enough as soon as we open the bag at the forest margin. Several Indians will be needed for the safety of the film team, and we should choose a spot carefully, where the giant snake can be easily recaptured.

That day we arrive at a little Indian village, its huts standing on stilts in a clearing of the forest by the river's shore. On the opposite bank are two further pile dwellings, near where we land. Pedro knows the old headman here, and after a warm welcome, it is obvious that this is where we'll stay. Mario hopes also to be able to film crocodiles, and whatever else might turn up. We see a crocodile for a short while the next night – but not with a camera; Pedro, who feels obliged to shoot at everything, does not hit it, luckily. Instead, with two shots, he brings down a thorn-pig or tree porcupine from the top of a forest giant: the animal splashes into the water only a short distance from Pedro. It is a doubly valuable trophy with its spines of more than thirty centimetres long – like black knitting needles. The 'pig roast' which the chief's wife prepares next day tastes great, despite the sinister fact that without its spines, the animal closely resembles a baby. It takes a great effort of will to bite into this grilled infant.

But you get used to it. Some things the Indians consume never cease to revolt you: bird-eating spiders, as big as a man's hand; ants with fat honey-yellow abdomens; and creepie-crawlies of various kinds . . . The ants taste of earth, and the spiders – well, I only managed to nibble at one leg; they are considered delicacies, but obviously I have not yet spent long enough in the forest. Porcupines from the grill, I can recommend, however, notwithstanding their appearance! The same goes for another speciality which from now on becomes our daily fare: fried piranhas! These notoriously bloodthirsty little fish still bare their teeth on the fire as if they wanted to strip an ox to its carcass, but of course they are harmless

in this state. Even in the water, they pose only a limited threat –
limited to the concurrence of blood being spilt. Given that, it is true
everything happens with lightning speed: hundreds of little jaws with
their razor-teeth snap and snarl, the water boils . . . and soon only
the bones of the victim are left. Even so, I cannot conceal the fact
that on this trip up the Maniti, and later too, several times I saw
Indios bathing without fear in the forest rivers. Mario swam across
the Rio Maniti and for a long time in the middle of the river eagerly
struck out against the flow. But Mario, well, is Mario. He is not to
be put off by crocodiles or piranhas – whereas I prefer to keep a
tight hold of the side of the boat whenever I cool myself in the
river. I do not let my bare feet touch the bottom if I can help
it, and never take off my bathing suit, having been warned by my
companion about two unsavoury inhabitants of such waters: one is
a fish which lies around on the riverbed and you run the risk of
stepping on its poisoned spine; the other – covered in sharp bristles
– deliberately seeks out orifices in the bodies of larger animals, in
which to enter as a parasite, and from which it is almost impossible
to extricate as its points are barbed like a harpoon.

You can take it from me that it had to be really hot before I let
myself slip into the water.

Next day, we head upstream in a dugout canoe; we have been told
of a little lake nearby, and Mario wants to see if we'll be able to
shoot our giant snake scenes there. This is a tipsy form of travel,
and you have to pay some attention to equilibrium. In front of me
an Indian is crouching with a short paddle, behind me sits Mario,
and then Pedro, who also has a paddle. For some days the Rio
Maniti has flooded its banks, enabling us to travel the whole way
to the little lake in the canoe – even across the rainforest!

It becomes a strange journey.

Sometimes Pedro points to one animal or another which has saved
itself by clambering into the high branches of a tree. Mostly, you can
recognise them only by a sound, or movement. The treetops, and
indeed the different layers of branches, are worlds in themselves,
and after we leave the river and penetrate the drowned forest in our
canoe, this becomes even more obvious. We zigzag between dense
vegetation, then high tree-trunks. There is no noticeable flow, and
everywhere smells of mud and the rotting leaves which are drifting
on the water. I am filled with apprehension: even as a tenderfoot in

the forest, I recognise how abnormal it is to be canoeing right across the forest floor like this. Besides gliding so mysteriously through the magic world of trees, you are moving in a different perspective, too, from at ground level. More than once I am tempted to ask the Indian in front of me to stop as we pass within reach of one of the fantastic red orchids with their darkly gleaming flutes, sitting on what would normally be the high branches . . . But it is just a whim; he passes by unmoved – to him it's just an everyday thing. The water is getting shallower and the tree formations sticking out of the water become increasingly bizarre. Indeed, can you still call such contorted figures trees? There is no word for this multitude of tangled roots and trunks and stems, all from the same plant, holding each other in tight, inescapable embrace, as if the participants in a wrestle for life and death had suddenly become frozen by a spell. Colourful orchids and ferns peek from the crooks and hollows. Aerial roots dangle down, and lianas . . . our dugout slides silently amongst these 'sculptures' – that is what they seem to be – groups of entangled Laocoon figures in ever-changing permutations, reminding me of the unsuccessful struggle of the father-priest and his sons of Greek myth, enmeshed by snakes. Sometimes the water gurgles gently at the dip of the paddle – the mirages of the tree-figures start to move and dissolve . . .

In front of us appears a clearing: the lake! A circular surface, surrounded by the walls of ancient forest giants, black water, like a lead mirror. All around it is still. Beside the boat, where the sunlight falls into the water, a transparency of dark brown to olive green dissolves into the black of the depths. You cannot see the bottom, and no animals are moving in this water . . . A sinister black hole.

Suddenly a swarm of parrots, with hellish squawking and whirling wingbeats, flap like beginners across the gap in the forest . . .

Mario decided this place was not suitable for our film. I had no objection. On the way back the man with the paddle sitting in front of me – speaking through Pedro – told us that a friend of his had died here recently, and he pointed vaguely to one of the twisted tree-sculptures: he was just ducking below the invasive canopy of leaves, when a little snake bit his head and it was too late to help him, it was a very poisonous one . . . The Indian's tale went on vividly, and all of a sudden Pedro laughed, explaining to us, 'The man did not suffer very much – he was drunk.' When I think back, I do not like this day at all. But that is how it was.

Finding a suitable location for the film turned out to be difficult, but then luck stepped in. At the edge of the clearing a new house was being built – that means a couple of poles had been erected with two cross logs fixed between. These provided a platform where our helpers could keep guard while Mario attempted to catch the snake below them.

On the day in question, even he seemed uncharacteristically tense and thoughtful, more irascible – not his usual prankish self. He knew that at the critical moment he dared not stumble, knew that the snake would only be subdued if he succeeded in grabbing it with both hands just behind its head, and pressed firmly. Until this moment, he had to beware at all costs of getting into an embrace! A bite from the reptile would hardly be worse than that of a dog – but a clinch could spell death. Why such a giant snake loses most of its force if you succeed in getting the correct grip around its neck is a puzzle to me. But all snake handlers know the trick. And what Mario needed to help him was a long, forked stick. He quickly cut himself one from the forest with his machete. I would also keep one of these sharp knives within reach during the ensuing film session; if things went wrong, I could enter the fray – and fast! That such swift assistance might be necessary was understood by the Indians as well. Even though they are accustomed to catching anacondas and boas from time to time, it doesn't always work out to plan – a man on his own is a weak opponent to a giant reptile!

I set up the big camera on its tripod about one and a half metres above the ground on the slatted wooden floor of a hut close to the one that was being built. I was four metres away from the ominous jute bag, lying now at the side of one of the new house-poles. From where I stood, I hoped to catch the whole scene with my zoom lens, secure a good overview from obliquely above and still be able to follow all the details of the action. In emergency I could easily leap down and weigh in with the machete – or, preferably, with my hand camera. Of course I felt some sympathy for Mario – at that moment he seemed a true hero to me, the essence of courage! And the sixteen million lire of his contract no longer seemed such a giant sum; safely atop my wooden grille, I felt quite content with my million. It is amazing how completely a metre and a half of extra height can change your perspective!

Not that you could say, of course, that you were really in a safe place up there: boas and anacondas are agile climbers and often found in trees.

The closer the moment approached, the more the white space of sky above the clearing seemed to disappear. The chattering of the natives died away. Even the forest itself stepped back . . . all my concentration was focused on what would happen in front of me.

It was the same for Mario: we had discussed all the eventualities and clearly knew what had to be done. Three Indians were sitting on the cross-tie of the new house. They would pitch in only once Mario had succeeded in locking the head of the snake in his special grip – he had hoped they might have been on the ground sooner, but they refused. Pedro was standing with a machete in the shadows behind another hut, ready to rush to assistance . . . We could start!

An Indian slowly and carefully loosed the string of the jute bag . . . and disappeared behind the next hut. The bag was lying so that its opening faced the forest and Mario.

For some seconds nothing happens. Then the brown fabric starts to move: evidently Margherita has noticed the glimmer of light penetrating the darkness of her prison. Slowly, hesitantly, she pushes her head into the open, as if dazzled by the brightness of the day.

I watch Mario: his face has frozen to a mask, his black eyes fixed, immobile, his glance nailed to the slowly emergent boa five paces in front of him. He has crouched forward slightly, like an animal about to spring . . . in his right hand he holds the two-metre pole with its forked end. Margherita suddenly stops. Has she noticed Mario? A forked tongue appears and flickers several times in front of the brown head with its shiny scales, licking the air above the ground. It is as if she is checking for hidden danger, and warning anybody from preventing her return to her forest. Mario still arches forward like a statue, 'frozen' in the sticky heat, sweat running down his face, eyes rivetted on the motionless snake. In the shade of the hut's roof, I too am bathed in sweat over my whole body – from excitement, from heat, from the effort of filming, from the concentration on what was about to happen next.

All is still and I can feel everybody holding his breath – even the Indios on the log; suddenly Margherita's decision is clear: with an agility and speed I could never have credited to a giant snake, she shoots towards the forest, not by the shortest way, but in a sideways loop, to outreach Mario . . . already I see her escape!

But Mario is not to be caught offguard: with a quick bound he blocks her path, standing in front of her once more, ready to thrust down the raised forked stick . . . And Margherita? Without hesitation, she adroitly changes direction, in a way which makes it impossible for Mario to realise his intention: her head slides back over the coils of her body, so that if Mario were to dive for it now, he would surely be caught in a suffocating grip. His situation has become unexpectedly tangled – taut and tangled in every sense of the words! He circles the sliding spirals at a respectful distance, yet close enough to take advantage of the moment when Margherita, in whatever direction, makes another break for the forest . . .

The boa has become slower now. Or is it simply an illusion caused by the many overlapping, overlooping coils of the scaly body? Now, at last, the giant snake must have understood that Mario is her enemy . . . more than a mere obstacle on her way to the forest . . . slowly, she now slides directly towards Mario, whose face betrays that he has understood . . .

Does he falter? Will he keep his nerve? Step by step, he retreats slowly and I see his hand clenching the stick so tightly that the knuckles have gone white – obliquely beneath me I hear the rustle of a sudden move as Pedro draws in from the side, but my full concentration is with Mario: he has lifted the forked stick and brings it down with all his force. Into the sand. He has missed the snake's head! The reptile makes a sudden move – Mario pants, he has lifted the stick again, I see how he trembles with tension in this uneven duel. He knows that he is not allowed another mistake like that! Again, he thrusts down – and this time he gets the fork exactly above the neck of the boa, nailing the head of the mighty animal to the ground. The six-metre scaly body starts to wind like a giant screw – a terrible sight . . .

Everything then followed at such flashing speed that it is all but impossible to describe it in sequence. A confusion of events, simultaneous, one after another and overlapping between: I see how Mario, hand over hand, comes down the stick as quick as a flash to the head of the snake. There comes a rough yell, from Mario or Pedro I cannot tell which. The Indios slide down from the log. Mario, having successfully secured the neck of the snake, now grips the boa tightly behind her head and, with all the strength of his arms and fingers, presses as hard as he can. He holds her head sideways now, half a metre above the ground. The Indios collect the still-writhing spirals of the reptile – but it is as if the energy behind the immense power of the animal has vanished under Mario's grip. Working in fours, the men now drag the snake to a large basket. I draw breath, but mentally only, because my filming goes on – it is truly unbelievable how the men succeed in stuffing the coils of the thick body into the basket, beginning at the tail. At last, Mario, with one swift gesture, tosses the head in on top of the giant skein – he had been holding the boa 'in grip' all this time. Swiftly, the lid is slapped over the wickerwork and tied securely. To me, it is inexplicable why such a strong snake does not simply burst or bite through a jute bag or a basket. But Pedro has repeatedly assured me that, cut off from daylight, these animals immediately curl up, as they would in nature in a hollow tree. Nobody has ever thought with the mind of a snake. I take a breath. Mario sinks exhausted on to a rush-mat: he is running with sweat, marked with strain.

'You did that well,' I tell him.

He nods and pants. After a pause, he suddenly says, 'And you? Did you do your bit well?'

The events of the last ten minutes flash past my mental eye. Exciting scenes, certainly an enthralling story . . . but every conscientious cameraman knows that you can never have enough material; such a truth one should not hide, not even in the case of a giant snake . . . 'Fantastic scenes,' I reply, seeing Mario visibly relieved, then – after a pause – I add, 'All the same, I could do with a couple of close-ups with my hand camera.' Silence.

'Are you serious?' Wide-eyed, Mario looks at me as if I'm a lunatic.

'You can never have enough material,' I insist, according to my conscience, and then I add with a benevolent voice, 'You can rest for a while!'

What Mario thought I don't know – at any rate, in the end he said, 'Okay, once more!'

Secretly, I want to add, at the back of my intention was the hope that Margherita might this time perhaps succeed in reaching the forest. I did not expect Mario to prevent her with the same resolution as before. But I was wrong: Mario subdued the snake a second time with his special grip! This time I was really close with my hand camera, 'skin-close'. Nevertheless, it all went so fast that I still needed one more take. After that, we were all exhausted. And poor Margherita? She had gambled away her third and last chance of freedom.

We stayed on a few more days in the jungle. We filmed the Indios, orchids, and several other things. Finally, we returned to Iquitos.

And Margherita?

Despite my protestations, Mario had presented her to the Indios as a gift. They killed and ate her. Mario said, 'We would have committed an unforgivable sin in their eyes if we had let her go.'

One of the laws of the jungle is never let yourself fall into the power of another.

*

I know this story of Margherita could have ended differently. Perhaps in a zoo in Europe, if we had brought her back to Iquitos. In those circumstances, I think what really happened was better. But why did we not let her go somewhere on the way back?

She had been promised to the Indians – and, once more, the rules of the humans prevailed over the rights of the animal.

It would be a pity not to tell how things went on with Mario . . .

We never did work together again. Not because of any flaws in the films we made. Well content with our success, we returned to Milan after our magic carpet had carried us 30,000 kilometres around the world. But there was a big catch to Mario's next project: not that we were supposed to spend a day with crocodiles on a sandy islet in some African river; nor even that on Kilimanjaro I was temporarily to pass my camera to my companion and perform a stunt as the star of the show – the script requiring one of us to fall over the edge of a snow or ice face (not to the bottom of course, we could use a rope. That was more my department, Mario said. It would be better for him to hold the rope). No, the real snag was that at the very start of the journey Mario wanted us to penetrate the Danakil Desert of Ethiopia. This, he hoped, would bring us into contact with an unchanged aboriginal tribe with some pretty strange habits. He had some telling photographs of women wearing necklaces made from the highly prized 'noble parts' of enemies of the tribe. This, I have to confess, did not endear these people to me. It may well be that they had now abandoned the practice, as was said, or that none of their trophies had ever come from Europeans . . . but it was enough: I had the uncomfortable feeling that my beloved Arriflex was not all I might lose there. Bloodthirsty stories abound in Ethiopian history: it is said that during the Abyssinian War some 3000 Italian prisoners were emasculated! Of course, that was a good while ago now, but even in 1969, when I traversed the highlands of Semyen just to the west of the Danakil, we heard from a very reliable source of one such act of revenge at the end of a fight between two locals. Mario, intrepid to the core, made out that his ruling principle in life would be compromised if he did not attempt to seek out this tribe, but by the time I had come to terms with the idea, and wanted a contract to cover all risks, Mario became suspicious. It rubbed him the wrong way, and when our wives then entered the argument, he became even more furious. One day I heard he was about to leave with a different partner. It wounded and grieved me, but I rang him to wish him good luck, even so.

Mario and his companion crossed the Danakil Desert, were captured at one stage, but got free again. Destiny caught up with them on Kilimanjaro, where they were forced to bivouac in a terrible snowstorm at almost 6000 metres. The end was bad – not for Mario, he has nine lives, but his companion had to be flown back to Europe with very severe frostbite. Mario called off the rest of the journey.

One fine day I was sitting in a pizzeria in Rome with Carlo Alberti Pinelli, a film director who wanted to visit the Indians at the source of the Orinoco River. Turning round, my eye was caught by an unusually lengthy corduroy suit, topped by a small rounded head. The man had his back to me, but that bristly haircut . . . the ostrich! It was indeed Mario. We had a pizza together soon afterwards and Mario told me that he was planning very shortly to parachute into the rainforests of South America. He believed he had finally discovered the lost city he had been hunting for so long. He said this with that same nonchalant smile with which he had once told me we were to capture a giant snake. It must make some difference, I think, if your grandmother comes from the Mato Grosso.

Perhaps I should add, by the way, that both of us ordered a Pizza Margherita.

Montserrat

'The serrated mountain' was how the practical Catalan farmers described these saw-toothed hills, long before scientists understood about the effects of erosion. Not a romantic name, perhaps, for such an outstanding work of nature, a composition of forms and figurines, shapes and silhouettes, unique in the world. Clusters of tall beings with curiously rounded heads, like a giant puppet show, some dormant, others in wild movement, all frozen to the spot by some mighty and irrevocable command.

The Romans built a temple to Venus here, the love goddess. And Catalan shepherds discovered a mysterious black Madonna in the year AD 880, which became the patron saint of all Spain. For more than 1000 years this place has held deep religious significance. At the bottom of a long row of rocky figures, there is a road leading to the monastery, whose church and the black Madonna are important sites of pilgrimage. Archaeologists think Montserrat has been a sacred place since primeval times. These strange and patently phallic rocks could have held only one meaning for our ancestors: a manifestation of the eternal creative force which maintains life on earth. A pagan fertility spot, no less. And so mystical, so holy, that its significance has transcended religious evolution, and even today, young couples – Catalans and other Spaniards – still come from far and wide to be married here, that their union may be blessed and fruitful.

To the climbers of Barcelona, of Manresa and other places around, the giant puppet theatre is a wonderful playground. What a joy, to hang between sky and earth as if amid the invisible threads of marionettes, what a lark to be played with gravity!

At first glance you would think the rocks of Montserrat were nothing but a mass of hand- and footholds, but a second look reveals that all the little rugosities are rounded, that hardly a grip is to be had on any of the violet, white, grey or brown pebbles which make up the reddish conglomerate of the mountain. This is 'puddingstone', resembling nothing more than a well-crammed cherry cake. And if, sometimes, with two or three fingers, you are able to gain temporary lodgement in one of the holes where a 'cherry' has fallen out, the general verticality or convex nature of the compact rock, and above all those rounded pebble-holds, demand an acute sense of balance *and superlative finger strength. Moreover, the last resort of banging in a piton when free climbing fails, is scarcely an option here: the conglomerate is far too dense for that. Who climbs at Montserrat needs a thorough mastery of his craft, and a rock-solid nerve. No wonder the area enjoys an international reputation in the climbing world.**

I could not help but be reminded of this requirement for steely nerve all the time on my first visit, inching my way up a vertiginous wall, my fingers clinging to two pebbles in airy space, the tip of my boot perched on another pebble, while with my free foot I groped for some 'cherry hole' in that perpendicular cake. All around wafted the marzipan-sweet smell of acacia, waves of it welling up on the breeze from the foot of the rock towers. Hey! Another pebble! The sun was beating down, and the rocks reflecting the heat, as I fingered my way higher, surrounded by a landscape which Picasso might have designed. Climbers were calling each other from one hundred-metre puppet, 'la Bola', to another, just slightly lower, which resembled an oil bottle: or from the tip of a giant finger which held aloft an 'Easter egg' of many tons in weight (how long had it balanced there?), to a comparatively small cube, which none the less still occupies the space of a sizeable house.

'Aixo es el Daiet – lo vuoi provare?' says José, my companion, half in Catalan, his mother language, half in Italian, knowing I understand that better, and he laughs as if at some great joke. Then, he explains in German, his eyes twinkling with roguish fun as he indicates down towards the house-sized cube, that this Daiet goes by the innocent name of the Würfelchen, *or 'nice little cubelet'. Did I want to try it? And still he grins all the while as if trying to conceal something.*

Well, why not, I think, and agree. At this moment we are standing atop the rounded head of the Bidglia, a skittle-pin some eighty metres high, and the petty cubelet down there fails to inspire me with great respect. And of course to my partner, the well-known expedition mountaineer and international businessman, José Manuel Anglada,

---

* Later I learned that even here some people have drilled straight up-and-down lines of bolt-holes. Spattered with artificial anchorages practically anything becomes possible, and such gloriously fortuitous 'puppets' are relegated to little more than designer climbing walls. Of course, a number of extreme and interesting moves will be created, but at what cost? Of destroying a mountain's identity. Were these people not prepared to find their own holds?

whom you can often find climbing on these walls with his wife Elli, or with the film-maker Jordi Pons, and who of course naturally himself got married in the Church of Montserrat, certainly to him this cube should not represent any big deal. He has made a number of first ascents around here.

As we stand in front of it, the cube does look a little more commanding. 'É un buon quinto,' José winks, 'it's a good 5:1 or more!' and he approaches one of its facets. 'Not at all easy,' he adds, groping for the first hold. 'A friend of mine came off here recently,' and he raises his eyebrows, nodding emphatically. 'Two weeks in hospital, it cost him. He fell the full length of the rope; landed, luckily, in the bushes. But you met him, yesterday, didn't you, at your lecture?' Already he is hanging by one finger, and stuffing the next into a hole above, then, maintaining the tip of his suede boot on a small white pebble, he wriggles and winds himself higher in serpentine fashion . . .

'Ah, mmm,' I answer, watching carefully – and recall the guy with the plaster cast. José is climbing in shirt sleeves and braces, easily, fluently, seeming to put no more effort into it than a stroll in the woods. But he is all attention. The hospital . . . José's braces seem to bounce, he'll be up in no time . . . It is true, I think to myself, people who wear braces usually exude spirit, humour – and security – even on the vertical walls of Montserrat. But it may well be just that the owner of the braces was called José Manuel Anglada, and I was reacting intuitively to that. Anyway, it helped to know that the braces were above me at that moment, and I was not required to lead this pitch. I chewed over the problems of the cherrystone wall, and eventually worked my way up it.

Anglada looked at me with a crooked smile, 'So, how do you like our cubelet?'

The climb that I long for, even today, is a thirty-metre sphere, perched upon a sixty-metre pillar. That I covet. I would love to stand on its top, but it has never happened. Something always got in the way. But perhaps, after all, it is always politic to retain an unfulfilled wish at all the best places life offers.

Spain is one of the best places that I know. A wide, open country, full of colour, a harsh beauty. The sky above the Meseta's immense plains seems closer, and the clouds (if there are any) lower in the blue than elsewhere; I remember pale desert areas and meadows full of red poppies, and I return often to the Basque country – as green as our Austrian Styria. It feels familiar and yet different. The songs of the Basques, their yodels and dances, these I treasure, and the feasts we have enjoyed together. And the hours in the mountains, in Spain as further afield with Mari Abrego or Josema Casimiro on K2 and Everest. I can see the round, near-Styrian face of Patxi, President of the local mountaineering club, and hear his calming 'siempre tranquillo' amid the wildest, most rumbustious revels and at blow-out 'banquets' in high places protected with barbed wire . . . When it comes to calmness, only 'little Pedruccio' surpasses Patxi. The whole world seems to revolve around his prodigious form (well over a hundred kilos!). Only his wife is exempt from this revolution: she, too, weighs more than a hundred kilos. Together, these Basque stalwarts are what we in Austria would call 'true human souls'.

Home is not simply that place or country where you were born, or lived as a child. It widens . . . and as life passes, your roots penetrate the ground in a number of places. This becomes both a gift and a burden. The more and better you understand, contentment and longing become your inseparable companions.

*

I am sitting on the boulders beside the pier in Barcelona harbour. The waves approach, break and retreat . . . and my thoughts wander far beyond the sea . . .

PART THREE

Hindu Kush – two men and nineteen camps: the tactics of a mini-expedition

Mountaineering expeditions these days almost always have a definite summit in mind. Accordingly, all their planning is directed towards climbing it. If the peak happens to be in the Himalaya, the Karakoram or the Hindu Kush, then they are restricted to the terms of a permit, which must be obtained in advance from the government concerned – Nepal, Pakistan, China. They are obliged to keep to certain areas and named peaks. The small but extended Hindu Kush enterprise which Dietmar Proske and I undertook in 1967 was an altogether different proposition. In the first place, there were just two of us and we were not, officially, an expedition, but simply travelling as 'sporting tourists'. Secondly, in spirit, this was a wide-ranging foray involving climbing and reconnaissance. For Dietmar, it was his first experience of the mountains of High Asia; I had been three times already and, besides, knew the Hindu Kush from an earlier, similar journey to the mountains of Chitral. However, since my first visit to the Tirich area, things were beginning to change and to be without a permit now could land you in big trouble. This was the end of the era when you could climb wonderful peaks and explore unknown valleys without asking anyone.

In some ways, I consider this mini-enterprise to have been my most successful expedition. Hermann Buhl's alpine-style thinking, with which I became familiar on Broad Peak and Chogolisa in 1957, had left its influence on me. The concept, I believed, could be expanded to apply to a whole mountain area.

I do not intend a full narrative of events, but want to demonstrate, by means of a compressed expedition diary and a sketch map, the complete comings and goings of our trip, with its repeated setting-up of camps (and depots) for our various objectives. On top of that I will endeavour to give the thinking behind the preparations we made for all this activity to show how a small two-man expedition with multiple aims can work and, depending on circumstances, could be repeated. Of course, there were times when Dietmar and I had to make the best of our situation, and times when luck played no small part in the outcome – but then, on any trip, you will always need some luck.

*

Looking north from Chitral – the main settlement in the area of that name in north-west Pakistan – you see the shining snows of Tirich Mir, high above the valleys. This mountain massif is the highest in the Hindu Kush, a range that includes several 7000-metre peaks. Tirich Mir itself is 7706 metres. Like a bastion, the massif thrusts south from the main spine of the Hindu Kush which forms the boundary between the Wakhan in Afghanistan and Chitral in Pakistan. On closer inspection the bulk resolves into crests, groups and single peaks, embracing mighty glaciers. Glacial tongues push out even into the barren brown mountain valleys to its east, south and west.

The second highest peak of the Hindu Kush, Noshaq (7492 m), and also the precipitous Istor-o-Nal (7403 m) are both linked to this system of crests, which encircles the multi-branched Upper Tirich Glacier like a framework. This glacier is essentially the heart of the area.

It is not surprising that the seven-thousanders of the Hindu Kush and other fine peaks of lesser height in the area captured the interest of climbers, albeit relatively late. Not until 1960 was it possible to launch attempts on the main range from the Wakhan Corridor – that narrow strip of land bordering the Oxus River, and created as a sort of *cordon sanitaire*, a buffer zone between two areas of political interest, two empires, the Russian and the British-Indian. Well before this, however, British officers, maintaining the Gilgit Frontier, and surveyors explored the mountain world of the Hindu Kush from Chitral, which then came under British influence. And as early as 1929 and 1935 there had been attempts on Istor-o-Nal by British officers, although it was 1955 before an American team reached what it thought was the summit.* On Tirich Mir itself an attempt from the Owir Glacier in 1939 led by Miles Smeeton was accompanied by the twenty-five-year-old Tenzing Norgay, but the first ascent was achieved only in 1950 when a Norwegian expedition led by Arne Naess approached from the south.

When, in 1965, with Herwig Handler, Franz Lindner and my wife Tona, I pushed beyond Istor-o-Nal to the heart of the mountains of the Upper Tirich Glacier, we were pioneers from an alpinistic point of view. Only Reginald Schomberg before us had made a geographical exploration of the area in the 1930s.

We found ourselves entering a wide glacier floor within what could best be described as a circle of mountains, beginning with the Tirich North group to our left. From where we were standing, the long southerly arm of the Upper Tirich Glacier continued up towards the pre-eminent Tirich Mir, bypassing the granite castles of the Tirich West group. Rising beyond this glacier arm, to the west, were the white peaks of the Ghul Lasht Zom group, almost in front of us. To our right, Istor-o-Nal, with its steep flanks and flying buttresses, bounded the outgoing (eastern) stream of the glacier, which finally dispatched its meltwaters through the broad U-shaped valley of the Tirich Gol into the main river of Chitral. (This river changes its name from stretch to stretch: here it is the Mastuj.) A further arm of this intricately branched glacier system extended up between Istor-o-Nal and its close neighbour, Nobaisum Zom; another, in a wide sweep, flowed from the foot of the southern flanks of Noshaq and Shingeik Zom. The Anagol Glacier (yet another branch) derived from the watershed between the Tirich basin and the two Gazikistan glaciers to its west. I wondered if, in the old days, people used to cross a pass here, down into the Arkari valley?

We christened the confluence of all these sidestreams of the Tirich Glacier with a name borrowed from a similar, but more famous landmark on the Baltoro in the Karakoram, Concordia or, as we preferred it, Konkordiaplatz. Our 1965 expedition was crowned

* The real first ascent was made fourteen years later by a Spanish team. See Adolf Diemberger's article in *Himalayan Journal* 29. My father was fascinated by the rugged mountains of the Hindu Kush, becoming eventually a specialist on the range, even though he had never been there!

not only with the first ascent of the 6732-metre Tirich North, but of three further six-thousanders in the nearby Ghul Lasht Zom group. We also gained some remarkable scientific results: Tona, a geologist, did the preliminary research for the first geological map of the area. We discovered enormous intrusions of granite in the dark slates (which turned out to be Paleozoic); they had forced crystalline dykes into the sedimentary rocks which had once been an ancient ocean bed (we found fossils in some places). Beautiful minerals formed from this conjunction of rocks lay everywhere around: black-rayed 'suns' of tourmaline and rose-coloured flakes of mica, shimmering like silk. My heart, like Tona's, quickened at such fantastic finds – after all, had not my own path to the mountains begun as a young rock-hound so many moons ago? Alpinistic objectives apart, we could see there were geological enigmas in plenty awaiting resolution: clearly, a return visit was called for. Two years later I managed to come back.

But this time everything was different. Whereas before we had been the only people on the Upper Tirich Glacier, now, in 1967, the Tirich area was attracting the attention of many mountaineers. Two strong expeditions penetrated the southern branch of the Upper Tirich Glacier, one behind the other: Czechoslovaks, under Vladimir Sedivy, and Japanese, with K. Takahashi as leader. Both intended an attempt on Tirich Mir from the west (this would be a new route: the Norwegian first ascent in 1950 had been via the South Ridge).

Also busy in the massif was an Austrian group from Carinthia, led by Hans Thomaser. They wanted to open a steep route on Tirich Mir from the south-west, from the Dirgol valley. The leader and his companion died during the summit attempt, and it was not until 1971 that a Japanese team succeeded from this direction.

A three-man party from Salzburg exploring on the Upper Tirich Glacier, our area, included my friend Kurt Lapuch. This group climbed the North Peak of Istor-o-Nal; and Kurt and I stood together on the first seven-thousander of my Austrian Hindu Kush Reconnaissance, 1967. Technically, I was a one-man expedition – as lightweight as you could get – but I should quickly add that another solo party, the German Hindu Kush Reconnaissance, 1967 – namely, Dietmar Proske – was active at the same time. The two of us had made separate plans to come here, although we agreed to travel together. Not knowing each other beforehand, it seemed prudent to remain basically independent, leaving each of us free to team up with other parties or make solo ascents. In the event, apart from a couple of days, Didi and I were always together and the collaboration worked so happily that you might just as well consider us a two-man expedition.

And our goals?

One strong reason for my coming back was because the West Peaks of Tirich Mir, still untouched by man, beckoned along the southern branch of the glacier. Beautiful, wild seven-thousanders! There in 1965 we had cast the first exploring glances into the far reaches of the Tirich Glacier – and, not least, at the West Face of Tirich Mir. In consequence, Didi and I hoped gradually to penetrate this east-curving glacier arm, and climb several of the surrounding peaks in the process: in particular we set our sights on the beautiful pyramid of Dirgol Zom (6778 m) and one or two of the Achar Peaks – a silhouetted crescent of six-thousanders which separated the western rim of the Upper Tirich Glacier from the deeply cut furrow of the Arkari valley, 3000 metres below. It goes without saying that we also hoped for the chance to climb Tirich Mir itself – either by a route being pioneered by the big expeditions or, better still, a new one of our own. To our dismay, as I said, bureaucratic difficulties had arisen since 1965: the Pakistani government now demanded an official expedition permit for Tirich Mir. We wondered if, perhaps, it would be possible to ride on the coat tails of the Czechs or Japanese. We had no wish to upset the government, but my oh my! Tirich Mir was a most beautiful mountain . . .

What about the other peaks? No problems, there: as 'sporting tourists' the authorities in Peshawar had granted us a fine permit, rubber-stamped to allow us to fish, roam freely so long as our wanderlust held out – including in snow and glacier areas (be it noted!), and to explore possible ski areas (they said this would be good for tourism). I took it that we could also climb all those peaks which were not on the special list prepared by the Ministry of Tourism as requiring the standard expedition permit. But what peaks these were was for us then a matter of conjecture, and we were wary of asking too many questions. Unfortunately, everyone knew that Tirich Mir was an official mountain . . .

This, then, was the transitional period, with many things left open to individual interpretation. Were we an illicit enterprise? No, no, God forbid! Even so, there was the risk of surprises: my friend

Gerald Gruber, a geographer from Graz and a dedicated Hindu Kush hand, found himself one fine morning in a village where the local police would not allow his porters to go on. He had to call off his exploration. That is why Didi and I treated the liaison officers of the big official expeditions with the utmost respect. Twelve years later, in 1979, linked by friendship and a rope to our liaison officer Major Fayazz Hussain, I would break trail for many hours with him through the deep snow of an eight-thousander to share the joy of a summit success on Gasherbrum II. But in 1967, Didi and I could not bank on such harmony, nor hope that our happy-go-lucky wide-ranging (and, we hoped, high-reaching) sporting activities would be seen as a reasonable interpretation of our special permit. Hence, we hesitated before accepting the invitation 'Please come for tea' from a liaison officer down at the bottom of the Tirich Gol valley. That is to say, we accepted, yes, from the safety of our inaccessible glacier world, but then had to postpone the date, over and again, because of 'sickness'. We strung it out until we had 'hooked' all our 'fish' . . . In the end I did 'come for tea', but from the other direction, up-valley, having fulfilled my wish to encompass the whole Tirich Mir massif.

Nudging alpine-style a step further

Back to our plans! I wanted our climbs and exploration to include the opportunity to collect more rock samples for widening the geological map; I developed a special interest in the Ghul Lasht Zom group, because the old *kammkarte* of the area to the north of there, towards the Anogol Glacier, was definitely wrong. Also, the southern peak of that group, a six-thousander, was still virgin – the only one we had failed to bag in 1965. And incidentally, what was on the other side of the Anogol – could you climb down there?

So far, nobody had ever succeeded on the South Face of Noshaq. Nearby soared the virgin and nameless P6999 and you could elevate that to a seven-thousander with your own body. Aims upon aims, possibilities without end . . .

Ever since I was on the Baltoro Glacier with Hermann Buhl, I have been committed to alpine-style, even when, as on Dhaulagiri in 1960, I could not put it into practice. (The oxygen at least remained unused on that trip.) What handicapped us in achieving multiple alpine-style successes in 1957 were the many miles of moraine rubble and glaciers over which all the necessary gear and food for other mountains would have needed to be carried. But given the acceptance of a multitude of targets from the beginning of an expedition – and accepting, too, the premise that in the Himalaya all alpine-style mountaineers employ porters to help get gear and food to their Base Camp below the mountain – then it is clear what should be done: create an appropriate depot system at the outset.

As I said, in 1967 we had no shortage of aims or possibilities capable of being realised by just two climbers in alpine-style. The term nowadays is usually only applied to the *ascent* of a mountain; for us, it included exploration and discovery as well. To explore more than one massif, and include successful quality climbing, you have to push the style even further. You need a network of depots for your intended camps, that still allows you the option of adjustment where necessary. The better you plan this beforehand, the less will land on your back later!

For our multiple targets, we required elastic planning. We only had a very limited number of tents: a couple of bigger ones for normal camps and a lightweight tent for moving around at high level on steep mountainsides – a Desmaison design with two vertical tentpoles. This latter gave us extreme mobility. We could proceed for days, setting it up night after night at a higher – or at least different – place, saving ourselves from dangerous bivouacs. Hermann Buhl and I had already employed such a 'wandering high camp' in 1957 on Chogolisa, his last climb: it represented the lightweight extreme of our *west alpine-style* (no high-altitude porters or oxygen gear for the climb), and corresponded to the purest alpine-style, even by today's definition. This dynamic climbing technique – often embellished with the term 'bivouac', although the use of the tent demonstrates it cannot be that – proves wonderfully effective as well for traverses of every kind, and for far-reaching exploration. We used our lightweight tent in making the grand circuit of Tirich Mir, and it was equally useful during the climb of the mountain itself, as well as on Tirich West IV, another seven-thousander, and the aforementioned P. 6999. It would in any case have been utterly impossible for us to set up a chain of camps, in the way that big expeditions do. In a sense, we got close to the 'capsule-style' concept advocated by Chris Bonington, the British master of strategy.

*

Our self-sufficient little team made frequent use of depots. We cached a duffel bag or an aluminium box with food and equipment on the Anogol Glacier; on the southern branch of the Upper Tirich Glacier; two such caches on the Konkordiaplatz; another on the North Face of Tirich West IV; and yet another below Noshaq; as well as several more. The addition of a tent to any of these depots meant instant transformation into a camp. Conversely, if a tent was needed elsewhere, returning a camp to a cache was equally simple. Even a reader inexperienced in mountain craft will see how flexible an expedition can be with the aid of such relay-stations. It is incredible how much distance can be covered when the layout of these stations follows a logical pattern.

In the course of our two months' stay in the Tirich area we only employed a single porter, Musheraf Din and, even then, sent him back to his village for a holiday every so often! It did mean a lot of carrying ourselves. There had been twelve porters on the march in; they deposited our gear in more than one place and the subsequent redistribution we did ourselves. Obviously, the honesty of the porters is an integral requirement of this system, but that was guaranteed for us by Musheraf Din and his people. No less important was the fact that the porters of every other expedition came from the same village – Shagrom Tirich – and Musheraf Din was their mayor!

But now: how to proceed? More precisely: how to extend the lightweight strategy for a chosen climb? In the centre of your field of action – for example where the southern branch of the Tirich Glacier flows into the Konkordiaplatz – you convert a depot into a main camp. (Alternatively, the necessary gear can be brought from the nearest cache, or from the last point of action. There's no danger that things might become too easy – you'll always find some load or other that needs ferrying! Logistics can never be that fail-safe, especially when you have a limited amount of equipment. Once, we were faced with gathering what we needed from three different spots.)

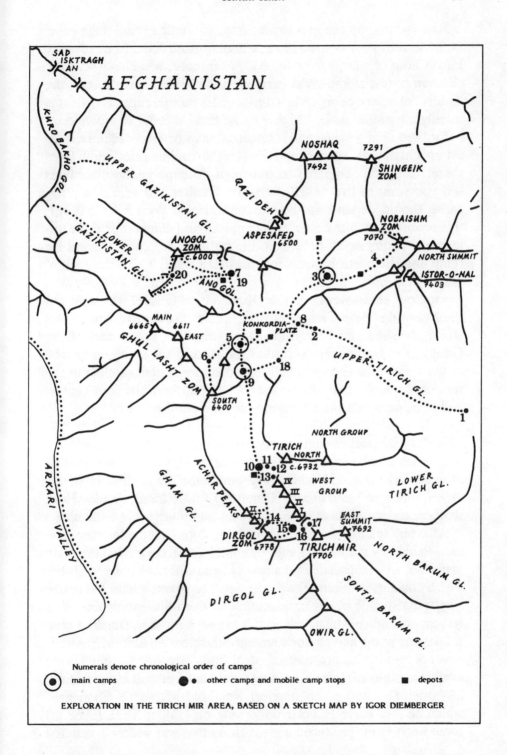

EXPLORATION IN THE TIRICH MIR AREA, BASED ON A SKETCH MAP BY IGOR DIEMBERGER

After setting up the new main camp, you add a small 'high base' at the foot of your desired peak, a miniaturised ABC (the Advance Base Camp of a large expedition). From there, you either start the climb in purest alpine-style, carrying just your lightweight tent, the 'ladder' of camps being reduced to a single mobile rung. Or, what is usually advisable, make a higher cache first, in order to reconnoitre before the final assault; and if circumstances or safety require it, to set up a high tent beforehand and start the 'mobile rung' climb from there. Common sense has to outweigh doctrine in the mountains – if you want to live to tell the tale. Whether and where to put a cache should depend on the situation. Tirich West IV (7338 m), this beautiful granite castle, was explored and climbed by us in this manner, taking seven days from the bottom. We chose a giant ice ramp and the north buttress for this first ascent.

During our seven weeks on the Upper Tirich Glacier we employed the following 'Base Camps' in turn: one at the foot of Istor-o-Nal (facing Noshaq and Nobaisum Zom); the next to the east of the Ghul Lasht Zom peaks; a third at the start of the southern branch of the Tirich Glacier; and finally a sort of permanent satellite in the remote Anogol basin. Altogether we established nineteen camps, and once occupied the abandoned tent of another party.

This elasticity worked well: we succeeded on three seven-thousanders – including Tirich Mir itself (7706 m). The other two of them were first ascents: Tirich West IV and Nobaisum Zom (the freshly christened P6999, which we found to be 7070 metres.) And to these, we added four six-thousanders. It cost us a lot of sweat and on-the-spot reckoning.

As a tiny team to have 'conquered' – or rather, made ours – the mountains of a whole area and, ultimately, to have circled the main massif; to have succeeded on a row of beautiful peaks on the Upper Tirich Glacier, with remarkable distances to cover; and to overcome all the logistical barriers in the course of this mini-enterprise – that was an adventure which, today, fills me with more satisfaction than if Dietmar and I had climbed an eight-thousander somewhere else. Several hundred more metres of altitude are fine, – but taking everything into consideration, that would have been less interesting, less original – and much simpler! Reinhold Messner's Challenge, which he and Peter Habeler undertook on Hidden Peak (8068 m) some years later, produced a great climb that was widely acclaimed as innovative. But the principle had been enacted earlier – more than once, on 7000-metre peaks, whereas Reinhold's 'bivouacs' were practically camps: the highest offered a double-fabric silk and perlon tent and sleeping-bags. Reflecting on the summer Dietmar Proske and I spent in the Hindu Kush, the difference, it seems to me, was merely a few pitches of rope, given the fact that Hidden Peak only just exceeds the magic 8000-metre line and its logistical difficulties were nothing by comparison. Reinhold, for his part, drew a not so apt comparison between his climb and the first ascent of Broad Peak in 1957. His 1975 expedition, he said, required only a tenth of the total weight in equipment and food that ours had done. Moreover, he had not taken a doctor. I could not resist a smile at that remark, at least. But for the mathematics, we had been four climbers, not two; we had been utterly alone on the Baltoro Glacier; and moreover, it had been almost two decades earlier. How many changes had taken place in that time, in equipment alone! On top of that, Reinhold used twelve porters to get to his starting point – just as we did in 1967 in the Hindu Kush. Of course Hermann Buhl's *west alpine-style* on Broad Peak was heavier and less elegant than Reinhold and Peter's method of climbing Hidden Peak, but the revolutionary concept was *his* and crystallised soon afterwards in the purest alpine-style employed on Chogolisa and Skil Brum. On Hidden Peak, an old style and an old concept had been applied – without question in a brilliant way!

After this 'spiritual excursion' to the Baltoro, let us return to the relative quiet of the Hindu Kush. Three eventful months – a great time!

An expedition journal

Dietmar and I met in early June to assemble the equipment. After three days the total weight of 500 kilos had been reduced to 420 kilos and strong rear-wheel shock absorbers fitted to the car. We drove for two weeks across Turkey, Iran and Afghanistan. At Dir, in Pakistan, we 'garaged' the car in what we hoped was a burglar-proof way by driving it on to someone's verandah up a ramp of planks knocked together by local men and then removed. We proceeded by Jeep for two days, hired donkeys for two more, then set off on foot with twelve porters to Shagrom and the Tirich valley.

Our objective was the Rhubarb Patch, known locally as Chur Baisum, where the Lower Tirich Glacier enters the valley of the Upper Tirich Glacier. The Lower Tirich is small and narrow, squeezed in between the North Face of Tirich Mir and the Tirich North group. This Rhubarb spot could be a good base for a first ascent of Tirich Mir's North Face!

The diary continues:

5 July Didi and Kurt pitch their tents some distance before the Base Camp already established by the Czechs.

6 July While Kurt is chatting in the Czech mess tent with them and their liaison officer, Didi, who has made an early start, passes with our porters. We march along the south flank of Istor-o-Nal to a spot shortly beyond called Nal, or Horseshoe. Years ago, according to the locals, one used to be able to take horses through from here to Afghanistan. Today the glaciers don't allow that.

7 July Didi and Kurt head on, turning right at the western edge of Istor-o-Nal to the northern arm of the Upper Tirich Glacier. This is where Kurt Lapuch's Salzburgers had their Base Camp for climbing the North Summit of Istor-o-Nal; they have now marched off to Shagrom. We set up our tents, and Lapuch arrives, following an invitation from Kurt. Nobaisum Zom (P6999) will be tackled from here by the two of them. After establishing a depot at Konkordiaplatz all porters except Musheraf Din are sent home. This depot will supply further depots to the south and west.

8 July Starting from Nobaisum Base Camp a high cache is established at 5800 metres.

9 July Lapuch and Kurt depart from Base Camp for their summit attempt and set up the lightweight tent at 6050 metres. The route for Nobaisum Zom will take the gap between this mountain and Istor-o-Nal, then follow the ridge to the summit. Didi makes a reconnaissance towards Noshaq – another possible objective of our enterprise – and sets up a depot.

10 July First ascent of Nobaisum Zom (7070 m by aneroid).*

11 July Descent to Nobaisum Base Camp.

---

* For me this was a hard struggle as I was not yet sufficiently acclimatised to such high altitude. In the same season (1967) Doug Scott, on his first expedition to Asia, was experiencing similar difficulties in the Hindu Kush in Afghanistan.

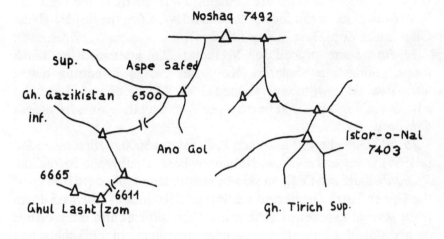

Sketch map of the Upper Tirich Glacier area before (above) and after (below) our 1967 expedition

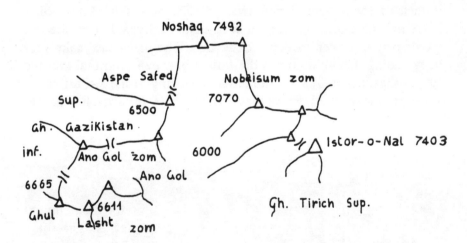

12 July Lapuch marches off. A little later a gigantic rockfall roars down the granite wall of Istor-o-Nal near Base Camp. Musheraf Din fetches the rucksack with our food, which had been deposited for the ascent of Noshaq. The reconnaissance has revealed the approach to the face to be too complicated and dangerous; Noshaq will not be climbed this time.

13 July Now the push into the Ghul Lasht Zom group must be prepared. Kurt will stay a short while at the Nobaisum Base because of phlebitis in one leg which has become worryingly thick.

Didi and Musheraf Din are bringing material from the depot at
Konkordiaplatz to the foot of the Ghul Lasht Zom peaks. Establish
Ghul Lasht Zom Base Camp (4950 m).

14 July Same procedure. Musheraf Din afterwards goes off
for a 'holiday' to Shagrom. Kurt's leg luckily is getting better
after treatment with several medicines. No ill effects. Later he
admits rushing up a 7000-metre peak immediately on arrival is a
dangerous error.

15 July Didi climbs Panorama Peak (about 5600 m, first ascended
in 1965). Kurt arrives from Nobaisum Base Camp.

16 July Kurt and Didi, on ski and skins, ascend the south branch of
the Upper Tirich Glacier, to a height of 5500 metres, then ski down
it for several kilometres. The run is very difficult and not worth it
on account of a long stretch of small *penitentes*. In 1965 there had
been excellent snow conditions on the southern branch, but we had
no skis then.

17 July Departure for exploring the Ano Gol, the north-west
branch of the Upper Tirich Glacier. The access to Ano Gol is
barred by an enormous icefall, which can be bypassed on the left
(southern) side over a steep rock section. The *penitentes* make very
heavy going. Climbing up to the saddle between Ano Gol and the
Upper Gazikistan Glacier, the latter belonging to the Arkari valley
side of the watershed. From the saddle (*c.* 5500 m) a knoll (5600 m)

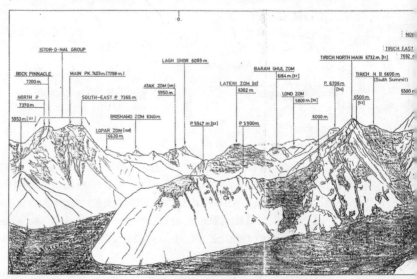

Sketch panorama of the Tirich Mir area from the Ghul Lasht Zom (NNW)

is ascended. This gives a very illuminating view: a descent from Ano Gol to the Upper Gazikistan Glacier could be possible, but very difficult. According to Schomberg, there might once have been a passage here for shepherds or smugglers down to the Arkari valley, and on into Afghanistan. Maybe ice conditions were better then. Another revelation is that between the Ano Gol and the glacier at the northern foot of the Ghul Lasht Zom group, there appears to be no barrier. Its ice flows for the most part down to the Ano Gol Glacier, and consequently into the Upper Tirich. Only a small amount finds its way into the Lower Gazikistan Glacier. The old *kammkarte* is wrong here. Interesting finds are blocks crammed with paleozoic crinoids on the left-hand-side moraine of the Ano Gol Glacier, originating from the southern precipices of the Asp-e-Safed group. Return to Ghul Lasht Zom Base Camp the same day.

18 July Day off. Didi gets some provisions from Konkordiaplatz.

19 July Start for the Ghul Lasht Zom group. Set up a High Camp (5700 m) in a glacial basin which is surrounded by Panorama Peak, Ghul Lasht Zom South, Dertona Peak and Ghul Lasht Zom East.

20 July First ascent of Ghul Lasht Zom South (6400 m) by Didi and Kurt from the High Camp. Great view of Tirich Mir and all the peaks around the Upper Tirich Glacier [see below].

21 July Descent to Base. Here Musheraf Din, back from his holidays, is waiting. He brought apples and needs new ski sticks.

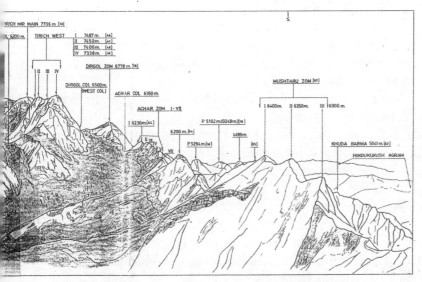

by Josep Paytubi, from photographs by Kurt Diemberger

22 July Start for first ascent of Ano Gol Zom. (The view from the top could be extremely revealing.) We set up a High Camp on Ano Gol Glacier (5700 m).

23 July From Ano Gol Camp to the saddle between Ano Gol and Lower Gazikistan Glacier, then ascent of Ano Gol Zom (6000 m), via southern ridge. Discovery of a promising descent possibility towards Gazikistan from the southern ridge. Whereas the saddle ends in a gigantic icefall, a passage seems to exist – though its lower end is not visible. Return by night, descending the east flank after an impressive view from the top towards Noshaq, Tirich Mir, Ghul Lasht Zom and to the Afghanistan peaks. Maybe a descent to the Upper Gazikistan Glacier would be possible, too, via a small peak and the north-west flank from the saddle we reached on 17 July. (Steep. Some crevasses.) Very late return to Ano Gol Camp.

24 July Establishment of a depot (Alu box) at the Ano Gol campsite for a planned crossing to the Arkari valley at the end of our activities. Return to Konkordia and establish another depot there near the Ghul Lasht Zom group and then ascend to our old Nobaisum Base Camp.

25 July Make two heavy carries from Nobaisum Base Camp to Babu Camp (at the south-west foot of Istor-o-Nal, a very favourable position). Flowers, grass, sun, a little spring. Height about 4900 metres. Babu was here as an Englishman's companion, so Musheraf Din tells us. Sleep at Babu Camp.

26 July Departure from Babu Camp to Konkordia, and then along the western moraine of the Tirich Glacier to the foot of Panorama Peak, erecting there a depot for our subsequent Tirich Mir Base Camp. Return to Babu Camp.

27 July Same procedure as yesterday. Now the Tirich Mir Base Camp is in place, and occupied.

28 July Rest day. Musheraf Din brings the duffel bag from Konkordia (edge depot). Moreover, all the remaining material is brought from the abandoned Ghul Lasht Zom Base Camp to our new Tirich Mir Base Camp.

29 July We arrive with nearly a hundred kilos of material at the foot of Tirich West IV and establish a High Base there.

30 July Musheraf Din takes material from Tirich Mir Base Camp and carries it halfway up, from where Didi and Kurt transport it to High Base. Musheraf Din goes back to Shagrom again, another holiday.

31 July Ascend with heavy loads (twenty kilos each) from the Tirich West IV High Base (or ABC) through a broad snow and ice couloir to the beginning of the big ice balcony, leaving a cache for our Camp 1 (and return).

1 August After dismantling our High Base, we climb to our cache and set up our two-man tent at 6350 metres, protected by a rock tower. An ice lake, some two metres long, and fifty metres below saves us having to melt snow! Explore along the big balcony to where it drops away at its eastern end towards the Lower Tirich Glacier. Impressive views down to the glacier, to the back of the Tirich North group and into the north faces of Tirich Mir and Tirich West. Spend a long time with binoculars scanning for a route between steep black slate and granite veins above us. The geological contact zone is like a huge spider's web made of dykes. Sleep in Camp 1.

2 August A reconnaissance push up the North Face (partly Grade IV), leaving a depot at 6650 metres. Return to Camp 1.

3 August Transport material to the depot. Return to Camp 1.

4 August Departure from there for a summit attack. With the lightweight tent, equipment and food, we climb to the depot, and then, with heavier loads, make a long traverse on to the hanging glacier. Benighted, we stay at a very uncomfortable place (6900 m) in a crevasse.

5 August Transfer everything into a capacious bergschrund (High Camp 2 at about 7000 m), there being absolutely no other possible site for our little tent.

6 August Go for the summit. First ascent. Difficult passage around the granite bulwarks on their east side and a steep firn flank. We reach the top (about 7300 m) in the afternoon at around 4 pm. Fine view to Afghanistan and closer Hindu Kush peaks. Take important photographs of the area and build a big cairn, Kurt finds some beautiful quartz crystals. Return to High Camp 2 in the bergschrund.

7 August Descend to High Camp 1.

8 August Bad weather, a real exception, not to see the sun. Extensive snowfall. Rest day.

9 August Descent from High Camp 1 with everything to the bottom of Tirich West IV. Leaving only a depot there, continue to the Japanese camp in the saddle between Dirgol Zom and Achar Zom I. Establish our own camp (nearly 6000 m) there.

10 August Rest day. Acquaintance and conversation with the Japanese.

11 August From the camp in the saddle ascend Achar Zom II (probably the highest in the long row of Achar Zoms, or perhaps equal in height to Achar Zom I, about 6300 m). Kurt – without Didi but together with two of the Japanese, Nishina and Takahashi (who is fifty-five years old) – makes the second ascent (after the Czechs). At the very top Kurt has a short fall through a breaking ice crust and is stopped by Nishina with the rope. He in turn holds Takahashi twice when he slips in the dark. Returns in bad mood to saddle camp.

12 August Kurt descends to Tirich Mir Base Camp for provisions. Nocturnal return to our camp.

13 August We go on to the High Base of the Japanese (6500 m) at the end of the southern branch and set up our own 'High Base' (One tent) close by. The Japanese politely decline an invitation to Kurt's sweet milk and rice pudding.

14 August Ascent of Dirgol Zom (6778 m) by Kurt, Didi and Masaaki Kondo, a strong mountaineer not included in the Japanese summit team for Tirich Mir owing to a broken rib, sustained in a crevasse fall. Return to High Base.

15 August Didi brings up supplies from the saddle camp depot. Kurt and Kondo establish a depot for the summit push on Tirich Mir at about 6900 metres on the slope which comes down from the gap between Tirich Mir and Tirich West I.

16 August Kurt and Kondo climb up to the depot and onto a 'pulpit' between two couloirs at about 7000 metres, where they spend the night in the lightweight tent. Didi was prevented by dysentery from taking part in the attempt.

17 August Encounter descending Japanese assault team after their fruitless summit attempt. Taking care of them delayed departure until 5 p.m. Difficult climbing in the eighty-metre chimney (IV, V), completed in darkness. Then by moonlight push up to the abandoned Czech tent on the saddle (7250 m) between Tirich Mir and the West group. Thus, we did not need to pitch our own tent, just crawled in theirs.

18 August Stay on the saddle. Short reconnaissance for the ascent. Masaaki barely understands English, but we manage somehow.

19 August Start at 8 a.m. for Tirich Mir summit. First follow the Czech ridge (North-West Ridge) to a height of 7400 metres, then traverse a couloir, climb a rocky face (III) to the western flank, traverse snow and blocks of rock diagonally to the right, up through the whole upper flank to join the Southern Ridge (where it makes its last kink), rest there for half an hour, then continue over the snowy ridge easily to the summit (but there were cornices!). Summit reached at 1 p.m. Stay there 1–1¹/2 hours. Great view over highest peaks and an ocean of clouds. Descend by the same route, getting back to Czech tent at 6 p.m.

20 August Descend to our Tirich Mir High Base.

21 August Descend to our Tirich Mir Base Camp.

22 August Descend, just the two of us, with ninety kilos from our now-dismantled Tirich Mir Base Camp to the Japanese camp at the south-east rim of Konkordiaplatz (4900 m).

23 August From there, to Babu Camp, and pack up. We prepare a box for the transport back to Shagrom. It remains temporarily at Babu as a cache. The remaining material is brought by us to the Japanese camp.

24 August Packing up everything at the Japanese camp.

25 August Musheraf Din appears with four porters from Shagrom and carries our luggage back there, where it is to be stored in his house until Kurt comes back from the other direction after his trip around Tirich Mir. Didi and Kurt depart for their crossing to the Arkari valley, arriving heavily laden at the depot on the Ano Gol Glacier. The Ano Gol camp is set up again (with the lightweight tent).

26 August The camp is dismantled. We move everything, tiresomely struggling across big *penitentes* to the southern ridge of the Ano Gol Zom, and up it to about 5800 metres. The tent is erected again.

27 August Pulling down the camp, descend over a long rib of slate to the Lower Gazikistan Glacier. Along it and on to its northern moraine, to a small pool with flowers (altimeter 4250 m). Sleep without a tent for the first time in eight weeks!

28 August Descend to the valley of Kurobakho Gol. Kurt goes up the valley alone and climbs on the Upper Gazikistan Glacier to 4300 metres to collect geological specimens and to photograph in order to clarify the question of the old crossing from Ano Gol to Upper Gazikistan Glacier. (It clearly is possible with crampons and good snow conditions. Impossible for horses. Steep.) Overnight stay in Kurobakho Gol. Food almost finished and no other humans for miles. We live on thin soup, rhubarb and wild onions.

29 August Descend out of the valley to Wanakach (3300 m). First inhabited settlement. Food! People are very surprised to see us.

Didi met up with the Japanese again a few days later, and when I also reached Chitral they obligingly included me as Masaaki's companion on their official paperwork for the Tirich Mir climb.

It had been an expedition with a broad range of success: we had achieved the first ski descent of the Upper Tirich Glacier and the first circumambulation of the Tirich Mir massif. We had corrected the map in the Ghul Lasht Zom area and made some important fossil finds – crinoids and the extremely rare Receptaculite, so far encountered in only nine places in the world. As for the climbing, I had made the third ascent of Tirich Mir, on a partially new route, with Masaaki Kondo; and with Didi achieved first ascents of Tirich West IV by a difficult route from the north, Ghul Lasht Zom South and Anogol Zom; the pair of us also did the second ascent of Dirgol Zom with Masaaki Kondo; and I made the first ascent of Nobaisum Zom (P 6999) with Kurt Lapuch and the second ascent of Achar Zom II with Nishina and Takahashi. The total duration of the expedition had been three and a half months. However, on our return to Chitral we had every reason to fear it might take longer . . .

Two chickens come home to roost

Sooner or later all the knots in a thread will arrive at the comb – that is an old weaver's saying in Italy. Sooner or later, boy, if you are up to mischief, they'll find you out! It's like British chickens coming home to roost though I confess, as an Austrian hearing that one over the phone for the first time, I thought it was 'roast' rather than 'roost' – what we would call a Wienerwalder Version. Audrey Salkeld, my translator, at the other end of the line felt the Italian comb version more aptly described Didi's and my touristic foray in the Hindu Kush, although when it came to our return to Chitral, it really seemed that all three of them fitted.

We had lived – one could modestly say – as if in the good old Age of Exploration. Even my eventual encounter with the Japanese liaison officer at the end of my circumperegrination of Tirich Mir had not gone off too badly: the storm, when it burst about my head, was dignified and flowery, while the local Chitrali were grinning and nodding at me, mumbling an appreciative *sot zom* . . . We had become famous with all the ibex hunters and smugglers of the area. *Sot zom* – that means 'seven peaks'.

However, on my arrival at Chitral, where Didi was already waiting for me, I sensed that something was smouldering. The political agent could not have been more friendly; he gave me the necessary signature and all good wishes for our return, but one of the other authorities was not so well disposed towards us. The Japanese may have helpfully declared me as one of themselves so far as Tirich Mir was concerned, but the fact that someone had climbed all over these 'hills', and then afterwards even gone round them, that had never happened before and appeared highly suspicious. Somebody wanted to pick a chicken, and we had just come home to roost! Or a roasting! I immediately began to tremble for my beloved stones and the photographs I had taken for the geological map – would all that effort be in vain? It was clear that we were not going to be allowed to leave here. No Jeep driver in the whole village would agree to be hired. A guard was posted outside our room. We were two quietly roosted mountaineers with a sentinel.

I was furious about the whole business, for what in the end was our mischief? I shaped a plan – and it worked. Outside the village, I engaged a lorry-driver with his vehicle, just coming up the valley, and told him that he must load all our stuff in a matter of seconds and leave immediately. There would be a bonus for this. The baffled sentry was quieted by the political agent's signature, which I thrust under his nose, then our bags and boxes were hurled on to the lorry and we took off. The two chickens escaped! We were jubilant . . . In Drosh, though, a small village further down, we found ourselves stopped by the police. After an hour of discussions, during which we refused all requests to get out of the lorry, finally the barriers were cleared. Mountaineers in Chitral had declared – thank God – that we were personal friends of the Austrian President. Apparently the telephone works in Chitral too – extremely well, indeed! The poor guard was badly punished, so we afterwards learned – but why had we been held? Did somebody suspect us of being spies? Who knows what goes on in the minds of military people. Of course, they only do their duty. I was later to be highly praised by Pakistani scientists, and a whole box of rocks – precious samples – now resides with the venerable Professor Desio in Milan.

*

Whenever I think of this expedition, a well-known Viennese joke springs to my mind . . .

A man enters a pub in a great hurry and calls, 'Quick! Quick! Give me a gin before the fun starts!' The bartender quickly fetches him a glass, and in next to no time the man has drained it. 'Quick, another one!' he shouts, 'before the balloon goes up!' And he swallows that one down as swiftly as the first. Feeling better now, he smiles at the host and says, 'Could I have just one more before all hell breaks loose?' And the puzzled barman fills the glass again. 'What is all this fuss you keep on about?' With the third glass empty, the man-in-a-hurry wipes his mouth with his hand and fixes the host with an even stare. 'The fuss is just about to start: I am afraid I do not have the money to pay you with . . .'

In place of money – or the lack of it – we had a very dubious sporting permit – and the question which we put to ourselves, up there in the glacier world, was: Do we go down now or later for 'tea' with the liaison officer? My advice was, 'Let's wait a bit. Let's grab another one before the balloon goes up. Better still, make that a double . . .' Tirich Mir!

The third eight-thousander?

'Kurtl, our third eight-thousander, let's do it together!' said Reinhold Messner at the Trento mountaineering film festival, always a good place to catch up with old friends. That was before the 1974 summer season. Wolfi Nairz was there as well, the Tyrolean climber and expedition leader. We were discussing an attempt on Makalu's South Face, which – if it succeeded – would mean a third eight-thousander each for Reinhold and me. The two of us had recently given a marathon joint lecture – organised by Charlie of Innsbruck – and entitled 'Four Eight-Thousanders' (Reinhold's two and my two).

That had proved very interesting, if long. I was convinced that with the exception of some experts, by the end of the evening nobody in the hall could have stood a further ascent, wanting, then, only to get home 'by fair means'! I think the lecture had lasted four hours. (The British have more endurance in these matters: at the mountaineering conference in Buxton in 1976, I delivered a six-hour non-stop slide and film lecture on my own, the longest so far in my career. It was, by the way, a very exciting meeting. At that time Cesare Maestri had just climbed the extremely difficult South American granite tower of Cerro Torre placing bolts with a compressed-air drill. He was there in Buxton, as well and, not surprisingly, stimulated a really animated discussion.)

In Trento, before the mountain summer of 1974, it certainly looked as if Reinhold and I would be climbing the South Face of Makalu together ('together', or one after the other . . . that would remain to be seen), but then one morning soon afterwards I received an official letter (and one could feel from its tone how hard it had been for Wolfi Nairz to write); it was an 'ex-vitation' (or whatever is the best word to describe a revoked invitation). Somebody on the expedition (or several) clearly did not want my presence. For me – who already saw the shining Makalu so close – this was a black day. It does not help very much now to go on about my thoughts then – the fact was it left me with very little time to wrestle the tiller . . . but I succeeded: I became instead a member of Gerhard Lenser's Lhotse expedition, which from the beginning was beset with bad luck and difficulties.

A big Spanish expedition held the permit for Everest, and did not want to share its climbing route with anyone – and the standard approach for the highest mountain of the world is essentially the same as that for its satellite, the 8511-metre-high Lhotse. (Only a saddle separates the two peaks.) This was a rich and influential expedition: the battery firm Tximist in Navarra was picking up the tab. Our protestations that we could peacefully coexist on the route were dismissed by the prestige-conscious Spanish, who feared a one-sided success. In the end, the Ministry of Tourism in Kathmandu told us: you have the permit for Lhotse, fine, but try the mountain from another side!

Hell, what kind of concession was that! Two years before, Gerhard Lenser had deposited in Lukla all the equipment suitable for a normal ascent of the eight-thousander.

. . . Or indeed, no less useful even for the South Face.

None of us, however, felt ready to venture on to this deadly face. Avalanches, avalanches, avalanches . . . a Russian roulette.

And so we came to the decision to try the Great Ridge: one of the greatest traverses in the Himalaya – not attempted hitherto, though perhaps possible – the Lhotse Ridge starting from the Barun Glacier. Given good weather, we reckoned we stood a real chance of getting over the two virgin 7000-metre peaks, Shartse (7502 m) and Peak 38 (7589 m), at least as far as Lhotse Shar (8383 m) . . . It filled us with renewed enthusiasm: such a wonderful route and – if it succeeded – a fantastic achievement! So we told ourselves.

We felt a little like pioneers for the future – even if we succeeded only in taking the first tentative steps towards what would doubtless be the ultimate, and far-distant challenge of this great ridge . . . You could project the line further, from Lhotse over to Everest, and from there down into Tibet to give you the greatest 8000-metre traverse in history. And including three seven-thousanders into the bargain. Such a feat would certainly need multifaceted military-style organisation, working on a number of different levels. Music for the future . . .

*

Our dream of doing the great Lhotse Ridge came true only in part – we experienced one of the worst pre-monsoon periods ever in Nepal. Scarcely any expedition was able to realise its high-flying project. The Spanish had to go home without Everest (which we wasted no tears over!) and Reinhold Messner was rebuffed on Makalu. I didn't reach Lhotse or Lhotse Shar. Neither Messner nor I got his 'third'.

But one mountain success did bless our expedition: Shartse – the first of the two virgin seven-thousanders on the ridge – the eastern corner of the Everest massif (Shar = east, Tse = corner, summit). It was the highest first ascent that season in Nepal, and proved extremely dangerous as well as much more difficult than I had thought. What I carried home from this expedition were friendships and the memory of storms and sickness. Extracts from my diary:

'If it goes on like this, we'll use up all our tents,' moans Gerhard Lenser. Never before has he experienced such a series of bad luck:

  In Camp 2 on a day of tempest there came a sudden retort, like a shot, and a wonderful Jamet Tent ripped open along its full length

. . . a stray gust had found its way in through the entrance, which happened to be open.

In Camp 3 wind-borne drift crushed everything, broke all the poles, and tore the tent. So often before, we had carefully collapsed it when we left, but this time, for some reason, did not.

In Camp 4 devils were on the loose. A cornice collapse destroyed the camp, burying it under tons of snow and ice. It was good luck only that nobody was there when it happened.

In Camp 5 the Schwabian, Hermann Warth and his companion Nawang Tenzing were buried during the night by a snow slide. Even though they managed to extricate themselves, they had terrible hours till morning. All the tentpoles were broken by the force of the impact. 'Many danger' smiles the strong little Tibetan, whenever the conversation comes back to that night. 'Camp 5, no die.' Perhaps we can repair the tent for a further summit attempt.

Only in Base Camp were no tents broken. A bad sandstorm had flattened them all – but it was not disastrous.

'In all truth, it was the most terrible season for weather,' complained Gerhard Lenser, and he should know if anyone does. He is more at home in Nepal than in Europe, so often does he go over there. It was no exaggeration: how many thunderstorms had we seen that set the whole night sky aglow over Makalu with continuous lightning-flicker – lasting hours at a time – a breathtaking firework display around that black silhouette. Around us on Shartse, fantastic snow shapes formed, magically created by this extraordinary winter: nuns' hats, on the ridge, all white and starched, fresh from the laundry, and forty metres high.

There was a giant snowdrop, and over on Lhotse Shar – you could see it really well through the tele-lens – floated an angel with spread wings.

Further down on our wild ridge, the wind played another of its jokes: a snowman was wringing his hands.

I railed at cruel fate because I was sick: was that the fault of the weather, or the big cornice which fell on my head at 6300 metres? 'My right lung feels like a sandbag, I am breathing mostly through the left side. But I don't have any fever. Nevertheless, it stabs so much . . .' I wrote. As it turned out, I had a broken rib, but that certainly was not the only thing. Even so, on 23 May 1974, Hermann Warth and I stood on the summit of the 7000-metre peak, 'our' Shartse, the first mountain on that mighty Lhotse Ridge. Our faces were bedecked with icicles (see jacket). We looked more like monsters than men and Hermann had two of his fingertips frostbitten during the summit climb.

This difficult mountain is only the 'first obstacle' on the Lhotse Ridge – we were happy that we had at least managed to bag that.

What else had this expedition given us? So much. The fact that four years later Hermann Warth, Nawang Tenzing and I were able to stand on Makalu is in no small part thanks to our epic on Shartse (I can't call it anything else), which left us such friends. Day after day we had pitted ourselves against an unkind destiny, that simply didn't want us to win through – against tempests and cornices. We had to endure so much. But we also experienced wonderful moments during this wild adventure. Sometimes, when towards evening the clouds were rising, that giant granite monolith with the name of Mahakala – a dark godhead – burnt like a sacrificial fire in the sky. Then we would urge each other to the entrance of the tent and look up through the icy silence of the evening till the light went out.

. . . Makalu . . . Mahakala . . .

At such moments this mountain is the most secretive place in the world.

*

One day before we got back to Tumlingtar – into the wide valley of the Arun River – as we were ambling along the path through the bramble bushes, stopping from time to time to pick a couple of the sweet, yellow fruits which are so full of taste, and when once again I was asking myself why in Nepal the blackberries are yellow – along comes the postman.

Mail from home! We bury our heads in the letters and read and read – at the same time I am still half-thinking about the blackberries because I know that Teresa, my wife, is coming for her first visit to Nepal, to wander with me, and she is crazy about blackberries. I will lead her into a great yellow bramble-heaven.

There, it is written: she has obtained her visa. In ten days she arrives! I open the next letter. Whoaa . . . What's this? I have been engaged to make a film in Greenland – in two weeks' time.

Oh, oh! Poor Teresa . . .

When will we finally wander through Nepal?

(We did succeed – many years later!)

Neck and neck with Reinhold

Before I bring the reader to Greenland, let us stay for some pages
in the great Himalaya. Five years after my return from the epic on
the Great Ridge – I jotted the following reflections:

Shartse: So much for my 'third eight-thousander' – it was not to be.
Could a person climb all fourteen, I wonder? Nowadays I think it is
possible. A lot of things and circumstances have to work together,
but lighter weight equipment and shorter approaches have increased
the probability. Luck you will still need.

Thinking it over today – and assuming survival – I could already
have climbed all fourteen eight-thousanders quite a while ago. In the
eighteen years' pause between the last 'young man's' eight-thousander
(Dhaulagiri 1960, at the age of twenty-eight) and the first 'latter-day
eight-thousander' (Makalu 1978, at forty-six) I would have needed to
climb one every two years in order to accomplish the nine I lacked
. . . such a thing is perfectly possible. Reinhold Messner has shown,
as I have, that you can climb three eight-thousanders within fifteen
months. Yes, at such a rate, theoretically you could snap up all
fourteen in a little less than six years. * *But I doubt if it would be*
much pleasure any more.

Nevertheless, I am sure there will be people who will succeed in
making the complete 'collection'. People who have enough time
and money, and certainly also a prevailing sporting attitude to
the problem. I think that Messner and I have already given the
broad indication that it is possible. For my part, I do not for a
minute regret my eighteen eight-thousander-less years during the long
pause between Dhaulagiri and Makalu. How much I lived in that
time . . .

I wrote that in my diary in 1979, having within a short while 'bagged'
Everest, Makalu and Gasherbrum II – all, as I said, within fifteen

---

* As a matter of fact, Jerzy Kukuczka needed just eight years. My forecast was
almost spot on.

months! At the time I could have entertained a race with Reinhold Messner, but I lacked the passion for it, as well as the necessary organisation and the money. It would have meant the end of a free life for me, and my untamed spirit would never have accepted such a bridle. I can well understand that many years later, when Wanda Rutkiewicz had attained eight of the highest peaks, she should want to cut the matter short by her 'caravan of dreams' – finishing off the rest in just one year. But she died on Kangchenjunga. And Messner himself, after reaching the goal in 1986, admitted to feeling 'freer than ever before'!

At the stage when each of us had five (different) eight-thousanders, the fact did not pass unobserved by the public (in the insider circle of the mountaineers, most already knew it). Moreover, my sudden, belated success on the eight-thousanders must have struck a little too close to home. How otherwise can I explain to myself that after Makalu my partner Hermann Warth (whose second eight-thousander it had been), was invited by Reinhold Messner to go to K2, but I, who had climbed my fourth, wasn't. Hermann did not accept the invitation. To both of us it smacked of politics. Doubtless Reinhold was already taking into account the possibility of becoming first up all fourteen eight-thousanders, rather than simply being a master mountaineer. He has always been an outstanding calculator, planner and organiser.

A journalist picked on the subject and wrote an amusing satire – through the eyes of an absolute non-climber – at the same time poking fun at the overall climbing scene. In the name of truth and objectivity, I have omitted a couple of the more unrealistic passages and below-the-belt fouls. Reinhold at any rate is well used to wrangles with journalists. But between its lines, this little set piece casts an amusing light on the situation in which we found ourselves then. Over a glass of wine on the moraine at the foot of Everest, Reinhold and I also spoke of the matter in autumn 1980. His suspicion, he told me, was that the journalists wanted to set us against each other: both of us had just suffered a defeat (neither he nor I were granted the summit of Lhotse). But we clinked glasses and drank to the future!

This intuitive piece of contemporary non-climbing writing was called: 'The Secret Fear of Reinhold Messner: has Kurt Diemberger been there already?' and sub-titled: 'Imagine the scene if the two best mountaineers in the world should run into each other'. It appeared under the byline 'Michael P. Winkler' in May 1980 in the German edition of *Penthouse* magazine. Having encountered the journalist Axel Thorer – who knows both Reinhold and me personally – in the bar of the Hotel Narayani I was convinced the story must have been propagated from his fertiliser! He has recently confessed as much, and allowed me to reprint it. Here, then, is the story of the journalist who was waiting to interview 'the best mountaineer in the world':

'Let us meet in the Hotel Narayani in Kathmandu,' he had said on the telephone. The Narayani in Patan is the starting point for most Himalayan expeditions. It is where the 'boys' kip in their last real bed before exchanging soft quilts for sleeping-bags for months on end.

In the bar of the Narayani all rules are dictated by a dark-eyed human penguin in a wine-red jacket, who whistles for taxis, and who greets you (as if by clockwork), 'Good morning, Monsieur.' In earlier times he used to include 'Mister' and 'Mein Herr', but that was before Pierre Mazeaud, the ex-Sports Minister of France, arrived from Paris with his Mount Everest entourage. Since 1978 it has been 'Monsieur'.

The Narayani Bar is square, and positioned close to the windows on one side, so that, after their tenth beer the climbing stars can belay themselves securely to the curtains. Coming in from the right in the half-darkness (low light is chic; almost no light is very chic, in Nepal) you presume, rather than make out the little tables, chairs and benches in the room. And you surmise rightly.

Some people are sitting there. They wear corduroy knickerbockers and bright red knee stockings. If one of them gets up to go through the glass door into the hotel lobby in search of the loos, it sounds as if a freshly shod carthorse is clopping over cobbles. Aha, nailed boots!

They will have been wearing them since Munich, even in the tropical heat of Delhi where they broke their journey. At worst, this will have cost them a few blisters, but think of the excess baggage saved! Yes, they are true lads of nature.

'Gin and tonic,' I shout. Devendra, the bartender, looks at me with astonishment while swiftly whipping away half a bottle of gin and three small tonic waters and concealing them in the ice under the counter.

'Hey, hey,' I warn him, 'I saw that. What are you doing?'

'Sorry, mister,' he excuses himself, 'Those are reserved for the best

mountaineer in the world.' Who's that? I feel tempted to ask, but I let it go. No point in starting an argument this early in the evening. Besides, several Italians are already looking up with interest. The world's best mountaineer, eh . . . theirs, or the one from Austria?

Toni Hiebeler's 'Lexicon of the Alps' cites two! On page 124: 'Kurt Diemberger, Austrian mountaineer and guide, born 16.3.32, from Salzburg. In the Alps he has mastered all the big north faces of Eiger, Matterhorn and Grandes Jorasses. Has climbed five eight-thousanders, among them the first ascents of Broad Peak and Dhaulagiri.' And on page 277: 'Reinhold Messner, Italian mountain guide from South Tyrol, born 17.11.44 in Brixen. About 20 solo climbs in the 5th and 6th grade of difficulty. Also, six big winter first ascents.'

Devendra, hardened by years of dispensing alcoholic treatment to mountaineers – like a football-masseur oiling muscles and limbs of the league champions – slides a beer towards me, foam spilling over the edge and dribbling in small rivulets down the counter. The beer is called Pink Pelican, and I feel really happy to be in a country which can apply such a name to a beer, even if there are no pelicans in Nepal.

From the ceiling three lamps dangle over the corner of the wooden bar. Their lampshades of woven wickerwork swallow half the light which the dim bulbs push out. Energy crisis on the roof of the world: more than three miserable forty-watt lamps and all the lights of Patan go out.

A few climbers are pressing in, others trying to get out. It's like a mustering: those in the lobby are staring through the glass door into the bar, and those inside keep looking out to see if they can recognise a familiar face. ('Ah! Old so-and-so from Innsbruck in here!') Every newcomer does what all the others did when they came in – set down their rucksacks at the entrance and raise a finger, 'Beer, please!'

Devendra in all seriousness asks, 'Pelican or Lion?' It seems in Nepal there are only zoological kinds of beer.

The air is getting thin. I am waiting for someone, who has decided to renounce all manner of oxygen gear for the rest of his life, from the highest peaks to the deepest valley. Thank God that every time one of the climbing stars comes in through the glass door, he fans some fresh air from the lobby into the bar. The buzz of voices in here is a babel of German-English-Italian-Nepalese-Japanese-French. Then, suddenly, everything stops as a reverent hush fills the room. The manager proudly leads a guest in through the glass door. At once, the whirr of voices starts up again, so that the newcomer does not immediately know he has been recognised. One admires him, but . . .

I had been told to expect a 'six-footer' and, supposing this to be the secret of his success, was disappointed to learn that in English this merely represents a measure of height rather than hexapodous endowment. The newcomer, then, is tall and lanky, and he wears modish 'New Man' jeans, a cotton shirt over his tee-shirt (leaving only letters 'rgst' visible), and embroidered slippers. The wide-brimmed hat, his trademark, he lets dangle from his left hand. Obviously he has no fear of excess baggage. The guy looks around, comes across and asks if the stool beside me is free; when I say 'Help yourself', he stands behind it. He has a slight lisp and a look of studied earnestness.

I would have liked to lift the fringe and peer behind the beard to see what he really looks like. Later, some associations spring to mind: a civilised yeti, perhaps, or a beautiful young man after a hunger strike. Some of the guests in the bar cannot contain themselves. Germans. They are storming out of the niches, boots aclopping, to surround the man. 'Reinhold!' one of them cries, 'Look – it's Messner in person!' 'What are you doing here?'

In impeccable High German he lisps, 'Holiday.'

Someone says, 'Did you hear about Hannelore?'

Reinhold looks really sad: 'Yes, but no details.'

I remember: Hannelore Schmatz, thirty-five years old, wife of a lawyer from Neu-Ulm; she was part of a group of three to climb Mount Everest on 2 October 1979, but died of cold on the way back, along with the American, Ray Genet . . .

I take a gulp of beer and timidly address the face behind the hair: 'Excuse me, what did they die of up there, those two?'

'Too old,' he replies, and strokes his beard. 'Genet was forty-eight, far too long in the tooth for such an undertaking.'

So that was it.

I look about. The people clustering around – are they all too old for the highest mountain in the world?

By and by I realise I have penetrated an elite group. You don't hear any surnames: they are all called Peter, Pietro, Pete, Pierre, Pedro. Or Luke, Jean-Luc or Luigi. Many of them seem to have invisible labels around their necks: 'First winter ascent of the Matterhorn East Face.' And: 'Three seven- and two eight-thousanders.' One calls to another: 'How was it on Lhotse?'

'I guess,' says the shock-haired lisper, *'that here in this bar'* – and he revolves on his heels like the official valuer in a dead man's flat – *'there must be about fifteen eight-thousanders.'* Pause. *'Without counting my six.'* Six?

That must be a dig at the man I am waiting for . . . Kurt Diemberger.

Devendra takes away the empties and serves new Pelicans. I ask: *'Is it really cold up there?'* and I point like an idiot at the ceiling of the bar as if Everest was lying just outside the hotel. The bearded façade with the peeling stucco of sunburnt skin replies that if the sun is shining during the day, and there is not too strong a wind, then with luck the thermometer might creep up to as much as −25C. Encouraged, I decide I will go and give it a try myself.

Then Reinhold continues: *'During the night it is somewhat cooler. Down to, maybe, minus 40.'*

I grasp my fresh beer. It feels like an icy rock wall. I try to withdraw my hand, but my fingers are already stuck fast, as if to frozen metal.

At such temperatures,' Reinhold recalls, *'you lose all sensation. My feet have frozen at minus 30.'* He looks down at me. My own right leg has gone numb, all the way to the knee. One of the Italians is taking interest and addresses the beard in his mother language. Reinhold answers in the same tongue. So, he is a South Tyrolean.

'That was on Nanga Parbat,' Reinhold continues, *'on 9 August 1978.'* My right upper leg has now lost all feeling. I keep kicking it with the left. Nothing. And my hand is still frozen to the beer glass. That's it, then, I have got frostbite from listening.

'I am just down from K2, over in Pakistan,' lisps the beard, pulling a nut from his pocket and hanging it around my beer glass – clearly to give me something to hold on to if I should fall. Then he goes on. *'That was in July, 12 July, actually, I reached the top without oxygen.'*

I draw a deep breath. *'Without oxygen?'*

'Mmmm, that's right. It's 8611 metres, quite high. Over 6500 metres the oxygen ration in the air is too low to sustain life in an unacclimatised person.'

'Oh . . .' I say.

'If you have bad luck,' he lisps on, *'your brain cells die away like flies on the wall. That's why mountaineers normally use artificial oxygen at these heights.'*

'But not you?'

He sees that I have understood, and continues my education. 'I have trained my body so well, that I can renounce this technical aid for a long time. Before K2 I climbed Mount Everest without oxygen. All in all, I have been up five eight-thousanders, and one of them even twice . . .'

I start to lie: 'No one will repeat that in a hurry, will they?'

Before Reinhold can answer there is some movement in the throng. Pushing through the glass door comes a small compact figure. He has receding hair, a bushy beard and the look of a crucifix carver who has fallen on hard times. The rucksack over his shoulder hangs as shapelessly on his back as do the cord trousers around his legs. Almost unnoticed, secretively even, he steers himself towards the last free stool at my side. Barkeeper Devendra pulls out the half-full gin bottle and the tonic water and fills a glass. 'Here,' he says, 'your drink.' Bald-pate smiles happily, thanks him, and puts it away in a gulp. I guess he must be fifty and wonder if that is perhaps the guy with whom I made an appointment in Kathmandu over the telephone in Munich.

A group of English, French and Japanese now surrounds Reinhold to my right. Five – sorry, six – eight-thousanders this guy has climbed. So often he's been to that altitude, which a normal earthling only ventures into by plane. Eight thousand metres. And every time without air. Beg your pardon: without oxygen.

Devendra tries to pull two pieces of chewing gum out of his hair, put there by a drunken American. The Christ-carver to my left demolishes his second gin and tonic with proficiency. 'Can you imagine,' I ask him, 'climbing an 8000-metre mountain and not carrying oxygen?'

'Sure,' he says, taking another slug. 'That's nothing unusual. This chap called Dacher from Germany climbed Lhotse solo without oxygen. But he did not beat the drum about it.' Pause. Then – a little louder – 'Reinhold is rather better in that department.'

An arrow has been released that is now sailing through the bar of the Narayani like a UFO before a surprise attack.

'Germany', the Christ-carver had said. Which makes him a foreigner. And 'Reinhold', he also said. So he knows him, perhaps? This really must be the Diemberger I am waiting for.

Just before setting out for Nepal, I met the Africa-explorer Heinrich Harrer, one of the first conquerors of the Eiger North Face; he was about to board a plane in Munich for Tanzania. He told me, 'This Kurt Diemberger from Salzburg was already climbing without oxygen twenty years ago. Not from any love of adventure, but because he could not afford the expensive oxygen bottles.'

About 800 Deutschmarks such a bottle costs today. And it lasts five hours. If you only take ten cylinders with you to Everest, you're still breathing a fortune! Dispensing with the genie in the bottle has become a matter of ideology among mountain stars and their fans.

I reflect whether I should ask this elderly gentleman at my side whether he is Diemberger, and whether he climbs without oxygen. But Reinhold Messner's words come into my mind and I don't want to be tactless. 'At forty-eight you are too old for Everest,' he had said.

A young climber from Tyrol, who told me yesterday that he had already climbed three eight-thousanders, joins me. 'You only managed your eight-thousanders because you are not yet thirty,' I venture.

'Mountaineering is not a question of age,' he corrects me. 'Messner is thirty-six now and has climbed five eight-thousanders.'

'Six,' I say.

'Yes, yes,' he answers, 'but one was twice.'

'I know,' I say, 'Nanga Parbat.'

'Diemberger, on the other hand,' he continues (the old man, that I take to be Diemberger, has meanwhile retired into a dark window corner) 'is forty-nine, and has also done five eight-thousanders. The last, Gasherbrum II, only this last August.' The Tyrolean is swallowed up again in the throng, but at the name of Diemberger, the elderly man re-emerges from his dark recess and is again at my side. Perhaps he likes me?

Fifty years old and still clambering around at 8000 metres in icy conditions. Fantastic.

'Fantastic,' I shout. 'Can you imagine that?' I yell into the ear of the gin and tonic guy.

'Sure' he answers quietly, pushing his glass forward for a refill.

'But without oxygen?' I forget my manners. 'Would you ever go without oxygen?'

'Why not?' he says. 'But with oxygen you get more out of being up there, because the fourteen million brain cells are more receptive.' This man understands something of medicine.

The fans have directed their attention away from Reinhold. He turns around, raising his glass to his lips – then, abruptly, sets it down.

'Kurtl,' he yells, 'Diemberger, Kurtl, where did you spring from?'

'Servus Reinhold! Nice to see you.'

Now I know for sure that the Reinhold is Reinhold Messner and the Christ-carver Kurt Diemberger. The youngest and the oldest best mountaineer in the world hug one another enthusiastically. Both, as I said, with five eight-thousanders behind them. Their closest rival only has three. Never have the two men climbed together. Each has Mount Everest in his swag-bag: but none of their others are in common. The last time Messner and Diemberger met was eight years ago, lecturing in Innsbruck. That was when they had each climbed two eight-thousanders and so split the evening between them. Afterwards, they swore to attempt the next Himalayan giant together.

'It should have been Makalu, 8475 metres high,' Diemberger remembers, 'but then your expedition dumped me, Reinhold.'

'That was a bit mean,' I say to Messner.

'Ach, leave it,' Kurtl interrupts me, 'they didn't climb it, anyway.' Diemberger has meanwhile added it to his tally, Messner still waits to.

With the appearance of Diemberger, which has been noticed by others in the Narayani Bar as well, a chillier, more combative atmosphere has descended, and this sense of an impending prize fight overflows from the bar, through the glass door and into the lobby . . . More knickerbocker-wearers, hitherto uninvolved, draw closer. They are expecting something to happen. It really is a historic moment when two such eminent alpine stars confront each other – even if no gorge separates them, only a hotel bar.

Messner, as the young climbers know – several of whom are now squatting at his feet so that the people at the back can also participate – this Reinhold Messner has climbed his five eight-thousanders without oxygen, Diemberger only has three gasless ascents.

'True,' admits the old man, 'but my record can never be broken: I have climbed two eight-thousanders as first ascents.' (None of the fourteen remains virgin now.)

A profound reverence charges the air. The lads cluster round with shining eyes – as happy as football fans suddenly caught in the same sauna as Kevin Keegan and Pelé, perhaps.

With this, in the international climbing standards, Diemberger has been elevated to the mountaineers' Valhalla, whatever Messner might still do . . .

Diemberger leans closer, sloshes gin and tonic on my trousers, and remarks innocently, 'Broad Peak and Dhaulagiri.' I don't understand.

Somebody else whispers: 'Those are the two summits he has climbed as first ascents.'

Ah, yes?

A stentorian shout issues from the darkness of the niche: 'Grö-ö-öbaz!'

Gröbaz? I know 'Gröfaz', the 'Greatest Field Marshall of all time' – it's code for Hitler. But Gröbaz?

Then it dawns on me: the 'Greatest Bergsteiger of all time' – Messner.

The man who called must be from the Diemberger camp. His acclamation has stirred the fans of both factions into frenzy. They are trampling on each other's feet. Why, can't be clearly made out; perhaps they have all risen at once, or is it because the hand-to-hand phase has started?

In another dark corner a muscular and chauvinistic Austrian adds his voice against Messner, the Italian. Taking the beer glass from his face, he hisses, 'Bivouac-merchant . . .'

Messner has not heard him. But Diemberger did, though he does not react. Something, therefore, must be hanging on that, or Diemberger would not accept a public detraction of his colleague.

In the bar the Messner supporters now crowd Diemberger and start having a go at him. 'You must speak slowly, friends,' he says, 'I have climbed too many eight-thousanders without oxygen.'

I am flirting with danger, here, because sudden laughter causes me to slap my hand on the counter and almost fall off my stool.

Did or did not Diemberger just insinuate that his competitor has suffered slight 'roof damage' from rushing without oxygen up the eight-thousanders? Including himself in that, too. For, if Diemberger claims roof damage after only three gasless eight-thousanders, and Messner has climbed five . . . I don't dare to think further.

[Note by K.D: I didn't mean it that way; if Reinhold really lost brain cells – they regenerated very swiftly!]

'What are the two of you doing here?' I ask.

Diemberger says he is earning money guiding a tourist group to the foot of Everest. Messner replies that he is exhausted from writing, and the endless driving from one lecture to another. 'Far worse, this rushing about,' he says, 'than any approach-march.'

Kurtl laughs, 'How would you know that? You always fly in by helicopter to Base Camp.' Touché!

The counter-blow comes from a Messner fan: 'And you have seventeen kilos of excess baggage when you set out.'

'Yes,' says Kurtl, and gets his glass filled again. 'But after fifteen days of foot-slogging and carrying forty kilos of luggage on my back up to 5400 metres, I am match-fit.'

The beer glass in my hand has meanwhile warmed sufficiently for me to free it easily.

'It's amazing that you can still climb so well at your age,' I praise Diemberger. 'What did you do last year?'

Diemberger starts counting them off: 'Gasherbrum II: that was on 4 August . . .'

'When I had just come down from K2,' Messner chips in.

'Diemberger continues: 'In spring '78 I was on Makalu.'

Messner moves in closer: 'That's when I was on Everest.'

The division of the Himalaya to the Kings of the Mountains continues briskly. Any more bids? Messner? Diemberger! 'Autumn 1978, I stood on Everest.'

A fan from the Messner side: 'When Reinhold was on Nanga Parbat for the second time.'

A further eye-witness chips in: 'Then, Messner was on Manaslu and Hidden Peak,' he declares.

Promptly from a niche, the echo arrives: 'But Hidden Peak is only sixty-eight metres above 8000.'

I stifle a sneeze. 'Anyone got a handkerchief?' I force out the words with my hand in front of my nose.

'Yes, here!' says Kurtl, fishing in his trouser pocket and bringing out a handful of coloured pennants from all nations.

'What use are those?' I ask, helpless, and rescue myself with a serviette from the table.

'Other people collect stamps,' says Diemberger, 'I collect pennants.'

'Which some poor sods have carried dutifully up an eight-thousander to record which country's sons have been up there?'

'Yes,' crows Kurtl, and blows his nose into my serviette.

Without doubt – this man in front of me is the most sacrilegious magpie of the mountain world. An American leans over to me. 'Believe, me, he doesn't just collect pennants, he passes them on as presents. Two months ago, he gave me one which I had myself stuck on the top of Makalu three years before!'

Kurtl tips more drink on my trousers and endeavours to order

*a new one, but the bottle which Devandra had reserved for him
is empty, so he wants to leave. But through the glass door – the
only way of escape – another tee-shirt walks in. This one, with the
words: 'Joggers make better lovers'. A sun-tanned Tyrolean en route
for Ama Dablam which, though not that high, is said to be the most
beautiful mountain of the world, an over-iced Matterhorn. Messner
– who sports a cryptic 'rgst' on his tee-shirt – also wants to go to Ama
Dablam. Perhaps the two are together?*

*I grab Kurtl by his trouser belt as a witness and ask Messner the
significance of his tee-shirt motto. 'It's a printing error,' he lisps. 'The
shirt comes from the USA.'*

*Now everyone wants to see what comes before and after the 'rgst'.
Reinhold unbuttons his shirt to reveal the chest, held by many young
ladies to be the most desirable bivouac site of the world. 'Bergsteiger,'
I read, 'make the very best lovers.'*

*Now Diemberger feels obliged to counter. He unbuttons, to reveal
no bivouac paradise, but a somewhat portly form, on which is written:
'Just a dirty tee-shirt'. Well, that's the way he is, Kurtl.*

*The Tyrolean with the competing shirt to Messner – Joggers v.
Bergsteigers – moves towards me and asks: 'Can I have your
autograph?'*

My God! What embarrassment . . .

I ask the reader: after this piece of theatre, should we guide the
said Axel Thorer up Mont Blanc and fulfil his secret dream? I, the
'pennant-pilferer' and Reinhold, 'the civilised yeti' . . .

I think we should agree in advance to procure some adventure for
him on the way. Though we can expect to chew our nails awaiting
his report of the climb . . .

Perhaps we had better take that old print-devil up.

PART FOUR

In the eternal ice – on the trail of Alfred Wegener

The helicopter thunders, it sings, as below us the outlines of mighty ridges and faces flow into one another, then extricate themselves once more. Oh, oh, you wonderful mountainland at the edge of the inland ice cap! Land of my heart! Another of those places in the world where I am at home.

A massive rock cliff appears. Qingarssuaq . . . the Summit above the Three Fjords . . . How fine it is! Suddenly an idea strikes me: I wonder if my cairn, my stoneman, is still there on top? 'Can we land on that summit?' I bellow through the helicopter's roar, shaking the pilot's shoulder to catch his attention and pointing downwards. Like a cathedral with yellow walls, the mountain rises vertically 1700 metres from the greeny-blue waters of the Kangerdlugssuaq Fjord, its finely detailed upper section dissolving into pulpits, ribs, flying buttresses . . .

The friendly Dane nods and gestures his agreement and already the motor begins hammering as we sink towards the peak.

The spire of the cathedral reaches out to us, daunting, incredible. These pilots are such gladiators, they can land anywhere! Squeaks of alarm issue from Anne at the start of our unscheduled descent, but her husband Robert, squashed in beside me, lets forth an enthusiastic roar. The tip of the spire draws closer.

'He's a crazy man, this Kurt!' Anne shrieks. 'One mad idea after another!' But I only laugh: I know the cathedral is not as sharp as it seems. Nevertheless, for a moment before we touch down, the aircraft tilts so steeply that all we see are the fjords which half surround us, and icebergs – looking no bigger than tiny sugar cubes, though they must be at least the size of apartment blocks. Heaven, I think as I stare into those dark sugar-studded waters, let there be no gusts.

A soft jolt: and we have alighted on the brink of the abyss. 'Watch yourselves, getting out!' I shout superfluously. But that applies only to one side – from the other, the summit can be reached easily. And there he is: my stoneman! I had already spotted him as we came down, and with a surge of sentiment – I am not ashamed to admit it – I watched eagerly as he drew closer, like a greeting, something of myself in this place – the memory of a happy day.

For some minutes I forget my friends, the pilot, the helicopter, everything. Approaching the cairn, I am tugged back into the past. We could have just built it – Bruno, Carlo, myself . . . the others. Gently, I slide away one of the rocks and the lady winks out at me, the little Madonna of Tortona, that strawberry town in the Apennines. Another greeting from the friendly earth. A small piece of Italy here in Greenland above the expanse of blue fjords. I nod to the stoneman: it is like dropping in unannounced on an old friend, and finding him as glad to see you. It is easy to imagine the stoneman happy that I have come. He has been on his own for eight years.

This is my third expedition to this part of Greenland. I came first in 1966, with the Italians – and I have told about that in my earlier book, *Summits and Secrets*; next was with Germans in 1971, the year I got to know Robert and Anne. We were wanting to climb other big mountains on the long Qioqe Peninsula, on which we now stand. This time – summer 1974 – one of our targets is the inland ice shield, where we hope to find traces of Alfred Wegener's last expedition.

Officially, we are the Second Hessian Greenland Expedition, and our leader is Robert Kreuzinger. Before we came, I spent weeks trawling through the yellowed pages of two old books in his library: *SOS Eisberg!** about a film expedition made by Dr Arnold Fanck to this area, and *Alfred Wegeners Letzte Groenlandfahrt.*† Kreuzinger wrote to all the survivors from the explorer's last enterprise of 1930–31, and I, in my role as film director and cameraman for

---

* Dr Ernst Sorge, *With Plane, Boat, and Camera in Greenland*, Hurst and Blackett, 1935.
† Else Wegener with Dr Fritz Loewe (ed), *Greenland Journey: the story of Wegener's German Expedition to Greenland in 1930–31* as told by members of the expedition and the leader's diary, Blackie, 1939.

Professor Karl Weiken and Station Eismitte, Greenland, 1930. *Below*, entertaining my Greenland friends, one-eyed in Umanak, after the filming accident.

The view from 1800 metres down to the Kangerdlugssuaq Fjord from the top of Qingarssuaq, our Three-Fjords peak.

Climbing one of the nameless mountains of the Qioqe Peninsula.

The inland ice, the immense white desert of the Greenland Icecap. Up to 3000 metres thick, it covers most of the earth's biggest island. This was the area where Wegener located his West Station. Eismitte was 400 kilometres further inland. *Inset*, his memorial plaque.

One of Wegener's propeller sledges on the icecap. *Below*, expedition members outside the winter house in 1930.

We found old gear from Wegener's time around the West Station. The gas from the hydrogen bottle served the weather balloons, the winch was for the kites. *Below*, The millepede casts its shadow on our environment. Is there no limit to the way tourism and technical progress invade our open spaces?

How long will fantasy keep its place between the dew drops on a twig?

the German television company ZDF, took myself to Düsseldorf to visit the white-haired professor, Dr Karl Weiken. This remarkably vigorous octogenarian gave me an eye-witness account of those dramatic days. Subsequently, every expedition box we found at the edge of the inland ice, every pemmican tin, every horse skeleton rekindled the long-gone events for us, and posed riddles . . . In Germany, Kurt Schif was able to furnish valuable information about the peculiar propeller sledges which were without doubt a fateful element in the course of Wegener's expedition. And BIBO-Film of Rüdesheim, who produced our ZDF film, even unearthed some ancient, faded but incredibly breathtaking fragments of film from the expedition itself! All these, associated with our own experiences, conjured up – and still conjure! – a 'word-film' before my spiritual eye, which I will try to realise in this chapter. (In order to make my mental leaps easier on the reader, I put historical events and all that is concerned with them in italics.) My admiration for the deeds of the old explorers is profound, and I am of the opinion that what we mountaineers do now on our expeditions to Greenland and the Polar regions does not remotely measure up to the achievements of those men, nor do we know anything of the privations they endured. They must not be allowed to fall into oblivion!

So, here we were, on a reconnaissance flight for the filming of *Im ewigen Eis* – having just made our unscheduled pause on Qingarssuaq summit. It was a happy day and I could not foresee that only a month later, while taking some of the final shots to illustrate Alfred Wegener's last journey, I would almost lose my own life. On this cathedral I felt only that something was linking me to the great explorer, perhaps the feeling of being at home in this barren, wonderful loneliness that is Greenland. Surely he felt that way about the inland ice, returning to it, as he did, time and again . . .

*

The helicopter lifts off again, Three-Fjord Mountain falls away, the ice cap extends immeasurably, limitlessly, appearing ever wider the higher we climb; firn basins shimmer, crevasse carpets spread, cloudshadows wander. The earth is full of secrets – to hold you in thrall for a lifetime.

The inland ice, the white desert . . .

I think back to that vanished time when our century had not yet
run a third of its course . . .

*On an afternoon in May 1931, a column of sledges stops some 190
kilometres from the western rim of the inland ice. Two skis have been
stuck into the snow, about three metres apart. Between them lies a
splintered ski stick. The men of the sledge column leave their dogs and
with picks and shovels start digging close to the skis, which obviously
represent some kind of memorial, or a marker, for a wayfarer perhaps
trying to cross the inland ice . . .*

*A reindeer skin is uncovered. Below it are more pelts, and a
sleeping-bag cover. And below them lies the body of a man, sewn
into two sleeping-bag covers. After cutting away the shroud they see he
is fully dressed, wearing fur boots, dog-skin trousers, a blue ski tunic,
blue waistcoat, a woollen jacket, wind-jacket, woollen balaclava and
a hood.*

*The face of the dead man is peaceful, relaxed, his eyes open. He
has been given a careful burial by someone who was a good comrade
and forced to leave him behind.*

*Those who opened the dead man's grave are also his companions.
They waited long for his return, then set out in search of him. He
is their expedition leader, Alfred Wegener. Now, they reinter him in
the ice, building a memorial from blocks of firn over the spot. The
skis are stuck back in the snow and a black flag attached to them.
Then the men head back westwards. They want to finish the great
scientific programme which their leader had planned and partially
carried out.*

Let us flash forward to the start of our expedition: after a four-hour
flight from Copenhagen we landed in West Greenland. On the
airstrip of Sondrestroemfjord, a staging place for Polar flights and the
most important civil airport on the island, we stand before a signpost
which points to the four winds and proclaims optimistically how, in
just a few hours, you could get from here to most of the big cities of
the world. But that is not what we want: we have been waiting since 8
o'clock this morning for the scheduled twenty-eight person helicopter
to take us to Umanak, 500 kilometres away. We – eight men and a
woman, hailing mostly from Hesse but including also one Austrian
and two Bavarians – are all enthusiastic alpinists with Greenland
experience. Our intention is to follow in the footsteps of the biggest

German Greenland expedition to date, that epoch-making venture which explored the island in the early thirties under the leadership of Professor Alfred Wegener. At the same time our mountaineering ambitions are not to be denied: we hope to make the first ascent of Agpatat, a mountain rising almost 2000 metres above sea level! (And that really does mean 2000 metres – unlike the Alps.) Agpatat is situated in the Umanak area and has already defeated two Italian attempts. We are sitting in the hall of the wide, low airport hotel, waiting and waiting. This is normal: Greenland schedules are rarely followed exactly. (I have been here for three days already!) I keep flicking through the folder of archive photographs which Robert has collected; one, more recent than the rest, shows a memorial plaque to Alfred Wegener, erected by his Austrian friends from Graz on rocks below the inland ice at the head of Qaumarujuk Fjord. Thoughtfully, I look at the picture of the explorer . . .

Who was Alfred Wegener?

Alfred Wegener, born on 1 November 1880 in Berlin, was a professor of geophysics and meteorology at the University of Graz.

The name Wegener became famous in 1912, when he sprang his 'Hypothesis of Continental Drift' on a startled scientific world. America, Europe, Africa and Asia were originally part of a single land mass, he postulated, only later drifting apart: America floating west, while part of India along with Australia and Antarctica headed east. Wegener's hypothesis was at first ridiculed by a conservative establishment, but later, as geologist H. P. Cornelius put it, proved the 'magic wand by which a number of partially heavyweight problems of geology itself, as well as various adjacent fields, could be seen in a totally new light'.

Alfred Wegener, however, was no mere desk-man; as a meteorologist and glacier explorer, he felt drawn to the eternal ice of the largest island on earth, to Greenland. Here were problems enough to satisfy not only glaciologists, but meteorologists too. The southern part of Greenland lies in the so-called 'Polar front zone', where cold and warm currents of air collide, creating vortices which move on towards Europe and greatly influence its weather.

Alfred Wegener went three times to Greenland, dying there on his third expedition.

The helicopter descends like a giant bumble bee. We clamber aboard, and soon see the land beneath us passing by in humps and waves, all smoothed and rounded by the action of ice – indication that the icy armour of Greenland once covered this south-west area also, aeons ago. Now, though, it is green, beautifully green! Reindeer throng down there; and Arctic foxes, not that I can see any this time round – I just know Reynard's home is there as well! From the distance comes the gleam of the inland ice – yellowish-white, whitish-grey, with hints of blue here and there; a person might certainly ask himself how Greenland came to be so called.

A green land?

People say Greenland acquired its name through a trick. A thousand years ago Eric the Red propagated the notion of a green and verdant land to attract Icelandic settlers to the country. In fact, the wedge-shaped island with a north–south length corresponding to the distance from London to the Sahara is anything but green. More than eighty per cent is covered by the inland ice, an ice cap which spares only a narrow coastal strip. Inner Greenland is a shallow bowl, and the ice contained within it is gently domed, achieving a thickness of as much as 3000 metres in the centre. Flowing slowly from this centre to the coasts, the ice becomes heavily crevassed towards its edges, before either breaking off directly into the ocean or sending glacial floes into the long fjords which articulate the coastline. What are known as nunataks – narrow hogs' backs of rock, or domes, or little spires – project here and there from the ice cap, though they are not usually very high. Around the coast, on the other hand, ranges of alpine peaks rise to as much as 2000 metres in the west, and more than 3000 metres in the east.

Thunderous roars accompany the famous 'calving' of the glaciers, when great masses of ice detach themselves to give birth to icebergs, and huge waves ram the coastline, sometimes causing havoc even in the villages. Icebergs drift through the fjords on carpets of broken ice, created under the shattering force of the calving waves.

The small town of Egedesminde has appeared in front of us, its painted houses tossed like coloured dice along the edge of sea. There are no big towns in Greenland, the whole island having only 50,000 inhabitants. Soon we are in the air again, flying on to the north. Below us now, in Disko Bay, numerous icebergs appear like floating castles – or like toys cast on the water by a fractious baby giant. I am delighted, even though I know that none will remain there.

Ocean currents carry the icebergs away, most notably the Labrador Current which flows southwards between Labrador and Greenland. Where it encounters the warm Gulf Stream waters, enormous banks of fog are created, especially around Newfoundland, compounding a notorious navigational danger. This is where the International Ice Patrol begins its operations, keeping drifting icebergs under surveillance on behalf of aircraft and shipping. It was an iceberg, appearing suddenly out of the night in 1912, that brought death to 1500 souls aboard the liner *Titanic*.

Doubtless the earliest inhabitants of Greenland observed the icebergs, too, understanding them perhaps better than we do. Nobody, however, calls these men explorers, even if, in their everyday struggle against the forces of nature, they were in many ways true discoverers. But scientific exploration also penetrates into those areas which are avoided by the settlers, and in doing so, takes advantage of local experience, where that can be useful to the realisation of its projects. Kayaks, fur clothing, igloos, skin tents and the winter huts of the natives all proved of great value to the pioneer Greenland explorers.

For science, crossing the big island was naturally a prime consideration. Fritjof Nansen was the first to succeed, on snowshoes, in 1888. Next came the crossings by Peary (1892–5), Rasmussen and De Quervain (1912) and the Koch-Wegener expedition (1913).

Origins of an expedition

Alfred Wegener, the greatest expert of his day on Greenland's inland ice, was asked in 1928 if he would lead a summer enterprise to attempt to measure the thickness of the ice cap. It was to be financed by the Notgemeinschaft der Deutschen Wissenschaft, an association founded in 1920 to benefit science during the post-war economic difficulties in Germany.

Professor Weiken explained to us how this work was achieved: 'By means of an explosion on the surface, you could create shock waves which penetrated through the ice to the rockbed below, from where they were reflected and returned. From the time it took for the waves to come back to the surface, it was possible to calculate the depth of ice . . . We made such measurements in many places.'

Why it was deemed so important to know the thickness of the ice sheet in Greenland was because geophysicists at the time wanted to extend their seismic techniques to prospect for mineral deposits in the earth's crust. *

Alfred Wegener – who was under the spell of Greenland more perhaps even than he was of science – grabbed the opportunity. His own agenda went even wider: with the help of kites and balloons, he wanted meteorologists to explore the temperature and movement of the air masses above Greenland. Glaciologists, besides taking their measurements of the ice, should also ascertain its structure and temperature at various depths. A very important point in Wegener's programme was to take gravity readings. This was to determine whether the Greenland massif was rising or not. If a measurement in a certain area shows a higher value of gravity than that calculated as normal for this point of the earth's surface, then a surplus of mass exists: in other words, the area is sinking. A smaller value signifies a deficiency of mass: the area is rising.

Wegener was fortunate: it was accepted that one summer in the field would be insufficient to accomplish his programme; almost two years would be needed. A special team would even make observations of the inland ice during the winter.

One of the proposed centres for scientific exploration was, as mentioned, in the middle of the ice cap (the Eismitte), at about 71° latitude. Furthermore, there were to be stations established on the east and west coasts. One of these two coastal stations would have to serve as the base for a push towards the interior and for the creation of Station Eismitte.

Only the West Station could support such an operation. Why? It was a question of time and distance. The provisions, fuel, scientific material had to be ferried over 400 kilometres to Eismitte, which meant starting the transport journeys as early as possible in the year. The west coast was known to be regularly free of ice earlier than the east. For this reason, the East Station was not established until later and worked totally independently of the other two bases. But that is to leap ahead: first, from where on the west coast should the push on to the inland ice be made? Wegener favoured the area around

---

* Later, similar methods came to be used by geological surveyors in Austria and other places to locate oil deposits.

Umanak, but the decision over exactly where would be most suitable would have to be determined on the spot – before anything else could be done. The resultant pre-expedition comprised, besides Wegener, a further three scientists: Dr Johannes Georgi from the Seewarte (Marine Observatory), Hamburg, intended to be the leader of the central firn station (Eismitte), Dr Fritz Loewe from the aeronautic meteorological station in Berlin, later organiser of the sledge journeys, Dr Ernst Sorge, who assisted Georgi in Eismitte as a glaciologist.

They were looking for a glacier that should not be too fast-flowing – not like the Rink Glacier, for instance, which according to Sorge's observations dispatched 400 to 600 millions of cubic metres of ice every ten to twenty days in mighty calvings! Moreover, for laying the ascent route it did not want to be too steep, because sharp steps create crevasses and séracs. Finally, the snout of the glacier should not be too far from the coast, since an approach over boulderfields and sand would be extremely tiring. The most appropriate glacier turned out to be the Qaumarujuk Glacier, which flowed in a south-westerly direction towards the sea. It was, unfortunately, also possessed of a sérac zone, but that had to be accepted. Access to the inland ice had been found. The main expedition could start the following year!

The voyage to Greenland

How different it was then! Today you step into a jet in Copenhagen and in a mere four hours are over in Greenland. Then? Well, everything ran to plan, at first at least – even if it was different from today: on 1 April 1930, the 'Disko', the biggest ship in the Royal Greenland Trade Department fleet, set out from Copenhagen, taking aboard twenty-five Icelandic ponies in Reykjavik, steaming around Cape Farewell, then north along the west coast of Greenland, to anchor in Holsteinsborg. From there, the journey to Baffin Bay continued on board the 'Gustav Holm', which was able to negotiate the drift-ice. The destination was to be Umanak, a small fishing village on an island at about 71° N. In order to reach it, the vessel had to turn east from Baffin Bay and enter the Umanak Fjord.

This is no simple fjord, rather an enormous bay limited to the north by two islands, Ubekjendt Eiland and Upernavik. From the east several peninsulas reach into the bay, amongst them the Qioqe and what would later be called Alfred Wegener Land. Everywhere are summits reminiscent of the Alps: a playground for mountaineers *of the future, stepping into the footsteps of the scientific pioneers. Uvkusigsat, a small village at the end of a long headland, dominates the access to the Qaumarujuk Fjord. It was to prove an important base for the expedition. However, then, in the beginning, on 4 May 1930, none of the islands, peninsulas and inlets could be reached by the 'Gustav Holm'. The sea was frozen! Still on 15 May the edge of the ice ran in a northerly direction to the west of Umanak, then curved sharply westward south of Qioqe towards Ubekjendt Eiland.*

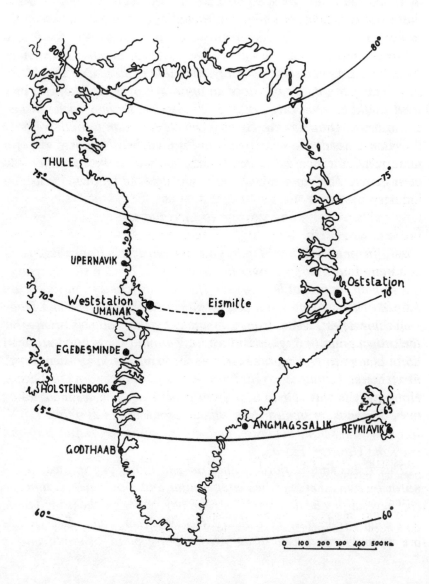

'Modern Times' in Umanak and Uvkusigsat

Umanak Mountain has appeared. I spotted it – my face pressed to the window of the helicopter; over there, it is diagonally ahead of us – a Greenland Matterhorn! A mountain on an island, the island consisting almost totally of this mountain. Greenlanders call the bold rocky shape 'the heart of a seal'. You need imagination to see that – something the Greenlanders have in plenty. Only minutes now separate me from that place which, on my first Greenland visit in 1966, could not be reached except by ship. Next time I came there was a helicopter pad. Everything here is in a continual state of flux . . .

Greenland has come a long way since the days of Alfred Wegener. As a base for the Allied Forces during the Second World War, it saw swift economic development, thanks to American aid. Few true Eskimos exist any longer. Plastic kayaks are part of the cultural evolution. And you hardly ever see turf huts any more: the Greenlanders live in prefabricated wooden houses, the raw materials for which are supplied by Denmark. One consequence of systematic commercialisation in sheep breeding and the fishing industry has been the replacement of small scattered hamlets by larger villages. The population has tripled in the decade and a half preceding our visit. Most of the Greenlanders live around the west coast, on peninsulas or nearby islands, like here in Umanak. All children must now go to school.*

Already I can make out the houses! Red, blue, yellow, green, orange – all colours, as if a slap-happy artist had been flicking his brush over the brown granite of the island! In front of the houses, on the coast, there is a small and miraculously sheltered natural harbour, which nonetheless cannot prevent some icebergs sneaking in to anchor alongside the ships. You find them in all shapes and sizes drifting over the wide surface of the Umanak Fjord!

* Postscript, 1994: Since 1953 Greenland, instead of being a Danish colony, has been an integral part of the Kingdom of Denmark, sending delegates to the parliament in Copenhagen; and in 1985 it was granted the status of an 'autonomous region', but with Denmark still being responsible for foreign policy and defence. In 1988 the inhabitants numbered about 54,000, the capital Godthaab; (Nûk in the Greenland language) accounting for 11,000. The most recent census of 1993 puts the total population at 55,000.

A fairytale image!

Umanak, once a tiny settlement, has become one of the district capitals of Greenland with 1000 inhabitants. Ice conditions mean the harbour can only be used from June to October, but it is nevertheless (in 1974) an important transshipment depot for the KGH, the Royal Greenland Trade Department which controls almost all business in Greenland.

Unlike Wegener, when he arrived in 1930, we can look down from the helicopter on to an open sea at the beginning of July; he was confronted by an ice-locked coastline after an ocean voyage of five weeks.

The rotor blades whirr, the motor stutters loudly, and we sink down. We are here – Umanak – the starting point for our expedition!

Word of our arrival spreads quickly, attracting the curious. Above all, countless children with their lively clacking-chatter (to me, Greenlandic sounds like a wild duck language) observe how the

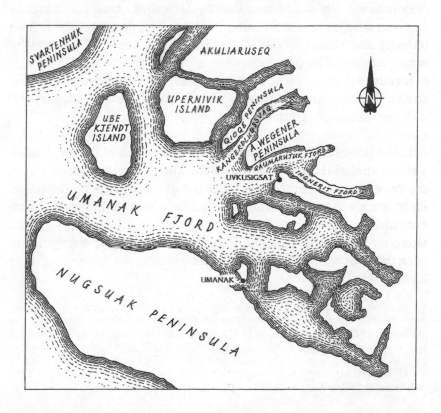

combined efforts of the eight of us eventually transfer our one and a half tonnes of expedition luggage on to a fishing boat. (The Wegener expedition, by contrast, had a hundred tonnes, the equivalent of ten railway waggons full! To be sure, they also had bigger aims than we do.) This boat has been procured for us by the ever-present trading company, and our smooth transit to the small village of Uvkusigsat, our next objective, does not come about by chance, of course. Long before being able to tread the Greenland soil, we had to obtain a visa and fix our expedition's route inside the country; moreover, we were obliged to raise a considerable insurance stake. The officials demand this safety deposit because all too often helicopters and rescue teams have to be called out to help expeditions in distress. The Wegener team in 1930 were reliant solely on their own resources – their safety lay in the knowledge and experience of their leader.

Our voyage to Uvkusigsat takes us through some fantastic ice formations – pyramids, archways, shining combs for fairy hair, armchairs, a giant grand piano, an enormous whale of ice . . . and whatever else you care to imagine (some people, it is true, may see only ice!). Before setting out, the fisherman in charge of our boat took aboard a sizeable chunk of fresh white whaleskin with its meat and blubber attached – and, with relish, he now chews on a mouthful of skin: it is a delicacy – for Greenlanders.

Uvkusigsat is to be a sort of central base for our ventures. We will set off for the inland ice from there, and for Agpatat peak and the Qioqe Peninsula (where we will of course have further camps; in all these places there will be no other people besides us). We are greeted in Uvkusigsat by a wave of friendliness, and an overwhelming smell of fish, which is everywhere hanging up to dry on high wooden frames. Large packs of sledge-dogs yowl and scrap – they are always hungry! And children, children, children, rampaging and laughing – Greenland is a happy island. Children make up about half its population. This may have something to do with the long winter nights, which counterbalance the endless days of summer.

As in Umanak, much has changed here since Wegener's day. Hardly a turf house remains. And the fish hall belongs to the Royal Greenland Trade Department, which buys all the catch – for vouchers, which the fishermen can use in self-service stores belonging to the company. Alfred Wegener had to bring in all his provisions, but we can go shopping around the corner – and find practically everything! The local luxuries are liquor, tobacco and cigarettes. A bottle of whisky costs about double what we would pay, but other food costs much the same as at home.

A fisherman in Umanak told Robert Kreuzinger that a Greenlander from the Wegener expedition still lives here in Uvkusigsat. We go to see him. The small, white-haired, seventy-two year old Fredriksen and his wife are round-eyed with astonishment and hardly able to contain themselves when they see the photos of expedition members taken by Weiken and Schif over forty years ago. In some of the shots they recognise their friends, relatives and children! They have never seen these pictures before.

It is on one of these days in Uvkusigsat that Robert, Anne and I are taken in a small helicopter belonging to the nearby lead and zinc Black Angels Mine and piloted by a friendly Dane for the recce-flight described earlier. By this time, I have already shot many reels for our Wegener film. And how did things progress on that expedition in 1930? The reader will remember we have left Wegener and his team at the edge of the frozen sea outside Umanak . . .

The difficult landing

The 'Gustav Holm' could reach neither Umanak nor the Qaumarujuk Bay. Instead, the ship rammed into the edge of the ice to create a provisional harbour for herself. Unloading was done directly on to the ice, whence dog sledges and horses carried all the gear to Uvkusigsat. The night of 9–10 May was the first passed on Greenland soil. The propeller sledges had been brought 'overland', by dog-power, directly across the sea-ice into the Qaumarujuk Bay. But the weakening ice could scarcely bear them. There was no way, either by water or over the ice, that all the Base Camp material could be ferried up into the innermost corner of the Qaumarujuk Fjord. From 10 May began a series of idle, nerve-racking days, spelling loss of precious time to the expedition. The men waited for thirty-eight days! It was 17 June before the expedition's 2500 boxes, chests and drums stood on the beach. These contained provisions, fuel, even blasting material for the seismologists, scientific apparatus, balloon envelopes, kite parts, and last but not least, hay for the horses. The team comprised eighteen members – German scientists, engineers and helpers – with some ten Icelandic ponymen, and a number of locals. Of particular significance *to the further course of the expedition were its two technicians, Franz Kelbl and Manfred Kraus, who drove the motorised propeller sledges and doubled as radio operators.*

Kelbl, after the transports were finished, was to man the radio station of the western party, Kraus the one at Eismitte – but neither radio operator Kraus nor his wireless gear reached Eismitte in 1930. Was this double-function role envisaged for Kelbl and Kraus one of the factors contributing to the tragic outcome of the expedition?

That was something we mountaineers of the German Greenland expedition of 1974 thought about often as we ascended towards the remnants of the West Station.

We gather in front of the Wegener memorial plaque in Qaumarujuk Bay. This is where the ship's captain has set us down after the short trip from Uvkusigsat. It will be our Base Camp for the forthcoming days while we establish a further camp about 1000 metres higher, from which to start the search for the relics of the Wegener expedition. We have small lightweight walkie-talkies with a range of a few kilometres only, but enough for us.

Eismitte Station, some 400 kilometres distant, lay beyond radio contact . . . was that the disastrous ingredient for the pioneers, or was it those new-fangled propeller sledges?

Dogs? Propeller sledges? Horses?

Kurt Schif, engineer, leader of the propeller sledge operations, had a meeting with Alfred Wegener before the expedition in the little Berlin hotel Westfalia to discuss his ideas for a mechanically driven snow vehicle.

Schif can vividly remember this first encounter: 'From the very start, I was impressed by this man with his shining blue eyes and direct gaze. He had modesty written all over his face, and you would never have known from looking at him that he already had two major Greenland enterprises behind him, and enjoyed such high prestige in the scientific world.'

What did the two men talk about? It was known that the Greenlanders managed to take their dog sledges over almost every kind of terrain, even if they preferred travelling over the flat frozen sea. Wegener had used horses for his Greenland crossing, and would employ them again this time as pack animals. But on top of this, he wanted to use mechanically powered vehicles. So far, though, all vehicles whose motive force acted directly on the ground (that is, via wheels) had failed in the snow, and contemporary caterpillar-tracked vehicles were too heavy for the inland ice. So why not employ propeller-driven motor transport over the snow surface?

There were already a number of propeller sledges in use in Finland. They were manufactured by the Finnish state aeroplane factory in Helsingfors, and employed during the winter months as a transport link between offshore islands. After his discussions with Wegener, Schif got in touch with the factory, which eventually agreed to design and make two propeller sledges especially for the expedition. A few weeks before the date fixed for departure, Schif went to Helsingfors to try to speed up their construction.

Spick and span at last, they stood there: red, shiny, awaiting only their final trials before disappearing into enormous packing crates for the journey. The bodywork was extremly solid, notwithstanding the lightweight construction: streamlined, with a cabin and seat for the driver and a roomy luggage compartment, the motor and propeller were mounted on the rear. Four broad strong skids of hickory wood were arranged in pairs on the two axles and well sprung on a rubber suspension. The front pair of skids could be turned, like the front wheels on a car. The air-cooled Siemens Sh 12 aero-engine had a horsepower of 112, and its fuel tank would hold 200 kilos (63 gallons). Would they work efficiently in Greenland? Before knowing that, they had first to be carried up on to the ice cap – with all the problems that entailed . . .

Ascent to the inland ice

The route was to take them to a nunatak of brownish rock, which divided two glaciers and probably for this reason acquired its name, Scheideck (Scheiden is to split or divide). These were the Qaumarujuk Glacier, up which the ascent was to be made, and the Kangerdluarssuk Glacier, upon which they would later erect the winter quarters.

'There was a serious obstacle on the Qaumarujuk Glacier,' Professor Weiken recalled, 'a heavily crevassed icefall which we couldn't get past. We had to construct a way through – had to keep on hacking and blasting a passageway through the ice – in order to get the heavy loads up, particularly the two propeller sledges, their motors and the winch. No sooner would we have it made, than it would be ruined

again because of the sun melting the glacial ice, and have to be abandoned.' Transport through the icefall was a test of power and patience for man and horse. Afterwards, the route was transferred on to a side moraine, but this route, too, had to be tailored to provide wide enough turning circles for the horses to negotiate. Above the icefall the loads were transferred from the horses and carried on by dog sledge.

To start with, at Scheideck, there was only the meteorologists' tent with those of a dog-sledge team nearby. Schif, Kraus and Kelbl started out in a camp south of the Scheideck nunatak, where the two propeller sledges were to be reassembled and made ready. It had taken six weeks to get them up here from the fjord. Later, to avoid constant negotiation of the crevassed edge of the inland ice, the sledge team moved to a depot which Karl Weiken had established twelve kilometres east of Scheideck. Here everything destined for Eismitte was cached, and it was from this depot, called Start, that the propeller sledges set out in 1930. Later on, the winter hut of the scattered West Station was situated a good two kilometres north of Scheideck on the Kangerdluarssuk Glacier, and this provided the base for the inland ice journeys of 1931.

First finds

Ahead of us lies a 1000-metre climb to Scheideck. At the back of the valley we see the tongue of the Qaumarujuk Glacier and the steep step up on to it, but neither will give us any problems! During the last four decades changes have taken place in the ice. We will carry provisions for five days, four lightweight tents and skis for a push on to the inland ice. Our backpacks are heavy – each of us is humping thirty to forty kilos! That is not counting the film gear, which nobody wants to be burdened with. Karli Landvogt, our doctor, volunteers to take the heavy tripod. 'A training exercise,' he says with a grin. You can hear the others sigh with relief. After a while everything is divided and we can start. That is just what Reynard, the Polar fox, has been waiting for. As soon as we are off, he comes visiting the tents of our Base Camp. We know him well by now: usually, he turns up with the twilight, looking for something to eat – and he is quite successful. His weakness is for tinned meat, but one enigma remains unsolved: why on earth does he keep stealing rolls of toilet paper? Now we wave goodbye to the slim, trusting little fellow, and are soon making our way around the strange collapsed ice bubbles of a fibrous structure which have formed over the valley floor to an impressive diameter of nearly ten metres. Then the gradient sharpens. Glacier ice and tiring loose moraine debris . . . blocks roll away under our feet . . . After two and a half hours of climbing Wolfgang Rauschl finds the first positive trace of the Wegener expedition: a petroleum can, probably lost in the transport. A few minutes later we are lucky again: Robert and Anne Kreuzinger discover a huge hydrogen cylinder, as tall as a man. It is astonishingly well preserved. Hydrogen was needed by the meteorologists for filling both the tethered and the mobile (pilot) weather balloons.

Our steps grow slower, our burdens heavier. It is hard to imagine that 100,000 kilos of material were conveyed up here by Wegener's pioneers. And what a much more difficult job it was then – I remember old film reels showing columns of men hacking routes through the ice, and the propeller sledges being hauled by winch up the steep sections, the men beating the horses to induce the monster sledges just a few more metres closer to the inland ice!

Of course, we make many pauses in our own ascent because of my filming. Towards evening we reach Land's End, at the edge of the inland ice, and spot a protruding dome of rock to the north-east. This can only be the nunatak Scheideck! It is too late to reach it today. We put up our tents.

Breakfast! We fortify ourselves for a dream of a day – the sun shines out of a cloudless sky, and we are full of expectation: ahead of us beckons the inland ice, surging into the distance in wide waves. But we can also see a barrier of crevasses. Four of us will venture on to the ice cap today. Somewhere around here must be the route the dog and propeller sledges took towards Eismitte.

After struggling through a real morass at the edge of the ice, our skis glide well. We have little hope of finding anything on the ice itself – like the winter quarters: too much time has passed. But perhaps our comrades who intend to search the rocky area at the nunatak will be more lucky . . . It will not be an easy job: they are without skis and will have to find their way there on foot through the deep watery slush. We see them become smaller and smaller dots behind us the further we press into the white of the ice cap . . . What a pity that there is not really such a thing as a time machine – we can only think ourselves back to those earlier days. How did it go, then?

1930: towards Station Eismitte

Station Eismitte was to be established about 400 kilometres from the westerly rim of the ice cap. It would need to be equipped with provisions, fuel and instruments so that a working team could overwinter there. Various calculations needed to be made: How much material had to be transported to Eismitte? How many sledge journeys would be necessary? Could the propeller sledges make a significant contribution to the effort?

Alfred Wegener had already pondered these matters back in 1929. He reckoned on a payload of 3500 kilos, which would have to be delivered to Eismitte between June and October.

Professor Weiken: 'Alfred Wegener had worked it out very precisely: three dog-sledge journeys would be required to take in all items essential for overwintering at Eismitte. The propeller sledges could carry extra items. Of course, further journeys would be needed the following spring to re-equip Station Eismitte for the summer ahead. These three dog-sledge journeys duly took place: the first in July and August, another during August, and the third from the end of August to 21 September. The propeller sledges were there primarily as an experiment – to see whether they could operate on the inland ice; Wegener warned everybody not to rely on them. That is why the essentials for Eismitte were to be entrusted to the dogs.'

As it turned out, however, far more material was found to be needed at Eismitte than had been originally assumed (particularly petroleum), and hopes were then pinned on the propeller sledges. They were incomparably faster than dogs and apart from fuel needed no 'food'.

We have reached 1050 metres above sea level! Robert glances at his altimeter. The surface of the inland ice is changing all the time, and we have to be very wary of crevasses. The wind has covered many of them with snow, so that frequently we only notice the dangers at the last moment. Naturally, we have been travelling roped for a while now. It is easy to envisage the difficulties the dog and propeller sledges must have experienced in this area. That is why most of the journeys started beyond the crevasse zone.

A slight mist rolls in towards evening – our altimeter now registers 1115 metres. We are increasingly overwhelmed by a sense of utter loneliness. Something similar, I imagine, to what it must feel to be on a small sailboat in the middle of a wide ocean. Here it is an immense ocean of ice which surrounds us, rigid, solid – but given a gentle dynamic by the slowly sliding shadows of clouds, and the ever-changing light, by waves of mist which form and dissolve again. Inland ice: home of the spirits, so the Greenlanders believe, and you feel tempted to believe it . . .

It can easily take you over, become an addiction, compelling you to go ever further into it, step after step, day after day.

A yearning.

But we turn back after twenty kilometres. For one day only we have felt ourselves the loneliest of people, surrounded by the eternal ice.

The sledge journeys

Reports of expeditions to the highest summits of the world very often carry charts illustrating their logistics on the mountain. Such a diagram is presented as a horizontal band of time, along which the heights achieved by individual members in their various ascents and descents are plotted vertically. There is a similar chart in the book of Wegener's expedition, but it shows, besides time, not heights but the distances covered by teams from the West Station.

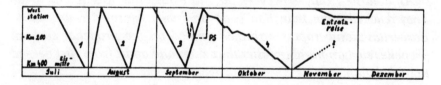

Extract of a diagram from the 1930 expedition by Dr Kurt Wegener (simplified).

You can see from the above the journeys made to Station Eismitte: 1, 2, 3, 4 represent four dog-sledge journeys and PS the soon-to-be-interrupted attempt by the propeller sledges. The Entsatzreise is the rescue journey in November–December. The line for the return of the fourth dog-sledge journey to Eismitte is a dotted one and cut short abruptly.

It was the end of the drama.

In the beginning, despite time lost on account of the pack ice, everything ran more or less according to programme. On 5 July the first dog-sledge journey headed out towards Eismitte. Loewe, Georgi and Weiken went with it, waymarking the route. They put in black pennants every 500 metres, and every five kilometres built snowmen with black fabric hoods. As much as anything, these were to pacify the Greenlanders among the party, since none of them had travelled on the feared inland ice before. Loewe turned back at the Depot Kilometre 200, as planned. Georgi and Weiken reached the middle of the ice cap on 30 July, along with four Greenlanders. Weiken then also said goodbye, leaving Georgi alone and out of contact with the rest of the expedition to establish Station Eismitte. At 3000 metres above sea level, this proved fatiguing work, but if men were to overwinter there it was important to make all necessary preparations. Wegener's plan called for him and Sorge, as well as a radio operator, to remain in the middle of this ice desert until spring 1931.

The second sledge train bringing material for Eismitte started out at the beginning of August. Wegener now had serious worries. The first trip had only delivered 750 kilos to its destination and, according to his estimate, almost five times that amount was needed. Under no circumstances did he want to relinquish this base, which was to be the heart of the expedition. Guided by Loewe, the second sledge party arrived on 18 August with a 1000-kilo payload. Ten more sledges set off on 30 August, accompanied by Sorge, Woelken and Jülg. They reached Eismitte on 13 September, where Sorge was to remain. Earlier, as they were leaving the Western Station, the men had seen the propeller sledges making their way to the Depot Start. They appeared to be functioning well. Everybody was optimistic that it would not be long before they were welcomed at Station Eismitte. But they never arrived.

The propeller sledge fiasco

Broken down into sections, the propeller sledges and their motors had been brought over the icefall to the assembling tent, and then put back together. The matron of a sanatorium (was that a bad omen?) had christened the two sledges Ice Bear and Snow Bunting when she came for a visit to Scheideck. Snowballs substituted for the usual bottles of champagne on that occasion.

Kurt Schif recalls: 'We were unlucky to encounter snow and surface

*conditions on the ice cap which were quite different from Wegener's
predictions, based on a crossing made with horses at a totally different
time of year. We experienced very uneven terrain, shot through with
crevasses, presenting very variable surface quality – one moment it
would be needle ice, then powder snow, and somewhere else snow
swamp. One look was enough to make me doubt that our propeller
sledges would prove as revolutionary as we had hoped. Initially, we
had no idea how we ought to address these difficulties, and quickly
decided to establish the starting point for the propeller sledges on
the inland ice itself, at a distance of some twelve kilometres from its
crevassed edge. Test runs showed that the sledges could only operate
when weather conditions were kind to us.'*

The gained speeds were, according to Schif, thirty to forty kilometres per hour, and it was impossible to reach Eismitte on a single,
full tank. Petrol depots would have to be laid in advance along the
route. During the seven days it took to do this, the sledges covered
a total of 800 kilometres. The depot at Kilometre 200 was especially
well equipped, holding also the reserves destined for Eismitte.

*On 17 September the propeller sledges left for the decisive push
towards Eismitte: 'We reached speeds of seventy kilometres an hour,
got to Kilometre 200 and passed the night there with Woelken and
Jülg, who were on their way back from Eismitte. We hoped to
continue next day at the same speed to Eismitte, but during the night
there was a terrible break in the weather – temperatures fell to minus
36° Celsius and we found to our consternation that the sledges simply
could not move any further. Nevertheless we sat it out, expecting an
improvement in the weather. Only when our rations had dwindled
so much that we had food for just two more days, did we decide to
unload the sledges and dejectedly to start back.'*

But it got even worse. Within thirty-nine kilometres of Depot Start
the motor of the Snow Bunting packed up: piston damage was
diagnosed, caused by insufficient cooling. Everyone piled into Ice
Bear, but eight kilometres further on, that, too, konked out. Piston
damage again! They were benighted on the spot. In the morning,
Wegener and Loewe suddenly appeared in front of their tent. They
were on their way with the fourth sledge journey to Eismitte. Wegener
now knew that he could no longer count on the propeller sledges for
this year, and that his fourth provision run for Eismitte was all the
more vital.

But the fiasco with the propeller sledges was still not over. There was no hope of encouraging Ice Bear an inch further. Two dogs collected on the way back were tied in front of a small emergency sledge, on to which a tent, sleeping-bags, some fuel and food were loaded. Severe blizzards hampered progress. It was 27 September before the team regained Station Start. They were absolutely exhausted.

Twice that year they tried to rescue the abandoned sledges, but failed to budge either of them: the ice held them fast. They would be there now until the spring of 1931.

Nunatak Scheideck, a treasure trove!

Sunshine on the glacier. The soft curves of the inland ice dazzle and shimmer, all around. Standing on the rounded head of the nunatak, you feel like the captain on the bridge of a ship sailing into a white ocean. The gnarled patches of swampy snow around the ice rim could be the foamy hollows between waves pressing towards the coast, just before impact. In one respect, however, the comparison falls down: the coastline here is lower than the sea. The white ocean in front of you – were it in movement – would sweep over you! It rises slowly, but steadily to a height of 3000 metres.

That is the feeling you get, looking over the prow of a nunatak.

The four of us returning from our inland ice ski trip rejoin Hans, Wolf, Karl and Wolfgang – our foot patrol. They had made a discovery while we were gone: a place marked with coal, in the ice just near the nunatak. Enthusiastically we all start to dig. We know that a year ago Danish search teams recovered one of the two propeller sledges for a museum, and afterwards marked the spot where they had found it. This is surely it! The second sledge must still be here, buried in the ice! We work fast, like moles who suddenly find themselves caught out in the sunshine. Soon, an edge of rusty metal appears. With renewed excitement, we dig further, but the deeper we get, the more difficult the digging becomes – it could take days to excavate the whole sledge. That at least is what the 'non-Austrian' majority thinks! Exasperated, all I can film is part of the engine-mounting at the rear.

But already, buoyed by the find, Hessians and Bavarians join forces and set themselves to work on the rocky hill and the blocks at its base. Shouts ring out! Every moment yields some new discovery:

here is the winch for the kites and balloons – it must be! Karli and Wolfgang joyfully wind the handle – the thing squeaks terribly, but turns perfectly! You couldn't expect more of it after forty years . . . Just as I am about to remind my energetic companions of the little matter of a buried and, to me, at least, magic propeller sledge – I did so want it on film in all its glory – Wolf Reute comes running over with a dog's pemmican tin. I sigh. Anne hauls over broken pieces of boxes bearing the inscription of the Wegener expedition. Will Kurt now, finally, forget about that damned sledge? Wolfgang procures horse skeletons, even discovers the foundations of a stable with some real hay in it. This country really is a fridge! The second biggest in the world after Antarctica. At any rate, that little rocky hill keeps us busy throughout the next day and the one after that – many finds and many rolls of film. Despite searching in the direction of the winter hut, we find no trace of it. The fast-moving glacier has engulfed it and in the intervening decades carried it God knows where . . . Sic transit gloria mundi. Thoughtfully, I look at one of the old photographs: expedition members and a smiling Greenland girl in front of the winter hut. The old white-haired man in Uvkusigsat, Jonathan Fredriksen, had recognised her as his sister-in-law Sarah, who was the caretaker. She's been dead a long time, as has his brother, who stood beside her in the picture. We gave him the photograph. I still remember how he took it back to his old turf hut, the only one left in the village.

Evening has come, the beginning of a bright night, which you cannot really call a night at all. I am standing on top of the nunatak, looking east over the inland ice . . .

Alfred Wegener's last journey

Would the propeller sledges make it as far as Eismitte? Wegener had some doubts about this after participating in their first test runs. Shortly after Sorge started on the third dog sledge journey, therefore, he decided to organise a fourth. He would undertake it himself, together with Loewe, with the main objective of carrying to Eismitte from Kilometre 200 the paraffin and other items still lacking there. Very soon after setting out they met Woelken and Jülg returning from the third sledge journey (Sorge had stayed behind at Eismitte). They brought two letters with them: in one Sorge gave a detailed description of the provisions at the base, and Georgi wrote that if they didn't get more paraffin and other essentials before 20 October, they would leave the station on foot with a Handschlitten, *a man-hauled sledge, and return to the Western Station. (Later on, the two changed their minds: the rooms of Eismitte which were excavated in the firn below the surface could be heated sufficiently with the existing paraffin; moreover, a return journey with just a man-hauled sledge seemed too risky. Wegener never learned of this change of plan. No radio message was possible because the apparatus and the operator were not there.)*

Wegener (as we have seen) encountered the Snow Bunting and Ice Bear stuck in the snow. All the more urgent now, he felt, to get his column to Eismitte!

But at that moment his Greenlanders went on strike, eight of them returning to the west. Four stayed with him for the time being, though he himself was later to send back another three. The reduced group that trekked towards Eismitte thus comprised just Alfred Wegener, Fritz Loewe and the Greenlander Rasmus Villumsen.

Wegener sent back letters for Karl Weiken with both of the returning Greenlander groups: in the first (dated 28 September) he still hoped to be able to ferry the necessary paraffin from Kilometre 200 to Eismitte, but in the second (of 6 October) he declares his desire to push on to Eismitte, even without a payload, so that he can at least bring dogs to Georgi and Sorge. Sorge's plan to leave Eismitte on 20 October by man-hauled sledge was held by Wegener to be unfeasible. They would never make it through, and freeze to death on the way. He and Loewe, he hoped, would eventually relieve Sorge and Georgi. Eismitte had to be manned over the winter at all costs!

In his last letter, Wegener requested that a small relief team go to Kilometre 62 to wait – until no later than 1 December – for the men coming back from Eismitte.

The relief journey took place: Weiken, Kraus and two Greenlanders set off on 15 November from Depot Start. At Kilometre 62 they built a snow igloo. They also set up two tight lines of marker flags, ten kilometres long, one towards the north-east, the other to the south-east, forming a rough right-angle and thus making it possible for anyone coming from the east to be guided into this 'corner' where the igloo stood, even in thick fog.

Every afternoon, as darkness began to fall, they would light a paraffin flare, which would burn for three hours.

However, on 7 December the relief mission was called off. It was impossible that anyone could still come from Eismitte. Storms were raging and temperatures had dropped to minus 42° Celsius.

*

The winter meant a long break in all activity outside the stations.

Did Wegener, with Loewe and Villumsen, make it through to Eismitte?

Yes, by 30 October, Alfred Wegener, Fritz Loewe and Rasmus Villumsen had reached the station. The temperature by this time had sunk to minus 50° and Loewe had suffered heavy frostbite; in his state a return journey was out of the question. However, inside the roomy 'cave-dwelling' which Sorge and Georgi had hollowed out below the firn surface the temperature was bearable. Here, they could continue their scientific tasks throughout the winter!

The 30 October was the only rest day for Wegener: it was as if he didn't feel comfortable in the firn-cave without any wind or snowdrifts, without the bitter cold. The extreme hardships of a journey lasting more than four weeks had failed to exhaust him. New projects for 1931 were discussed – two Greenland crossings! On 1 November, his fiftieth birthday, Wegener started out with Villumsen for the Western Station. Loewe could not go with them. All his toes were frostbitten. Some time afterwards they were amputated by Georgi – with a pocket knife and wirecutters. Loewe was obliged to sit in his sleeping-bag the whole winter, right into May, because it was too cold in the room for his damaged feet.

What was the situation meanwhile at the ice rim, at the Western Station? Karl Weiken continues his description: 'Wegener never arrived with us; we waited for him in vain – and we all hoped, therefore, that Wegener, Loewe and Rasmus had remained in Eismitte with Georgi and Sorge. If they lived frugally and also ate the dogs they had brought with them, they could last out there till May, even five of them.'

Spring 1931: at the Western Station operations for the current year were being organised. The propeller sledges were meanwhile functioning without any problems. Everybody was oppressed by a single worry: Alfred Wegener – what had happened to him?

The first sledge journey of the year, therefore, had to be to Eismitte: a dog-sledge group led by Weiken set off on 23 April. The propeller sledges caught up with them at Kilometre 330, just short of their common destination. They spent the night there together. On 7 May the propeller sledges were the first to reach Station Eismitte . . . Where was Wegener?

'He left last year with Rasmus Villumsen, on 1 November; he was heading for the Western Station . . .'

Only then do the men of Eismitte and Western Station understand that Alfred Wegener and his companion must have died on the inland ice.

The search started immediately . . . Wegener and Rasmus had left Eismitte with two sledges and seventeen dogs. If they lost a considerable number of dogs on the journey, they intended to go on from Kilometre 200 with only one sledge. Rasmus was to drive it, Wegener follow on skis.

At Kilometre 285 a box of pemmican was found, at Kilometre 255 a sledge, at Kilometre 189 Wegener's skis standing in the snow. A preliminary dig when the earlier team passed this spot on their way to Eismitte had turned up only a pemmican box. This time they dug deeper and found Alfred Wegener's grave. He had died, they supposed, from exhaustion.

Rasmus probably took Wegener's diary, gloves, pipe and tobacco with him. After burying him, he would almost certainly have continued westwards.

They found two of his campsites. At Kilometre 170 he might have spent a longer time. An axe from Eismitte was found on the spot. After that, nothing.

Kraus had established a small radio transmitter in Eismitte. On 8 May he radioed the message homeward: Wegener and his companion had perished on the ice cap.

The work of the expedition continued. Kurt Wegener, the dead man's brother, took over the lead. Even today in Greenland the name of the peninsula Alfred Wegener Land commemorates the great explorer.

*

Qioqe, Agpatat and – the final take

We packed up and abandoned Scheideck. During our days there
we had found much, even if not all that we wanted – the events
of a long-gone time had woven themselves into our consciousness.
Robert and I, in our thoughts, were still decades back on the inland
ice when we descended to Qaumarujuk Bay. We had so identified
with the events surrounding the last journey of the great explorer
that it was hard to put it behind us. It almost seemed absurd that
from now on there would simply be normal mountaineering.

When we reached Base Camp our friendly Reynard, the arctic
fox, was waiting, already impatient. Wolfgang immediately opened
a tin of meat for him! Next day we left the bay on board the cutter.
Reynard stood on the beach and followed us with his gaze. I believe
he thought it unfair of us to go . . .

Increasing numbers of small mountaineering expeditions visit Greenland nowadays for its carefree climbing on fascinating coastal
mountains – so different from the Alps, with the climbing from sea
level, on uninhabited peninsulas and islands, and in the everlasting
daylight of the Greenland summer. Under the low rays of the sun
at midnight, when it stands in the north – and during the bright day
when the seagulls circle above the fjord and dive for fish.

You could write a whole book simply on the fascination of
climbing in Greenland.

It has its special adventures: just pull an iceberg ashore and melt
it down if you cannot find fresh water. Or sit on a summit, as if it
were the middle of a sundial, and watch the shadow of your mountain
circling way below, like the hand of the clock – hour by hour over
icebergs, sea, glaciers . . .

When we reached the Qioqe Peninsula we experienced all that.
It was the third time I had been here. And it was, as I said in the
beginning, a piece of home to me.

After several first ascents we turned to our last objective.

Agpatat is the highest point in Alfred Wegener Land. Its summit,
1922 'true' metres above sea level, was still unclimbed. Twice it had
been attempted. It is a mountain of many ridges, subsidiary summits,
buttresses and enormous fins and flakes – which quite often conceal
the main summit from the fjord. A strange, complicated structure,
as we had already ascertained from the aerial pictures given us by

the geodetic institute in Copenhagen. However, we finally worked out a possible line of ascent from the south – where we are now.

Colourful flowers bloom in the rocks of the cliffs – daisies, willow-herb, bellflowers . . . Lichen, bilberries and pillows of moss higher up . . . after that for two hours we encounter nothing but boulders: and what boulders! Extremely steep moraine debris. Stones keep rumbling away into the depths. Today I have given the tripod to Anne – as everybody takes good care of her – the camera I carry myself. When we arrive at the base of a massive, vertical corbel of eroded, rotten rock, suddenly, lit from above, it glows beautifully green: malachite probably. A really big patch of it. Unfortunately, it is not possible to get at it. We penetrate a high valley, a sort of amphitheatre: rising in the background, above a steep snow and rock face, is a pinnacle that could well be the summit. There is a glacier in front of it. Before going on to the ice we find a flat spot, dotted with mighty blocks, an ideal place for a high camp – and with water, too! Eleven hundred metres above the fjord we erect four lightweight tents, pop into them our sleeping mats and bags and the camp is ready. Tomorrow, the summit of Agpatat will be ours! Eight hundred metres more – no problem. Tomorrow, we will build another stoneman on the highest mountain of the Wegener Land and feel happy . . .

Brilliant sunshine, indescribably clear air, the unspoiled nature of Greenland. Already we are being treated to summit views. Of course there are still riddles to be solved, alpinistic ones; we can see that . . . but that is part of the fun!

It turns out to be no fun at all. The next day begins with bad weather. Humid, cold winds, dark banks of cloud; and then it snows, and it snows, and it continues to snow – for fourteen hours. You are tempted to forget this is summer in Greenland. Finally, things look brighter, and I set off at once with Wolfgang in order to film the 'bad weather version' for the end of our film – in case we do not make it up Agpatat. Our companions consider that a bad omen. They are right, of course: within a short while the weather is again so foul that the scenes of 'the retreat' look very authentic!

And so, Wolfgang and I lie down in our camp fairly well satisfied, under the circumstances.

It lasts four days . . . Mostly, we sleep or toss from one side to the other. Then, even the most optimistic among us are fed up.

Defeated, we descend to the sea. There, it is raining. Sometimes for long stretches, sometimes shorter. I work away imperturbably at my bad-weather ending. Most of my companions have started to swear whenever I call them for the next take. Suddenly, I hit on one last, grand idea. Please, good friends, it really will be the last! It's Joerg who makes the sacrifice: he agrees to descend on a rope from an overhanging wall, directly towards me, coming to a standstill exactly in the focus of the big camera lens! Not a problem for him: he climbs from the other side until he's at the top of the wall, hammers in a piton, passes the rope through, and rides down the doubled rope in a sit-sling. And I? Of course, I am not standing below him for reasons of safety. Joerg comes down twice more, kicking out every loose stone on his abseil route – I had always hoped I would grow old . . . Right! Everything is ready. Joerg is sailing down, directly into the camera. 'That was no good,' I yell at him. 'We need more action,' and I keep looking through the viewfinder. Now even Joerg is swearing – it is the fourth time he's come down the rope. Normally he is always so patient – it must be the weather. Still, he runs up again, mumbling to himself that this time he'd show me. He seizes the rope. I'm convinced that now he'll come down elegantly – just like Rébuffat – you only have to activate those energies which lie sleeping in everybody. Already I see the silhouette in the viewfinder. (I am ignorant of the rock poised obliquely over my head, six metres further up the wall, as big and heavy as a typewriter.) 'Bravo, Joerg. Bravo. That was good!' (Not really like Rébuffat, more a wild horse in a harness, but never mind . . .) I keep my finger on the button, the camera whirrs, Joerg's outline in my viewfinder swings out sideways, comes in again . . . Suddenly: all is black! CRAAACK! A terrible blow in my face knocks me down, and it feels as if I have lost my head, an unbelievable impact, an enormous weight – I sink to the ground, dropping the camera at my side – Joerg bends over me, I hear yells from the camp, running footsteps – then nothing. Almost immediately, it seems, I am awake again: see Karli, our doctor, and feel blood running down my face. I cannot see anything out of one eye. It is as if the violent blow had frozen into my face; it is still there, particularly on the upper jaw . . . Ah, there is a faint gleam, fuzzy shapes . . . Yes, I can make out something with my left eye. 'What's the matter with my eye, Karli?' I blurt out – I think I'm wafting off again.

'Don't worry. Your eye's fine, but you're a lucky sod: without that camera in front of your face, you'd be stone dead by now,' he says, and bandages me up. 'We must give you an eye patch for a while. My, that looks elegant.' And he doesn't know how much he calms me with that; if Karli is launching into his Bavarian good cheer, then he must think I'll be okay.

In the background I hear somebody mutter: 'My God, look at the camera. Total write-off . . .'

The Arriflex which saved my life was cracked through; two of the optics looked like squashed top hats. Joerg was devastated, not because of the camera – that was insured – but because of me. It wasn't his fault. His fatal sideways leap had really been caused by me. From the distance comes the throb of an engine. The fishing boat, thank God! But I cannot manage to lie down on board: throughout the whole journey I remain on my feet in the cooling wind, as the pain hammers away in my eye and my jaw.

My companions are kind to me, helpful as never before. I think now they would even excavate the propeller sledge. It is good to experience such care. But I also notice that obviously as a self-made film director, I must have been too hard on them sometimes. Because, as I am lying on the divan in our room in Umanak, already feeling better, Robert turns up: 'If one doesn't have to carry your tripod, you are a nice bloke,' he says, and gently adjusts my head to the correct position on the cushion.

Karli joins us with a grin. 'Take Six,' he says, and puts a new tape over my eye.

'This cup of tea – I hope I only have to bring it to you once!' says Wolfgang drily, but one could guess what he meant. (How many takes did I put him through again?)

And Anne? Anne strokes my face kindly and asks, 'How are you? Better?' Even if this had nothing to do with the film, it was very, very pleasant.

But then, what does she say? I hear her laugh softly. 'Kurt, it is a fact that since you stopped filming, we all like you much better.'

There must be some truth in that.

And by the way – just because there is a grain of truth in it – I want to describe one small episode of this film production. We needed a crevasse fall. (Why in films do they always want crevasse falls?

Just one of those things? Whatever, there it was in the script which the production company had given me: Scene 15 – crevasse fall.) I decided to film it on the inland ice. That's where it was supposed to happen in the film. After some research we found a suitable place about a mile from the spot where the Hessians and Bavarians had refused to dig out the sledge. (During my fever dreams after the accident, sometimes the expedition appeared coming home in a triumphal procession; marching in tight double rows, two and two together, and carrying on their shoulders a golden propeller sledge!) So, anyway: I had the crevasse – blue, neat, commodious, ideal – but neither Hessian nor Bavarian wanted to jump inside it. You can understand why. Jumping with crampons is dangerous; to jump without them . . . can be quite uncomfortable afterwards. Best not to jump at all. That's what my companions thought, too. But finally, Wolfgang Rauschl sacrificed himself – give the guy a medal! While he was hanging in the crevasse and being held by Hans, the latter yelling into the abyss (a tremble of excitement in his voice: I am a tough director), 'Wolfgang – I've got you!', at exactly that moment, the batteries of my recorder ran out. Damn. Not now! There is no other solution than to fake this scene later on.

Although it goes without saying that the whole accident was phoney (did you ever hear of anyone filming a non-intentional fall into a crevasse?), it embarrasses me to have to confess to additional fakery with camera and sound. But when, a fortnight later on the Qioqe Peninsula seventy kilometres away, Hans was standing 'at the edge of the crevasse' (actually, at the edge of a granite boulder above a green meadow by the beach) and in his trembling voice yelled towards the crevasse victim (who was relaxing in the grass), 'Wolfgang – I've got you!', a sudden suspicion came into my mind that perhaps Hans had worn a hat in the original take. Bloody hell! (There are no patron saints for film directors to call upon.) I tell him, 'Hans, we must shoot the whole thing again. Weren't you wearing a hat?'

Hans, who already had pearls of sweat on his forehead (he was at 1000 metres on the ice rim, and heavily clothed), stuttered, 'I have three different hats . . .' and as if my misfortune wasn't sufficient, he continued, '. . . and I cannot remember whether I was wearing my goggles or not either.'

The tumultuous laughter of the Hessians and Bavarians echoed from wall to wall along the Kangerdluarssuk Fjord, and no doubt all the way to the inland ice. Various more or less 'ambitious', more or less volunteer tripod- and film-box porters made pointed remarks about film directors – I was destroyed. By the sweat of our brows (mainly of Hans Lautensach's, but also my own) I committed all possible permutations on to several rolls of film (Hans, a person of pedantic precision, only a bit distracted, had meanwhile remembered something else: did he wear gloves, or not?)

The subsequent laughter in Rüdesheim carried from the studio across the Rhine. You couldn't hear it from the inland ice, but certainly as far away as Mainz. On the cutting table: Hans with fur hat, without goggles, with gloves . . . trembling: 'Wolfgang, I've got you!' Hans, with beloved woollen Peruvian bonnet, with goggles, without gloves: 'Wolfgang, I've got you!' Hans, dripping with sweat, without hat, without goggles, with gloves: 'Wolfgang . . .'

Now I always carry a notebook in the pocket of my jacket. But only the spirits of the air know whether I'm wearing the right jacket.

Eruption on Stromboli – the crater works like a valve on a pressure chamber.

The fantastic Diamir Face of Nanga Parbat.

Umanak, town and harbour at 71° north on the west coast of Greenland as we saw it in the summer. Not far from here was Alfred Wegener's starting point for his legendary exploration of the Inland Ice.

PART FIVE

A night on Stromboli

Stromboli – the only continuously active volcano in Europe. Also one of the seven Aeolian Islands to the north of Sicily. The island bears the same name as the volcano, since that is all there is: the steep cone rises straight out of the sea. Its top is 980 metres high, but what the visitor sees, approaching by ship, is no more than the very tip of the cone: the roots lie 2000 metres lower, on the bed of the Mediterranean.

Stromboli will disappoint nobody. Like a kind of 'Old Faithful', its craters spew thundering fire fountains into the air as regularly and reliably as the whistle on an overheated pressure cooker. Anyone on the summit is treated to a spectacle of indescribable power, so frightening and fascinating as to touch one's innermost being. The intention may have been to spend just an hour there, but one finds oneself staying a full night.

Sometimes though, the fiery soul of the mountain is stirred with an overwhelming force, which sends a glowing lava flow racing down the black burned slopes of the Sciara del Fuoco and into the sea. At those times it is better not to make an attempt on the otherwise benign summit. The local guides know the moods of their mountain and will certainly warn anyone when it is unsafe.

A number of fishermen and their families live on the island. More precisely, there are two small villages – San Vincenzo on the northern coast and Ginostra in the south-west. They are built on old lava flows – and sitting in their squat houses spooning their fish soup, folk often hear above them the rumble of the mountain. They have got used to it.

To a rock climber, Stromboli is of no interest. It is for the adventurer. British mountaineers attempted the traverse of the steep north-westerly coast, from one fishing village to the other, at sea level, passing below the Sciara del Fuoco, the 'course of fire'. Threatened by lapilli slides, they struggled forward, sometimes in, sometimes out of the water, through niches and caves, moving across sand and ashes until, blackened but happy, they finally reached the other side. It was never repeated. For their part, the fishermen hold such goings-on as madness, and prefer to travel by boat. Only very rarely does anyone cross the island by climbing over the mountain.

I met one of the British 'madmen' once on the cliffs of the Welsh coast: Dennis Kemp, an excellent climber and mountaineer with a lot of experience behind him, though white-haired, was full of youthful enthusiasm. We spoke about the beauty of different places around the world, where the sea and the mountains meet, and while we were sitting on our airy pulpit, with the surf pounding the slabs below us, he told me about Stromboli. Near us, meanwhile, a pair of climbers moved slowly on tiny holds across the Dream of White Horses, the famous traverse high above the foaming crests of the waves. Surrounded by all these impressions, a plan ripened gently in my mind: I would experience the volcano for myself. The opportunity came sooner than I expected. When I returned, somewhat battered, from Greenland, my daughters hugged me and scolded: 'Papa, we're not letting you go off again for a while.' Teresa thought the same. No doubt they were right: it was time to stay at home. But hardly a week had gone by before I was conspiring to make my convalescence rather more eventful . . .

Black sand, glittering and overlaid with a yellow-gold shimmer when viewed into the sun; black, rotten lava monsters emerging from the foam of boiling waters. The dazzling houses of San Vincenzo, the narrow coastline around the island. Higher, the dominating mountain skyline, rusty and black, with patches of dark green on the lower slopes. Fast moving clouds – drifts of smoke? A distant rumble, echoing down from the sky . . . the volcano.

'. . . *è normale!*' It's normal, an Italian fisherman comments with a smile. Another wears an apron, which boasts in big red letters: I TALK ENGLISH EVERY INFORMATION. A handful of tourists cluster round him – the old sailor (I take him for that), home from the sea, has managed to find a way of using his experience to augment the meagre livelihood of an islander. But the tourists soon return to the ship which brought us here from Naples, and continue on to Lipari, to Panarea, to Vulcano . . . Only a few remain on Stromboli.

We find a room to stay, very cheap, with old bedsteads and mattresses, but breakfast is included. What luxury! We spread out our sleeping-bags – Karen and Hilde, my two daughters, only eight and fourteen years old, Teresa from Bologna, and me. We are very excited, delighted with the island, and do not hide from our hosts that we want to go to the top of Stromboli tomorrow, and overnight there. Overnight, as of course in the dark you can watch the eruptions so much better.

Our hosts, though, meet this announcement with an expression of sorrow: only last week there had been an accident. A boy lost his way, coming back in the dark. He fell over a cliff. Dead.

Fall to one's death on this mountain? Such a possibility had never crossed my mind. We have hard hats with us, sleeping-bags, a bivvi bag, a stove, torches . . . but no rope.

Next morning we buy a hemp line from a fisherman, not very long, but tough . . .

Clouds are racing over the ridge up there, sailing by incredibly fast. There's a strong wind from the west. Patches of sunlight and shadow dance across the steep slopes. It looks unfriendly. Some tiny dots are moving up on the skyline. Somebody, then, has gone up . . .

We don't get away till afternoon. The wind has died down and the sun is now shining pleasantly, warmly. A comfortable mule track leads through the tight Mediterranean scrub . . . Spanish broom; metre-high spheres of spurge, what we call Wolf's Milk; and in between, the countless blue and white flowers of rosemary, with its characteristic scent; pink blooms, too, and greenery . . .

The black sand and the lava cliffs become inkier and inkier as they recede into the depths, and the sounds of the sea soften to a murmur. In the end, only the hum of insects and the sweet smell of the maquis surround us. We meet some islanders descending to their village, and a group of young lads with enormous rucksacks and colourful anoraks overtake us as we move leisurely upwards.

Clearly, they want to pass the night up there, too. Soon they are lost to view. A jungle of tall, yellowish cane, which covers the slopes now, has swallowed them up.

It is getting steeper. The mule track has given way to a narrow path which winds in a tight zigzag up between the shrub and cane. Sometimes it is deeply incised in the soft ground, then dissipates into vague traces across loose rubble and dark volcanic rock. Leaning on our sticks and ice axes, we gradually work our way up, following a rounded ridge that is flanked on its right-hand side by a sheer drop. Obliquely below us, we can see the steep, grey course of the Sciara del Fuoco. The sea is shrouded in a yellowish haze, and to the west a grey bank of cloud has built, getting darker all the time. 'What do you think about the weather?' Teresa asks anxiously.

'Not much,' I reply, but continue upwards. When we stop for a breather I address my little crew: 'You had better know that I'm in no mind to carry this enormous pack up, down, then up again. We have got everything we need for a fine bivouac, and if the weather turns bad, we wait till it gets better.' No objections are raised to that. They have never bivouacked before, anyway – high time they did!

The strong wind blows up into a storm. Whenever we draw close to the exposed edge, sand whirls about our ears, blown uphill from the depths of the Sciara del Fuoco. We put on our pullovers and anoraks. The branches of the bushes bow low before the wind's blast and Hildegard's long blonde hair streams like a battle standard. She leans into the wind with all her might, but little Karen has pulled her hood over her ears and does not look at all convinced . . . Teresa takes her hand and coaxes her gently upwards, quietly, patiently, as always. Coming from a big Italian family, she is used to having other people to take into account, many others, and is resigned to not always being able to do what she wants. Probably she would prefer to be down at the bottom now. But – turn around here?

Shouts from above, trampling in the bushes, two figures appear. One of them, a bearded guy, stops. 'You're not going up now?' he yells at me, staring at the children. 'Not in this storm, for heaven's sake?'

I protest that he doesn't understand. 'We're keeping an eye on things. If it doesn't improve, we can still go down!' The bearded man throws me a glance as if I were mad, and hurries after his companion.

'These people obviously haven't come prepared with bivouac gear,' I reassure my troops. Maybe they have, I think, and just don't like bivouacking . . . but I keep that to myself. It is good for the children to get used to storms.

Another group clatters down. '*Mamma mia!*' and '*Padre impossibile!*' yells a dark Italian woman, regarding our slow-moving party with wide eyes. An impossible father . . . But my children, of course, know that already. 'Papa, perhaps we had better go down,' a small voice issues from under Karen's hood.

'Wait a bit, sweetheart. It's not raining yet.'

Is that more trampling and shouting from above? Somebody else about to undermine our resolve? 'Come on, let's tuck ourselves in the bushes for a rest. We can wait till they've all gone.' And I distribute nuts and – chocolate – a good father. (I'm having to polish up my image.) As we sit in the scrub, the last group scampers downhill. Now we have the mountain – and the storm – to ourselves. All possibilities open.

Perhaps we can still find somewhere to bivouac that has a view of the eruptions, as we planned to. Some little niche higher up, out of the wind? I rather doubt it: already it's beginning to get dark. But to sit it out here and see nothing – that would be totally boring. We're all agreed on that. So then, higher! Unfortunately, it really is dark now. We get out the torches . . . A little later, at a steep rocky section, the hard hats and fisherman's rope are pressed into service as well. With care, we manage to get across, but it's worse on the other side: no bushes, not even smaller plants, nothing to slow down the wind, and no trace at all of somewhere to bivouac. In these gusts, the occasional rumble of the volcano can hardly be heard, it sounds like collapsing séracs on a glacier . . . I admit defeat! 'Okay, gang. We'd better go back. We can't stay here . . .'

Down in the groove of the path, we find a spot where it is horizontal and smooth, sheltered from the wind among the canes, and tucked into our sleeping-bags, down jackets and bivvy bag, preparing something hot to drink becomes more interesting to everybody than any eruption . . .

*

The moon draws a glittering ribbon across the sea. Incredible. The wind has vanished, and the sky is clear! Suddenly, just like that. How long was I asleep? 'Isn't it beautiful, Papa!' whispers Hildegard. She has raised herself on to her elbow and looks down. Karen and Teresa do not stir. Above, a thunder-roll makes the air tremble. A small cloud takes on a red glow for a second or two.

'Wait! I'll creep over to the edge and take a look!' Another thunderclap . . . followed by a whoosh! Beyond the black silhouette of the ridge glowing spheres rise into the sky, silent, then gently float down again. I grope my way back. 'Hilde, come . . .'

The spectacle bewitches her. 'Papa, we must get higher!'

Stromboli's craters lie on the north-west side of the mountain, somewhat below the summit and directly above the Sciara del Fuoco. The higher we can climb this ridge, which is blocking the view to them, the closer and better we should be able to see the eruptions. I wake Teresa. 'The weather is fine now! Hildegard and I will go up a bit higher. We'll be back in a couple of hours. Then I'll take you and Karen up. We couldn't go all together, not in the dark. You sleep for now. *Buona notte!*'

How different everything is without the storm. Hildegard and I are roped up, it is true, and we are wearing our helmets, but the difficulties are minimal, elementary you might even say. Nevertheless, we must not fall. To each other we seem only unreal shadows, as we feel our way up the black rocky step which stopped us before. Again, I can't help thinking: how different without storm! How lucky we are . . .

We gain height briskly. Even at fourteen, Hilde is almost as tall as I am. She was only seven when we climbed the Gran Sasso; later other interests took over. With mounting excitement we grope higher towards the invisible thunder, which emanates from somewhere behind the dark rock. What will we see? Above us, the outline of the ridge stands out clearly, so it cannot be far now. Another loud rumble. Instinctively, we quicken our steps, as if we might be missing something irretrievable, and pant up the last few metres, moving as fast we can.

The ridge. All is quiet. We are standing on a horizontal shelf. Soft moonlight bathes the dark bulk of the mountain, as it does us; it draws our shadows out as silent companions on to the rocky, sandy ground. Deep down, almost intuitively, we sense a mighty semicircular cauldron, which must be where the Sciara del Fuoco begins. Beyond it, considerably higher than we are now, is the summit. It still seems a long way off, unattainable and dream-like. In a wide curve, our ridge, seamed with black shadows and indistinct obstacles, leads up to it. As far as that? I am surprised.

Suddenly there appears below it something like a giant flower of fire, trembling, opening, blossoming within seconds high into the night sky! A thunderous roar . . .

We are both speechless.

It is so beautiful that at this moment I feel no regret that we failed to establish our bivouac on the summit; on that so distant spot . . .

Although . . .

'Papa, that is magic! We have to get up there!' whispers Hildegard.

'Much too far at night.'

'But I want to get to the top!' she insists. 'We've got this far . . . and there's still plenty of night left.'

Perhaps my daughter is right. Nothing is unattainable, except what you have already relinquished. 'Okay, then. Let's give it a try!'

I realise something, and it touches me in a strange way. I was almost prepared to accept the situation, to give in . . . Not Hildegard! Joy seizes me, a sort of exultation that I cannot explain to myself – as if something would come of this night, something to link her and me in a vitally new way, different from before. It is true I am in front, leading, but for the first time I feel my daughter is an equal ropemate. More than that, it was she who made us continue.

We are feeling our way along the ridge. It is wider than we expected. Many of the obstacles turn out to be shadows only, and we are able to detour a real rocky barrier. To our left, the ground plunges away, down, one imagines, to the fishermen's village of San Vincenzo. All of a sudden the earth below our feet changes to a fine, soft, yielding sand! It gives the sensation of trudging uphill through heavy snow. Above us, the summit outline has noticeably altered. Another few steps and it has changed again! That means it cannot be much further now – it is just the moonlight that makes it seem so far away!

'Hilde, another half an hour and I think we will be up . . .!'

We whoop for joy. The mountain is ours, already it's ours . . . has been all the time!

And the magic of this night. Again and again the explosions come,
every quarter of an hour . . . In between, the volcano bubbles and
sloshes in its mighty pots: liquid lava, the red glare of fire in the
darkness. We see them diagonally ahead, and much nearer now.
Phew! What a stench of sulphur! Acrid fumes engulf us, blowing
over the sandy ridge from the craterfield. And there is a prickle
on the skin, like a million fine needles. We hurry on through it.
Steeply now we are plodding up the last few metres. The outline is
quite different now – it can only be a few more minutes . . .

A fire fountain, very close. We stop. It is so beautiful; you could
never get used to it.

It is two o'clock in the morning: the ground becomes hard again.
Lava slabs, a curving crust above the void. We take the last steps
to the summit.

Here it is!

Who could have imagined that we would still make it up to this
spot tonight? The moon, the sea, the silhouetted coastline of the
whole island below us, the red glow from the craterfield, the tangled
contours of the mountain . . . over there, on the other side, outlines
of ridges and troughs. Far to the south some twinkling lights and a
shadowy line of coast: Sicily! A cold wind is blowing up here. We
might even walk over to the other side of the crater rim . . .

We follow a sort of track that appears to lead down into the
craterfield. It is a real temptation to keep going closer – but at a
bivouac wall with inviting stone 'seats', we stop. The mighty pots
are simmering and hissing – still some distance away. Nevertheless,
the next explosion almost yanks us from our perches in fear and
excitement . . . With a deafening thunder-roar, a cascade of liquid
rock, white-hot, one or two thousand degrees in temperature and
weighing many tons, shoots skyward just in front of us, splitting
into a giant bundle of rays, parabolas, and a hundred ribbons of
light, arcing back to earth. Rocks patter as they strike the edge of
the crater, a fiery rain that continues to glimmer on the ground,
changing from white-yellow to orange to red, to crimson – till all
the dots of light go out, disappear, and only the dull glow of the
bubbling lava, reflected up from the depth of the craters, penetrates
the darkness.

We wait for the next eruption.

Somewhere deep down on the ridge Teresa and Karen are sleeping
in their bivouac. They cannot imagine what we are experiencing at

this moment . . . but, they could not have made it this far at night. Perhaps tomorrow morning?

It is such a pity they don't see this.

Of the five craters down there, three are active – and the largest of them erupts regularly about every ten to fifteen minutes. This is the one we are specially waiting for! Its fire fountains may reach one or two hundred metres high. The second crater only erupts now and then. And the third is a real character: we call him the Swindler. This hooligan is the noisiest of the lot: he roars like a jet testing its engines, only louder – he roars, and roars . . . yet nothing appears, until shortly before the end of his performance, he spits, one by one, three or four red glowing tennis balls at crazy speed, diagonally into the dark, where they rise higher than all the other missiles from the craters. It looks so funny for all that noise to produce so ridiculously little, and whenever he does it, we can't help laughing. For all its otherwise fantastic show, the Stromboli Theatre has its clown, too. Once, he even seems to respond to Hilde's shouted encouragement and spits five balls!

Cold creeps into our bones, but how can we ever drag ourselves away from here? Every so often we reassure each other that it is not that bad – but next time we will bring a sleeping-bag with us. Next time? Who knows when that will be?

One thing is certain: never in our lives had we dreamed of such a night. Perhaps it is the more impressive because we are here totally on our own. And because we had to fight our way up here. And . . .

Many things are possible only once in life – you have to seize the opportunity when it comes.

*

While we descend to Teresa and Karen, it is as if we walked slowly out of a strange dream. We have to keep telling ourselves it is still true. For how long? Words and pictures encompass only a space; inside that, reality gradually dissolves, like smoke.

Later on, while Hildegard catches up on some sleep at our bivouac, I climb up with Teresa and Karen to the shoulder of the ridge. We see a couple of wonderful eruptions – and Karen hugs us both with delight. But the dawn is gradually creeping in, covering mountain and sky in pale blue, draining the shine from the glowing shells . . .

There is no point in going on to the summit any more. 'From up there,' Teresa says wistfully, 'it must be even more beautiful.'

Another time.

'I canali' – the channels

There is one landscape in Italy that could be called a mountaineer's nightmare: the channel country near the mouth of the Po River . . . For centuries people here have been draining the swampy ground, tough people reclaiming land while the mighty river continues dismantling Alps and carrying them to the Adriatic, pushing the coastline further and further eastwards. Porto Maggiore, as its name implies, once the biggest harbour, is now a small rural town more than thirty kilometres inland – as the crow flies . . .

And crows, that's another thing. There are literally hundreds of them in this land of pulverised peaks. Normally I like birds and their songs, and I certainly don't go along with those people who see the crow as a bird of ill omen, but even I consider there are perhaps too many in this flat land, which has unexpectedly become an important station along my life's way, and very much a proving ground. Here is where Teresa was born, grew up. Her mother, too.

*

And the channels? This is a landscape you cannot hurry through: wherever you walk, wherever you go, you soon come to a dyke or channel far too wide to leap across.

A weird sensation for a mountaineer.

There is something else, too: the Padrona di casa – a special and peculiarly Italian figure. The literal translation 'patroness of the house' does not really get you very far. Since I have had the benefit of a growing personal experience, I will attempt to describe the phenomenon more exactly.

In appearance, usually as solid as the farmhouse she rules over.

Once you have entered the house, you are in her domain. Woe to the person who dares sneak something out of the fridge at night (admittedly a shortcoming of mine!). It is for the Padrona to decide when people eat. She keeps all objects and subjects under her control. Night and day.

Never wash the dishes, nor the plate or cup you have just used. Don't try to be helpful – leave well alone; thus you avoid offending the Padrona.

She does not care whether Mount Everest is in Africa or Asia, or if India is in South America – or not; just so long as the borders of her property are right (and respected).

No matter how the watchdog howls and lunges on his chain, do not set him free. The animal might dig up the lettuces, or even run into the house . . . a terrible thought for the Padrona.

She is busy in the house from morning to evening, cleaning, cooking (great!), and dealing with the laundry. Like the Forth Bridge, as she finishes one end, she starts again at the other. Anyone who expects to find a speck of dust in the Padrona's house is sadly mistaken.

Entertainment during the day for an Italian Padrona di casa is provided by visits from the scattered clan of relatives, the network of which is almost as intricate in the surrounding area as that of the channels. On these occasions, the normally sacrosanct 'best' rooms are thrown open.

And, finally, since anyone who comes within her circle of might will do his utmost to follow the Padrona's unwritten laws, for fear of provoking her indignation, inevitably all outside connections, contracts and relationships cease at once to be valid. As the husband of a Padrona's daughter, you are not competent to make decisions – indoors or out – however much you grind your teeth. It is the Padrona who has an absolute claim over love and respect.

On the other hand, if you manage to observe all her rules, you can be sure she will do everything for you . . .

For a mountaineer, that is not, as we in Austria say, an easy tart to swallow. Knowing what to do in a sudden breakdown of weather, or how to avoid stonefall, to face the dangers of a mountain – none of these prepares you to cope with a Padrona di casa in the network of channels of the Emilia-Romagna (a district, incidentally, where Mussolini was born).

To be sure, my mother-in-law is a helpful person, but I do not think she considers me much of a catch for her daughter . . . and one has

*to understand that. In this channel landscape, I fit about as well as a
Matterhorn in a cabbage patch.*

*So, we are not always in harmony: especially when she keeps the
shutters closed all day long . . . she loves the dark, and I the sunshine.
It must provide an entertaining spectacle for an observer: a house
where the venetian blinds snap up and down continuously. Two tough
characters fighting for the light of day . . .* (from my diary, 1980)

Thinking back now, I realise how much better things have become
since we built a big, new, roomy house on top of a hill near
Bologna, a house for six people, including Teresa's sisters! Half
of the shutters stay closed and the other half open, and we respect
an invisible borderline, as it were between England and Scotland.
Two dogs run freely together and mother-in-law generously feeds
everyone in style, tends her flowers and, well, is the boss on her
side of the house. We can smile now at the old trench warfare.
Still, anyone who imagines the Italians as an easy-going people,
knows only half the truth. And a Padrona di casa is a very special
regional delicacy . . .

In the interest of my fellow mountaineers, who might find
themselves marrying in Italy, let me return once more to the
entrenchments . . .

*Besides my wife, there was the dog who demonstrated himself in
favour of my visits: he jumped for joy whenever I arrived, knowing
I would cast off his chain, at the same time urging him not to
exhume any more lettuces! Of course, I wouldn't leave the door
open and give him the opportunity of slipping into the house – I
was full of high endeavour to keep the peace! And, though things
changed only slowly . . . my wife assisted me and I admired her
for her patience. I knew she would never turn into a Padrona di
casa (at least, Good heavens, I hope not!). Two full summers I
endured in the landscape of the channels for her!*

*It was not just stoicism that kept me there, we were extremely fond
of each other. Even so, I felt that the striped pattern of the venetian
blinds so perfectly echoed the watery network outside. That I did
not end up a 'pulverised' mountaineer, is simply because I could
not give up the hills.*

Even today, in Bologna, I live far from real mountains – they are in these pages as I write, and frequently I long for them. Months and years are in these pages – you give up a lot of present for the past. But in the channel landscape I learned fortitude.

Ceci, my son, was born there – he is stubborn and full of fantasy . . .

Some things never change, even today: without warning the Peuterey Ridge suddenly erupts out of the vegetable garden over the hills . . . and I am off again! Teresa and Ceci know that I have to go whenever too much time has passed. It is the other life. Father will come back, sooner or later. That is the way it is with mountain guides, sailors, cameramen – their home has no walls and no fence.

(Will mother-in-law still feed me? Perhaps I had better scrap these pages in the Italian edition! After all, in Italy, they know well enough what a Padrona di casa is . . .)

The millipede

It is huge, living amongst us, and proliferating with the speed of a swarm of locusts; it munches, munches everything before it . . . The legs of this replicated monster cast long shadows across valleys and forests, into once lonely cirques, over alpine meadows, plateaux, even over the summits of some peaks. Or the monster turns into an apparently harmless slow-worm, winding its way steadily, and gently covering more and more of the green with grey. Highway millipedes with concrete legs, asphalt snakes with their offspring, parallel and diagonal links, countless poles of cableways . . . entire 'zip-fasteners' opening up our alpine homeland. And not only there: the millipede threatens the forest areas of Germany, no less than the mountain world and high valleys of Austria, Switzerland, Italy, France. Stay away from a place for ten years, or even less, and you will be surprised when you return. If we do not act quickly, the millipede scourge will march inexorably on. You can always find a reason for it, be it a wish for comfort or the commercial interest of a group of people – local or urban outsiders. It might satisfy some person's justifiable need, or the country's economy, or the image of a politician, seeking to improve his chances in the next election; sometimes, people merely feel left behind by the burgeoning progress they see all around them. There is increasing art and cunning in the destruction of our landscape: people have no trouble finding more than one justification for their own pet millipede: economic, touristic, development, redressing competitive disadvantage, capitalistic – for investment, or because it deserves to be done – or to bring full employment . . . And at the back of it is always a political motive, because somebody will have a personal agenda. Consequently politicians either have little regard for landscape (especially mountains), or at best find themselves in a big dilemma – more bluntly, you could say their personal freedom of choice is compromised.

So, we should not be surprised when yet another fresh weal disfigures the earth's countenance, another cord is added to the ever-constricting network that strangles air and liberty and living space. It is like a fungal disease ravaging a face, and spreading relentlessly – fed by an amalgam of power, greed, technical progress and indolence. It is the cancer on the skin of the world.

On this increasingly comfortable globe, where today you can travel almost anywhere quickly and without effort – but where in so many places it is no longer worthwhile to go since everywhere begins to look the same – if we do not stop and protect what remains, all that in the end will be left are apathetic idiots and a handful of specialists. Should we then be surprised, and would it even matter, if one fine morning the second Big Bang overtook the lot of us?

Does it have to come to that?

Who is there to help, disinterestedly and honestly, pushing personal interest aside? In the summer of 1980, when I entered these thoughts in my diary, I came to the rather sceptical conclusion: Except for some single outstanding individuals, statistics show that people's trust in the honesty of others is very far from encouraging. I quote from the 'Neue Kronenzeitung':

> *The American psychologist Dr Julian Rotter interviewed 4000 people in New York on what they thought of the honesty of those engaged in twenty different professions. He found that doctors and judges were considered to be the most sincere. Then priests and teachers. At the end of the honesty scale were ranked television technicians, plumbers, second-hand car dealers. The least trustworthy of all, in his researches, were – the politicians.*

As I said, not an encouraging picture. Along with the vested interests of industrial and agricultural development, it is the politicians who, in the end, decide the matter by making laws and directing funds. Without engaging their interest, no one will get anywhere . . . True, Dr Rotter's was a North American statistic, but it makes you worry about the situation in Europe, too. At least there is some hope: in my Salzburg country, thanks to politicians, a high mountain plateau has been saved from development. But, recently, I heard of a project for a new cableway on the Grossvenediger. It makes you weep . . . Heavens above, don't we have far too many cableways already?

One of my friends from Canada – Herbert Kariel, a professor of economic geography at Calgary University – studied the alpine situation. As a result, he issued a terrified warning to the Canadian Alpine Club, begging them to ensure that development was never allowed to get that far in their own country.

Thank God that today such voices can be heard in increasing numbers on both sides of the Atlantic, as well as in the Himalaya, and a general conscience for the protection of the environment has begun to take shape. Yet it will be a continuous battle, with some successes, but many defeats. I remember my own fight against Russian helicopter transport of tourists to K2 from the Chinese side, as well as against a cableway project in Spain. I was supporting my friends of the Collectivo Montañero por la defensa de los Picos de Europa, who with the sterling help of a British climber, Robin Walker, finally defeated the financial interests.

The growing number of expeditions and treks also contribute to the despoliation of some of the most beautiful places in the Himalaya. New roads and a number of accompanying facilities increasingly erode the natural barrier of fatigue; no wonder that more and more people arrive. In Biella, in 1987, at an international meeting of mountaineers in which Lord Hunt and other eminent climbers participated, we founded the movement Mountain Wilderness for the protection of the mountain environment. Along with Chris Bonington, I am still one of its guarantors. A number of interventions have taken place since then – in the Alps, the Apennines, on K2 and other places of the mountain world. For too long we climbers have taken insufficient care of our mountains, have committed desecration simply by going to them and opening up the area to outsiders.

PART SIX

A new world

Beside me, Chic Scott gnawed on his pipe and gazed over Salzburg's many churches, its fortress, and the grey-green ribbon of the Salzach River flowing through a scattered sea of houses. The town lies plumb in the centre of a wide bowl which stretches from the gently undulating plain and alpine foothills to the north to the massive limestone outcrops of the Kalkalpen. We were standing in a meadow on top of the Gaisberg, a hill of about 1000 metres, and my silent friend, who is Canadian and had been working in Europe as a climbing guide for a year now, was letting his eyes range back and forth over my home town and out to the abrupt line of the Untersberg plateau, with the dark woods at its foot. 'It's nice here,' he said at length, taking the pipe from his mouth and pointing to the dusky rim of flat land below the limestone cliffs. 'See that forest?' He drew a deep reflective breath, which sounded more like a sigh, before continuing, 'Where I live, the forest just goes on and on and on, if you can imagine that. In the Rocky Mountains, everything is so much bigger . . .' Then he clamped his teeth around his pipe once more, not appearing to notice that it had gone out long since. He was homesick. That evening, when we were climbing up from the banks of the Salzach to the rocky fortress of Hohensalzburg, he spoke of Canada again.

Considering the many expeditions I had made around the world, it may sound strange that the North American continent was a blank on the map to me then. I had trodden its margins years ago when filming the Labrador Eskimos with Mario. That was all. Today, when I feel perfectly at home in the Grand Canyon and have flown many times through the skies over New York, it is hard to imagine that my knowledge of America at that time came solely from books, postcards, and a few Westerns. Of course, I knew this was a gap in my experience, a serious neglect on my part, but I could see no practical way of rectifying it. Apart from Alaska, North America is not somewhere you make expeditions to, and where was the adventure in going with a group of tourists? How was I to get there? Everything changed for me when I met Chic Scott.

He found Europe attractive, and sympathetic, but very small, very limiting. After his visit to Salzburg, I drove him back to Leysin in Switzerland, where he was working. Karen and Hildegard, my daughters, came along for the ride, and Mama Tona was alerted to pop one of her special giant pizzas in the oven. We would take the route via Varese, even if this was by no means the shortest way to Leysin. During the long ride the conversation ranged over all manner of things. We spoke of *The Eiger Sanction*, the latest Clint Eastwood thriller, which was pulling in audiences on the other side of the Atlantic, and making the Eiger's notorious North Wall even more infamous. Chic had worked on the shoot for this film along with a Salzburg friend of mine, Norman Dyhrenfurth. We spoke, too, of the Himalaya (which Chic had yet to visit), and about Canada (which I told him I regretted not having seen).

Suddenly he said, 'Why don't you come to Canada, and tell us about your expeditions?'

Could I do that? Was that the way? 'I'd love to,' I told him, 'really love to! But how would I go about it?'

'Oh, I'll take care of that,' Chic replied, and he said it with such nonchalance, you would think it the easiest thing in the world. Even though the North American continent was so large, he told me, Canadian climbers, from the east coast to the west, all knew each other. The Alpine Club of Canada was an extremely well-knit association, its sections keeping in close touch with one another. That certainly proved to be true. But, as I found later, it can be a different story in the United States. You are made just as welcome around that enormous country but, to arrange a lecture tour, have to negotiate individually with all the local clubs along the way. It becomes very difficult to plan a rational and cost-covering route with the vast distances involved.

Chic Scott returned to Canada soon afterwards, and I waited on tenterhooks for news. Would he be able to pull it off? Would I get to tell of my adventures in that land of opportunity between two oceans? Months went by . . . while in Banff, right in the heart of the Rocky Mountains, Chic and Evelyn, the Alpine Club of Canada's secretary, worked on my itinerary. When the letter finally arrived, I could not believe my eyes. I was invited to travel all over the continent, from Toronto to Vancouver, with a trip to Los Angeles thrown in. I had mentioned to Evelyn over the phone that I knew a philatelist there, and by chance he turned out to be the main organiser of events for a local climbing and rambling club, the Vagmarken – or Milestones. But more of them later.

I was overjoyed! Never had I believed such a thing possible. Now I burned with excited impatience. Once more, I had seen living proof of how doors open up for someone with foreign languages. If you know five, even if you do not speak them all perfectly, you can regard yourself as a citizen of the world – even three may be sufficient to get you by. I was interested in more than just 'getting by'. When you give up a secure life in favour of freedom and uncertainty, among the advantages to this often difficult freedom is being able to talk to people of other nationalities about their lives and perceptions, besides enjoying the opportunity to convey something of your own experience. It is quite wrong to say that in a civilised country, there is nothing left to discover – the jungle and the Arctic are not the only places where you can go exploring!

A new world! As far as I knew, Gaston Rébuffat had been the only other European mountaineer to make a lecture tour in North America, but that was many years ago. Later, I learned that Dougal Haston, too, organised an extensive circuit in 1974. My visit was in 1975, when I proudly presented my 'show', *Summits and Secrets*. From one lecture venue to the next, I covered enormous distances: the equivalent of several times across Central Europe! Altogether, from my departure to return, I travelled 29,980 kilometres. The tour did not end as planned, just kept extending and extending . . . Even if the earnings were melting away under the southern sun before I could get them home, it was an adventure I would never have missed. To feel in tune with a whole continent – is a wonderful thing! For that, I shall always have Chic and Evelyn to thank.

*

A glittering sea of lights below the plane's wings, a carpet of twinkling lights, some amber, others nearly white, like luminous pinheads closely packed on a dark pincushion. Street blocks become strange trinkets and there are bright islands down there – impossible now to say what they may be . . . New York is sliding away . . . I am already on my way to Toronto. I have lost all track of time. I don't care. I'm here now. The shiny red Beetle outside the little airport in Luxembourg, my friends Klaus and Brigitte, who had driven me there, waving and waving . . . I can still see them . . . Then Iceland, with its fog banks and dark grey-green patches of land between . . . the east coast of Greenland, a Milky Way of broken pack ice along its length, like disintegrating nebulae seen from up here at 10,000 metres . . . Greenland's chilly peaks, the inland ice, fjords . . . so many hours jumble in my head.

Gradually, the chain of images sorts itself out in my brain, and I am landing in Toronto. Skyscrapers, spattered with lights, thronging streets, yet a strange calm at the heart of it all – it's like one of the Wonders of the World, comprising a quiet Austrian engineer who whisks me home to stay with him. Next day, like a sleepwalker, I take my first steps through a suburb. The trees are in bloom. Springtime in Canada! But towards evening it turns cool, and grey, and a few snowflakes tumble from the sky. 'There's a blizzard on the way,' the engineer announces drily. More snowflakes flutter down, and more. I deliver my lecture, experiencing a little stage fright at the beginning. 'Jolly good! Super!' the people say and begin to stream out of the hall . . . we follow them out, the engineer, some American friends and I – to find it snowing in the streets, just like Christmas! Tomorrow I have to give my talk in Ottawa.

A blizzard rages outside as I stand in the departure hall of Toronto Airport. Everything is white, except for the small dash of colour provided by the maple-leaf device on the Air Canada planes – all of which are grounded. There's no doubt about it: Ottawa is cut off by train, road and air. I have to cancel the lecture. Springtime in Canada!

Two days later I am in Montreal. A train managed to plough its way through the snowdrifts, often barely able to move at all. A friendly Canadian in a fur flying cap, down jacket, and a pipe in his mouth, picks me up at the station, saying, 'There's been a newsflash on radio and TV, telling everyone to stay at home!'

Cars have been abandoned all over the place, almost buried under snow. Most of the stores are closed since nobody could get into them anyway with snow up to their doorhandles. But I give my lecture – fifty people turn out for it! Not a lot for a town the size of Montreal. This is a good start, I think to myself. The New World is certainly full of surprises!

I am in high spirits. Below me unfolds the country of the Great Lakes. Like oceans, they epitomise the spaciousness of this Canadian landscape. I am getting into the spirit of it now, taking in more, and more: these endless dark woods, studded with thousands of little lakes, and huge fields – one after the other – like a snowed-in chessboard. For hours and hours, they slip below me. Somewhere in the middle is my next stop, Winnipeg. Mountaineers here always complain about how far it is to the Rocky Mountains. No wonder, even in a straight line they are some 1000 kilometres away. And to get here from Montreal has been 1500 . . .

I am taken on a short cross-country skiing trip while I am here, along a frozen river. All is flat, as far as the eye can see. This country wouldn't suit me at all.

On again. Endless farmland beneath the jet's silver wings: this is where all the Canadian wheat comes from, and cattle, too. At last, the Rocky Mountains! A dark indigo ramp on the horizon – not a series of peaks like our Alps, but a multitude of parallel ranges, one behind the other, great arcs of mountains, each with its own name – the Selkirks, the Coast Ranges – until you get to the Pacific Ocean. The main spine of the Rockies, however, towering up here to the west of the Great Plains, extends from north to south throughout almost the whole continent, from the Yukon to New Mexico. It is about 4000 kilometres long. Here on the prairie, where the buffalo herds have long since vanished except for sad remnants, surrounded by fertile agricultural land, lies Calgary and, a hundred kilometres to the west, among the limestone peaks of the Rockies, Banff, main settlement in a large and famous national park, seat of the Canadian Alpine Club and later, home to a great festival for mountain films. Most of my Canadian friends live here – Herb, a geography professor, Pete and Judy, and, above all, Chic and Evelyn, who were responsible for my tour. In those first days after I landed in Calgary, of course I could not have foreseen that I would come back here time and again, that the mysterious curves of the

Rocky Mountains would resolve for me into peaks with individual characteristics and very special adventures of their own – just like my summits in the Alps. I have now seen the Rocky Mountains in every season: I know they have their own Matterhorn, Mount Assiniboine; that the rocky citadel of Castle Mountain could easily be in the Dolomites; and that Mount Temple richly deserves its name. They rise from the dark pine forests and I can understand why Chic Scott was so homesick in Europe for his native, immeasurable woods.

Chic was waiting at the airport to drive me to Banff. He stopped off to show me a tiny church on the way, near the Bow River, introducing it proudly as a 'historical monument, very ancient'. Perhaps seeing me had reminded him of the many churches in Salzburg. This modest chapel was called the McDougall Memorial Church and was built in 1875, one of the first churches in this whole area. Chic explained how it was originally intended for the Indians of the Stony Tribe.

When, a little later, we came to a railway line taking trains across the Rockies to Vancouver, he told me how important the opening of this communication link had been at the end of the last century, adding – again, not without pride – that his grandfather was an engine driver on the line back around 1910. I was touched by how gently, step by step, he was presenting his homeland to me, to this Austrian confronting the wide-open spaces of Canada for the first time, having travelled so far to be here, with what seemed only short airdrops into the other cities on the way. Driving towards Banff felt a little like approaching the Salzburg 'basin' from the plain, only to find everything changed. But, as Chic found something to tell me about every landmark on the way, I fancied we were merely continuing the conversation about the great Canadian forests that we had begun on the Gaisberg. Pine woods – spruces and fir trees – were the dominant features, with small maple woods in between, and my friend conjured up for me visions of rich autumn tints in these blue limestone mountains. But here on the Bow River, it was springtime at last, even there banks of ice still stood beside the water and isolated patches of old snow dotted the bright landscape. There was no trace of the blizzard that had struck the east of the country. It was sunny and warm.

In Banff, to my great surprise, Evelyn – dark-haired, shapely – sat down at a grand piano and played Chopin. Maybe one pays more attention when you are a long way from home, but in any case I was enchanted by this melody in the heart of the Rocky Mountains. It seemed strange to be hearing the familiar notes in this Canadian wilderness, where frozen cascades still hung from the mountain walls, where one peak followed another among the infinite forests. The notes pearled away carrying us out of time . . .

The mood was interrupted by the sudden arrival of Evelyn's sister, a wiry grey-eyed woman with dark blonde hair and an extremely dynamic personality. I at once declared her the archetypal Canadian Woman, which prompted some hilarity. Later on, she and Evelyn took me for some fantastic white-water canoeing trips. Certainly, you could traverse all Canada with a woman like this! Definitely an original. I spent several days in the area, lecturing at Banff and Calgary, from where Herb took me off into the prairie to a place where dinosaur bones had been found. Imagine the ecstasies of an old fossil-hunter presented with that! But my programme tugged me on to the West Coast, with its deep bays and countless islands – to Vancouver, Victoria, Seattle (the stronghold of alpinism in the Pacific north-west, where more than 800 people came to hear me and afterwards I climbed with Bill Sumner, Dusan Jagersky, and fourteen-year-old John on their local crag – Mount Rainier, a 4393-metre extinct volcano. From a distance it looks like a *Gugelhupf*, covered in whipped cream, rising above the immense pine forests. We reached the top, with one bivouac, by the Liberty Ridge). Later, I moved on to Los Angeles, 1500 kilometres away, then in three days was back another 2300 kilometres to Edmonton – only 300 kilometres, a catspring away, from Banff, my Canadian 'Salzburg'. There, I gave some hard thought to what I should do next. My final lecture was only a month away – a restaging of the one cancelled because of the blizzard in Ottawa, back another 3000 kilometres therefore to the east coast. Meanwhile, I had developed a taste for this country: couldn't there be something for me, too, in the Land of Opportunity? But what? Lectures . . . adventures . . . mountains . . . The American west lay open before me, and I had the feeling of a good time waiting there for me, if only I looked hard enough.

How to catch a millionaire

Whether Gordon from Nevada is really a millionaire or not, I cannot say with my hand on my heart, but he certainly looks the part. Greying slightly at the temples, a high, intelligent brow, and an air of cool determination. He can be pensive, then suddenly become more full of beans than you would credit a man in his late fifties. He has that certain something, a combination of sensitivity with the raw toughness of a penetrating intellect, which marks out the real businessman. I don't know what his business is – he used to run a flying school. He is a self-made man and, as I said, projects an air of great wealth. He certainly owns a mountain, and an observatory, and he lives with his young and pretty wife and their family in a wonderful house, built of sweet-smelling wood, and overlooking the deep blue Lake Tahoe. Because of prodigious snowfalls that hit the Sierra Nevada, it is often impossible to get to his house by any conventional means of transport. The nearest road is miles away. Gordon has equipped himself with three huge caterpillar-tractor snowmobiles to maintain supplies; on one of these his son is driven every day to school. The boy could take one of Gordon's many horses instead, but with those masses of snow and the humid air blowing in from the Pacific, the snowmobile is probably safer.

I am staying in the house for the time being, but, knowing myself, realise it will be for only a few days. Before this I was in Colorado, where the indefatigable Steve Komito repairs boots for all the mountaineers in the American west in his shop near Denver, and where Michael Covington and his mountain guides take hundreds of people every year to the summits of the Rockies, some by extremely ticklish routes. It has been snowing there a lot, too. When I climbed the East Face of Long's Peak with Michael (a crest more than 4000 metres high), it was more like a winter ascent. And it's partly on account of the snow that I am living now in the millionaire's house . . .

Flashback to Banff: Mountain Holidays, a wilderness outfit run by a couple of Austrians, invite me to go heli-skiing in the Selkirk Mountains. 'That's a rich man's sport,' Evelyn tells me. All the better that it's gratis, then, I think – and we both go. I take a box of slides with me. In case . . .

And so we abandon the hard climbers – all away at the moment, climbing frozen waterfalls – for a life of luxury. (Incidentally, some of those waterfalls are incredible formations – like the Pilsner Pillar, a column of ice some eighty metres high. You can walk right round the bottom of it, a cascade paralysed by frost. It is climbed with the aid of crampons, ice-screws, and most particularly, short axes. You have to stop the minute the weather warms, otherwise the whole flimsy chandelier might suddenly collapse, along with its human pendants.) Another speciality here is skiing on slopes of just a hundred metres high: you have to keep clambering up on skins – very tough and traditional, very Canadian. But, today, Evelyn and I are on easy street. The helicopter, which in the crowded Alps is seen as such a disturbing nuisance, causes little intrusion here in the expanse of the Canadian Rockies. The Bugaboos would hardly be accessible without it, because of the avalanche danger in narrow V-shaped valleys. A splendid, comfortable lodge greets us – you could not call it a mountain hut – ski instructors, a few helicopters, and long, beautiful downhill runs all round us, up to thirty kilometres at our disposal – including the glaciers.

'Try and get in as much downhill as you can manage,' Leo, the stockier of the two Austrians, advises, nodding in my direction. He's going to stay in the lodge. I certainly will! I'll keep it up until my knees turn to jelly.

Which they did.

Seven thousand downhill metres in a single day! I had no idea where I was at the end of it, and that's the truth. You can put that down completely to the helicopter. No sooner are you at the bottom of the hill than it whisks you off somewhere else, up among the peaks – and you peer around you, trying to make out where you have just been. But already, you cannot work it out. The helicopter sets you down again, its powerful rotorblades churning the air. People rush out, ducking low into the snow – despite the need for speed, no one wants to lose his head! Then, off you go again, down a different run, behind an ace instructor, over pristine snow where no one has been for weeks – because the area is so massive. You can enjoy powder snow or firn, and have it to yourself all day! A skier's paradise! No wonder it is not cheap . . . a day here would even then cost you 200 dollars. But there is no shortage of takers. They come from all over America: some are certainly mountaineers, others could be honeymooners – I try to sneak a good look at my fellows during the short breaks, but there's so little time. Over there, another helicopter touches down on a peak. And it's downhill again, down, down! Bend your knees . . . There's snowdust in the air, flashes of crystals. Don't lose sight of the others, most of them racing like champions! Bend those knees! Peter Habeler was rude about my style when I took the guides' course – 'archaic', he called it – but at least it keeps me on my feet. Watch those knees! . . . And we're down. Another trice, we're up again! And once more it's: Remember to bend those knees! and, Keep your head low, watch out for the rotorblades – you don't want it sliced off! How many times have I heard that today? Always somebody says it. A grey-haired man from Nevada whispers it to a pretty young thing next to me in the snow. She is Janice, he Gordon – a nice couple. Then there are the honeymooners: a helicopter ride is scarcely long enough for a kiss . . . but there are plenty of them! Evelyn is streaming down the hill like a goddess – no wonder, with that long Canadian winter!

My knees increasingly feel the strain. That's no wonder either. Perhaps I should have listened to Peter and changed my style? I can't seem to make it work today. Back in the helicopter again; it roars, and up we go. The honeymooner is kissing her millionaire; she beams with joy, no doubt, congratulating herself on her fortune. My God, I suddenly think, that is just what I need. A millionaire. But how to catch one? Then I have an idea (America prompts good ideas): remembering how *The Eiger Sanction* has been enjoying such success in all the cinemas, I think: I know! I'll give a free lecture at the lodge tonight on the Eiger North Wall! I've got some of the slides in my box, and my other pictures can just set them in context. Only today, I won't play it modestly: I'll be a real hero! Superman on the Eiger!   So, I give my lecture that evening, in a style I would never dare at home, and hardly have I finished when the gentleman with the distinguished greying hair sidles over. He comes from Nevada, he says, near Reno: where there are no mountaineers, but it would be extraordinarily interesting if I could give a lecture there. (My heart leapfrogs for joy.) And, why not at Lake Tahoe as well? I am aware that this is the area where the big ski centres are, as well as all the casinos . . . I ask him about the gambling casinos – he doesn't sound too happy that I brought them up – yes, there are plenty, but I am not to worry that it might affect the attendance: he will personally guarantee a respectable minimum fee! He eyes me expectantly, and after a short deliberation, I accept his offer.

Aha! – I think to myself – here's my millionaire! Now, *I* have one.

It's something to sing about – not a woman's prerogative! And the mind dreams up untold possibilities: pretty soon it is raining dollars! From now on, the only way is up: America will lie at your feet! But gold does not rub off easily, it says in the old proverb, and you need more than luck and good connections to become a millionaire. You must practically be born to it, for it means hard, very hard work, and always being on your guard. You have to sacrifice a lot. That I don't find so appealing.

So my golden Icarus-dreams are doomed from the start. And besides, it would be too boring in the long run. Really, it is more interesting to dip into all manner of lives around the world, making your own at the same time. But you are allowed to dream: my new friend Gordon could not know what raptures of imagination his timid request unleashed in me – I took care not to let it show (I didn't want that to lower the price!). Later on, I manage to arrange an evening in the American Midwest, 1500 kilometres from Banff, and I seem on an inexorable rise: it's Hollywood, Los Angeles next stop. (And speaking of Los Angeles, the Titian-haired club chairman has already enrolled me as a member of the Vagmarken, the Milestones.)

Will I have to act as my own agent when I get there? I wonder with a sigh. Maybe, I am not born to be a millionaire. Steffi, the Vagmarken redhead, has fabulous hair that reaches to her knees, full and thick – a striking chairman she makes. What a club! A long way from the *Alpenverein*!

'It's a long way from LA to Denver . . .' John Denver sings on the radio, homesick for Colorado . . . indeed it is – about 1600 kilometres. He is singing of Aspen, of the forests of the Rockies, of the waterfalls and the white bark of the aspens.

Sixteen hundred kilometres, then, the other way round, from Denver to LA. Perhaps I should visit my club?

Meanwhile I am staying at Gordon's, in Nevada, with him and his family. They are very friendly and kind, and hardly ever talk business or money. All that seems to belong to some former life of Gordon's. We speak of the universe, and on clear nights observe sparkling clusters of stars and spiral nebulae above the Sierra Nevada. Thousands of wonders up in the sky and thousands of questions to ask. What about black holes? Will a new universe develop after this one has gone?

We are sitting in Gordon's observatory, looking up at stars which perhaps do not exist any more; we are surrounded by pricks of light, each one standing for another time, depending on whether they are near or far in the cosmos. We are posing unanswerable questions in a web of light-years, worlds apart. I want to say that in the end, here at Gordon's place, my dream of a new career appears futile – so insignificant in view of the fact that is constantly borne home to me: the sheer fortuitousness of being alive!

After all the different kinds of skiing I encountered in the last weeks – with sealskins, cross-country, with helicopters – here I become acquainted with a new one: Gordon loads the whole family into one of the big snowmobiles and rattles up to the top of his mountain. There is a fine vista over the undulating crests of the Sierra, down to the deep blue surface of Lake Tahoe, that marvellous stretch of water in the mountains, its far bank in California. There are only young trees in the landscape; Gordon explains that the forests all vanished down the pit shafts during the gold and silver rushes. He points eastwards to the brown hilly country of the Nevada Desert.

Some days later I go into the desert with a new friend, a college lecturer. Near Virginia City, a ghost town, we discover an old gallery, bearing the nameplate HOWARD HUGHES. We can't resist it and drag ourselves along on our hands and knees into the bowels of the earth. Three hours go by before we blink back into the daylight again, covered in dust from head to toe, and not a single crumb of silver or gold the better off. Still, a nugget as big as a man's fist was found by a daytripper last week in a nearby shaft.

In the meantime, the leaves of my calendar are falling as the day of my lecture approaches! At Reno and Lake Tahoe, my *Summits and Secrets* is up in coloured lights. Many people must see it as they hustle to the casinos below, but of course the throbbing illuminations for The Golden Nugget and other such attractions also exert their pull on the passers-by. I am anxious to see what the outcome will be. The great day comes. In the red plush seats – fifty people only. Nearly a black hole. The Golden Nugget has won. Gordon sighs, and says that it is a hard lecture to start with in this part of the country, compared to the Eiger thriller, but I should not abandon hope. Nor should he, I tell him, we can try it again some other time. And he nods sympathetically.

Then, he hands over my agreed minimum fee.

A few days later we are passing the packed gambling halls of Lake Tahoe, just before my lecture; regiments of slot-machines rattle and jingle and occasionally spit out money with a great fanfare, but most of the time swallow it up relatively soundlessly . . . We are prepared for the worst . . . it turns out to be a very pleasant, if intimate evening. Gordon and I exchange smiles. 'Not to worry,' he says calmly. All the same, I don't think we'll be taking it to Vegas.

Milestones in California

'Hi Kurt, can you hear me? How are you?' On the phone is the chairman with the red and wondrous hair. 'We'll be delighted to see you in Los Angeles again,' she tells me. 'Listen, we'll pick you up in Jack's plane at noon, at the Carson City Airfield. Be there!' I am overwhelmed, overjoyed that my suggestion to return to Los Angeles has been taken up, even if there is to be no lecture. Who cares about that! This is almost too much to take in straight away: only in this Land of Opportunity could anyone say they would pick you up by plane! It's a distance of – I don't know – it must be at least 1000 kilometres, yet to them, it seems, no more than we might say at home, 'Wait on the corner, I'll grab a taxi and be right there.' My heart leaps sky-high. The chairman of the Vagmarkens, those oh-so-sympathetic Milestones, is still giving me details about where we are to meet. In the background I can make out a deeper voice, her husband, sending me greetings. It is the voice of a big man, gruff, bear-like. I sigh. Nothing is perfect!

I bid farewell to my millionaire, to Janice and the children. It was so nice staying with them. An hour and a half later and this Austrian mountain-adventurer stands expectantly on Carson City airstrip in the Nevada Desert, heart thumping, hopes high, a rucksack full of slides, and head craned back, scouring the skies for his 'lift'. It comes! Twin-engined, with twin tail booms, an odd-looking craft, one engine in front and the other behind the passenger's cockpit – a Cessna Skymaster, Steffi had said. It loses height, touches down and taxis to a standstill. The Milestones tumble out – a representative selection at least, nothing in the least 'stony' about any of them, or at all angular. Besides Steffi-the-Red, there is brunette Donna and blonde Renata. The pilot, Jack, clambers down, too, tall, smiling, waving cheerily. It is his plane. I could not wish anyone a warmer welcome. The Milestones hug me, relieve me of my backpack and usher me aboard.

Yippee! California, here I come!

The blue surface of Lake Tahoe disappears behind us, as ever more grandiose mountains march past. Looming ahead, the Sierra Nevada! Valleys filled with forest, mountain wilderness, the dark eyes of little lakes – then a magnificently incised valley – Yosemite! That fantastic dreamland of granite, beloved of climbers . . .

As an extra treat, Jack flies us in close to the Nose of El Capitan, we skim over Half Dome's bald pate, see a gigantic cascade pouring in to the 1000-metre-deep valley. And then? (Even today, a flush of vertigo washes over me as I remember that ride, such electrifying havoc was played with the senses.) Jack whisks us the full length of the Sierra Nevada, swooping over towers and minarets, soaring around a Californian 'Matterhorn', showing us proud Mount Whitney, one of the four-thousanders and the highest summit of the United States outside Alaska.

Those mountains of Sierra Nevada are so beautiful. Now, that – I think to myself – is somewhere I could live! At the time I had no inkling that for the next few years California would turn out to be my second home, almost indeed a second life, quite separate from the one on the other side of the Atlantic. How often are you reborn, once you have come into the world?

A dismal valley, with only meagre splashes of green, passes below the wings as we head east from the mountains. Steffi explains that Owen's Valley was a verdant paradise until the people there began selling water to Los Angeles. The thirsty megalopolis, pushing out its boundaries and growing thirstier all the time, has so lowered the water table that today almost nothing remains of its once-green splendour. Owen's Valley. Lawsuits rumble on, and you can still see pieces of waterpipe, blown up by demonstrators. Soon we will be landing on the outskirts of Los Angeles.

'Seven million people!' Donna says. She is small, dark-haired and with an Italian air about her. 'That's more, isn't it, than all the inhabitants in Austria?' chips in Renata, in German. She is a new American. It is certainly difficult to grasp how vast Los Angeles is, for you never see all of it, on account of its size, and there are very few skyscrapers. They emerge, two or three stumps here and there, from an immense field of lower houses. The buildings are light, simple and uncomplicated, the majority single-storey or at most one other floor. That is enough with the earthquake danger. The San Andreas Fault runs to the north of the city, that great dislocation in the earth's crust between San Francisco and Los Angeles, rendering the whole area seismically unstable.

We have landed. In one of the many districts of this urban sprawl. My companions deliver me to the home of my philatelist friend, Gordon, a retired postmaster. It is thanks to my long correspondence with him that I met up with the Vagmarken. (I do not collect stamps myself.) So, now I know two Gordons here: a millionaire and a former postal official – how different life can be! The night grows cold, as it does in the desert, but there's nothing to be seen of the desert here. Yet the Mojave begins just outside Los Angeles.

Gordon's wife Norma, a friendly motherly woman, has put an electric blanket on the bed for me. I snuggle under it, switch it to the top setting, and dream of Madam President.

Fifty-six steps around a general

Ever since I was in California, all other generals in the world have lost something of their stature, no matter what decorations on their chest or how many stars on their epaulettes. There, it took fifty-six steps to walk around a general, touching him all the time. Nowhere else will you find a brass hat to match that! General Sherman in the Sequoia National Park.

*

It was the middle of the night when we arrived at the big trees. Steffi had this idea that nobody could comprehend just how big they were merely by looking at them. It was something much better achieved by touch, by walking round them in the dark.

A strange idea, maybe, but that is Steffi: she is herself a natural wonder . . .

How she managed to get away, I'll never know . . . from all those down parkas she has to sew – and from her husband (whose giant presence kept intruding in my mind). Bud, his name is. He reminded me of the calm and well-weathered hero in those romantic old Westerns with bodies all over the place, the tough guy who never loses his cool, and still manages, in a matter of a moment, to fell three men with a single move of his hand. His grey eyes, set between impressive side-whiskers, looked friendly enough, rather thoughtful if anything, but it would clearly be no joke to have him mad at you. Steffi always treated him with the greatest respect, I had noticed that. John Wayne or not, those dominating whiskers commanded deference!

I wonder why natural wonders have been distributed so unevenly?

Natural wonders: vast tracts of country can boast nothing of consequence – just fields, fields and more fields . . . Of course I know it is possible to see something in every blade of grass . . . but, well, in the long run . . . it is a pity, I think, that the real phenomena are sometimes so close together. This was to give me a bit of a headache later on. But that is still in the future, and another story.

So, it is night and Steffi has suddenly stopped the car on the winding uphill road. 'Out you get,' she says. 'See if you can find the big tree. Then, walk round it. And touch it – don't forget to touch it!' She sends me off with a sweet smile. That's how I come to be going round in circles in the dark, all round an invisible monarch.

Steffi is full of ideas.

Though I can hardly see a thing, I succeed in finding the tree, and set off walking. Round and round, careful to maintain contact with the rough, fibrous bark. It feels like fur, or the hide of a horse – and more like being beside an animal than a tree, a calm, docile animal that lets you stroke it. Something huge, a dinosaur, almost – no, bigger even than that! Fourteen steps bring me back to where I can see the rearlights of the car once more. Steffi has left them on to give me one point of constancy in this pitch blackness. Fourteen steps around a tree! 'Why, that's only a baby!' she sings, and I hear her laughing.

A baby, eh? So how big is this General Sherman? After that night I knew it: fifty-six steps it took, my hand on the general, till I was back where I started. This time there were no backlights to guide me, but Steffi waiting in the darkness. We called them the friendly giants, these trees. Each one was an individual. You could imagine them talking to each other at night – and even to crazy visitors like us.

*

Monorock. A spire of granite. A giant figure with a weathered face. (No whiskers, though!) We parked the car close by, just as dawn came up, reclined the seats and fell asleep. Next thing I knew, the sun was high . . . Steffi slumbered on beside me. I looked at her . . . soft and warm in her wonderful down parka . . . and so close. I had sunk into those downy billows when I fell asleep, and even now remained comfortably afloat, supremely content with America (as you can imagine) – oblivious, then, of its darker sides. Steffi stirred lightly. 'Whaaat's the time?' she blinked, still heavy with sleep.

'Nine o'clock,' I lied, and she whispered, 'That's all right, then. We can sleep a bit longer,' and, with that, my down-swaddled wonder snuggled against me once more, devastating me with her soft eiderdown warmth, and those long, straight, beautiful red tresses, winding and smooth. Ah, Steffi! And I sank again into the blissful softness, wishing that every time I wrapped myself in eiderdown concoctions on the high summits in future, it could be like this. Some while later I sensed somebody peering in the car window at us, some visitor to the National Park, no doubt, but I kept my eyes tight-closed.

It was around noon when we woke properly. Steffi flung the door open with fierce energy. 'Dammit! How could we sleep that long?' She commanded respect, too, did Steffi . . . definitely a no-nonsense gal. When you are married to John Wayne, that's how you have to be. Even her strength was impressive. And she had that swing of the hips, which in Italy we call *la mossa*, a scintillating move of southern women, which switches the heart of the dark cavalier to high frequency . . . she not only knew how to achieve this swing, but to such effect that it could be dangerous to be standing next to her at the time – *la mossa* could toss you against the nearest wall! I dare say John Wayne, that rock of a man, never found himself hurled to the wall, but with lesser guys Steffi is not so pernickety. No wonder they made her chairman. But the last thing I want to do is convey the impression that she lacks charm. She is very feminine and graceful.

In these American forests, which to a newcomer from Europe seem to burst with wildlife, I never felt anything but safe in Steffi's company. It was as if all the animals respected her. Even bears? Well, if there were bears in Sequoia National Park, I am sure even they would have been teddies that day. In her home Steffi has a great raven flying about the place: he bit me on the finger at first sight, but with Steffi he is as gentle as a canary.

We came to a grove of sequoias some way from the others, five or six giants towering above the universal conifer canopy – which here seemed mere brushwood by comparison – and we sat down among them, cradled in their friendly atmosphere. Their rusty bark, I noticed, exactly matched the colour of Steffi's hair . . . I risked a sideways glance, then ran my hand over those marvellous locks, which here, among the giants, were so completely part of nature. Slowly, the big trees moved their massive arms . . .

One of them triggered something in my mind. Dark beards of moss trailed from its branches, grey, intermingling fronds . . . looming over me, like side-whiskers . . .

'Watch out!' Steffi warned me at that moment. 'If one of those sequoia cones clocks you after falling sixty metres, you'll think you've been shot by John Wayne!' She said it in a low voice, gentle as the breeze stirring the branches over our heads. But there he was – John Wayne again! What prompted her to bring him into it?

'I think we had better go,' I said. 'This particular monster is not as friendly as the others.'

In the years that followed we returned several times to our friends in the grove, the friendly giants. We spoke to, or listened to them. But that first time – perhaps because I had never before made the acquaintance of such beings – I was a bit nervous. A crackling in the undergrowth made me jump out of my skin! A bear? No, a bulky figure in a brown uniform: a warden. 'They patrol the National Park,' Steffi explained, 'to see nothing happens that shouldn't.' I took a deep breath. The man passed by, smiling and waving in sociable fashion. He had a weather-beaten face and side-whiskers. And he moved with a slow rolling gait. Like John Wayne.

Later on, in California, I wasn't so twitchy.

Grand Canyon – a sunken world

A dense grey fog hangs over 'the Valley' (as the inhabitants of Los Angeles like to call their home territory). It is not always obvious to the seven million people who live under this noxious canopy, because of the sheer extent of the city, but you get a better idea from the air, from where it appears as a brownish, barely transparent stain, enshrouding the whole town. In the distance, mountains and knolls rise from it, like a coastline. Sometimes the smog covers them, too. To be sure, there will be rare days when you are able to see the impressive ocean of houses, Los Angeles clear and distinct, like an interminable field. Then you are treated to the best view as the jet makes a wide loop over the Pacific before descending into Santa Monica. The majority of the time, though, only the roofs of enormous industrial complexes, aeroplane factories and other bright reflective structures glint up through this cover of haze. Most people here have never seen the Grand Canyon, only 400 kilometres away as the crow flies.

*

We are sitting in Jack's Skymaster, passing over the barren brown landscape of the Mojave Desert. A short while earlier Jack dived towards a green oasis in the midst of this pale sandy expanse and landed on a small, clean concrete strip to refuel. Around us are brown hills and black mountain ranges – probably solidified lava. We still have a long way to go: to fly the full length of the canyon means another 300 kilometres each way. So we crowd back into the plane, where I am sitting next to Chuck, a young Vagmarken climber, who is supporting his hand rather awkwardly. It was put in plaster last weekend after he attempted something ambitious at the local outcrop. The pilot, Jack, sits diagonally in front of me, a man coming up for forty now, I guess. His sharp aquiline nose has the effect of accentuating all the checking glances he casts out of the window, between giving his eighteen-year-old daughter some advice about flying. She already holds a licence, but her father thinks there remains room for improvement. At the moment, one of his three planes languishes, wingless, in the cellar of his house – but that is not something daughter Beverley likes to be reminded about.

Word has it that she was doing fine until a friend kept her waiting at an aerial rendezvous. When, suddenly, she realised her fuel was running low, there was barely time to put down in a cornfield, which is where her troubles started. The corn was unusually tall, much taller, it seems in this field than in any of the others, and when the plane came to a standstill . . . Whoops! No wings! Completely sheared off by the cornstalks! She must have been coming in at one hell of a lick!

'It's no problem,' Jack had said when I coaxed the story out of a reluctant Beverley recently, 'I can fix it.' He is an aeronautical engineer – or, more properly, was: now he produces sporting goods, designing new models with a refinement that only an aircraft engineer can give. He makes streamlined tents, all gleaming and metallic, which in their styling and fabric look like futuristic flying machines. And sophisticated sleeping-bags, with built-in mattresses, yet still ultra-light. Multi-layered clothing systems to meet almost any requirement, the ingenuity of which only Jack can explain. You think, surely there has to be some button that serves no practical purpose, but no! Every feature is vital and performs a variety of functions. Jack, in short, is an inspired inventor. Though he does not consider himself well-off – three planes notwithstanding – that doesn't bother him. He is one of life's realists. I sincerely believe that anyone who feels at all depressed or mixed up would only need to meet him for things to resolve themselves immediately. He radiates convincing optimism, and however much we Europeans may scoff at what we see as the American laid back attitude, Jack, inventor and philosopher, could prove in a few words (or a lot, maybe, if that's what the occasion demanded) that everything would come right in the end. You will get through, if you want to, if you are prepared to rationalise your way out. Jack laughs a lot; you rarely see him without a smile on his face – as if this in itself were part of his philosophy – unless he is lost in thought.

Now, as Jack talks to his daughter and Chuck dozes, it is my turn to be buried in my own thoughts. A perfectly straight line runs below us across the desert, like a double black thread – we have been following it for most of the flight so far: it is the highway from Los Angeles to Las Vegas. Microscopic cars move along it. Occasionally, you see houses by the wayside, or a square or circular green patch, and for the rest, just pale, desolate sandy plains, shimmering in the heat, with mountains of shattered rock like ruins in an endless brown sea. The great spaces of North America with their diversity of scenery, like their people, are difficult to describe in just a few pages. A single visit gives only a small idea, but it does show what a cramped world we inhabit in Europe, where so much has become impossible. Gazing out into these endless spaces, you feel you have stepped from what was your life into another, wider one. Even as a visitor, here only for a short time before returning home, the door never closes. The fascination which this continent exerts – despite the darker aspects of the American way of life – few European can deny who have been there.

The plane is shaken by some hefty turbulence. Father and daughter – both of them? – busy themselves at the controls, minimising its influence. 'The desert!' Jack laughs shortly, casting a glance back at me. I nod back. Yes, the desert! Hot air currents rise from every mountain ridge – here comes another to rattle the plane, and another. It must be an oven down there. I cannot help remembering how yesterday we were sitting in Jack's Jacuzzi, the whole family: Jack's wife Joan, with her long sleek hair, and several young men – not all at once, of course: the family is very big. This circular hot tub, about three metres across, is set into the floor of the living room at just the right depth for you to be able, sitting in hot water up to your chest, to reach over your shoulder and pick up a drink. If you wanted to eat a meal in it, the water would have to be lowered slightly but, basically, anything is possible, says Jack. You could even wear a swimsuit, if you had a mind to, but that seems a rarity in this house. When I walked in with Jack the first time, I was taken aback at being introduced to an Austrian pilot and his fiancée soaking in the pool. 'Servus!' I stuttered, bowing to the naked nymph. But a few more minutes saw us exchanging all the Austrian gossip, as if we were in a Viennese café.

Jack's latest invention is another pleasure pool, which he has constructed from an old boat. This small craft penetrates the outer wall of the third floor of the wooden five-storeyed house which he and his family have been sawing and hammering away at for two years now. The stern projects into the open air, while the bulk of the boat resides in the living room. Every evening, this cheerful family and their guests relax in the airy and unusual construction. 'Well, I couldn't fit the whole boat in the room,' Jack explained to me. What would our building regulations make of that? I wondered. But the house that Jack builds stands in the beautiful maple woods of New England on the East Coast. (Yes, like so many Americans, Jack has moved home once more!)

Las Vegas has come into view! By the bright light of day, the sparkling gambling town with its famous shows looks disappointing. Small pale squares in the brown of the desert – nothing more. But a short while later we see a stretch of the most heavenly deep blue: a lake pushing its many fingers into the desert valleys, like a skeleton-leaf of blue water. 'Lake Mead,' Jack tells me. Small boats are buzzing about on its surface. How big, how branched this lake is – incredible! The course of the old river and its tributaries have been flooded by the waters of the Colorado behind the colossal Hoover Dam. The main valley has long since vanished under the immense reservoir – so many indignities this Colorado must suffer on the long journey from its source in the Rocky Mountains to the Gulf of California, 2000 kilometres away in Mexico. From the reservoirs, water is drawn off for irrigation; the biggest vegetable-garden in the world, the Imperial Valley in California, is exclusively nourished by Colorado water. Only a fraction of the river, a pathetic remnant, reaches the Gulf of California not least because of the enormous evaporation during its long passage through the deserts.

The famous Grand Canyon of the Rio Colorado would not exist today, would probably have been filled with water like Lake Mead, had it not been protected from economic exploitation in the past by being granted national monument status. Most people are unaware that Lake Mead is a drowned canyon of the Colorado.

The Grand Canyon . . . 'We'll be there in a moment!' Jack sings out and starts nosing down. We are gliding over a bay, an arm of the lake, towards the entrance to a gigantic chasm.

I am staggered! Overwhelmed is no word for it! And anyway, there's no time to be overwhelmed when new sensations are continually bombarding you, shaking you, grabbing your attention, whetting your appetite for even more unexpected thrills. You are looking ahead, back, down, as gigantic buttresses sweep past, pillars and palaces of red rock, side valleys opening and closing, the terrific gorge agape below you . . . You are flying through the biggest trough on earth. All the pictures I have ever seen of the Grand Canyon are forgotten. They are tiny facets, mosaic pieces, nothing more – I see that now. No human brain can comprehend this intricate labyrinth which is the Grand Canyon. It is a world.

'A sunken mountain range . . . a submerged land', is how Indian tribes in ancient times are said to have described the colossal chasm. We are flying now at low altitude over an immense, wide valley, bordered to left and right by relatively small walls . . . flying like a midge over a blanket.

The bluffs on either side sometimes draw more closely together, then pull apart, periodically yielding to tributary valleys – in places there may be fifteen or twenty kilometres between the two sides of the canyon . . .

'The outer rim,' I hear Jack say, indicating the upper edge of the canyon, to our left and right, just a little higher than we are flying. Then he points obliquely downwards, where a deeply incised chasm running more or less in the direction we are following, creates a jagged edge in the wide red bedrock below, 'And that is the inner rim.' He pulls the aircraft closer to this incision, so that the view into its depths really opens up. You could imagine an angry giant having slashed the ground with an axe, in a frenzied, zigzagging fashion. Steep vertical walls drop away to bottomless depths: it is a terrible abyss, at least 1000 metres down to the Colorado River, which appears now, far far below, as a small greenish ribbon, filling the narrow base of the cleft. Jack banks steeply into the chasm and we follow its direction as best we can. This inner gorge of the river has many twists and side valleys, cutting the rocky surface of the Esplanade, as the wide course between the outer rims is known. Table-like mesas, which occur in many places as a result of the erosive action of the side canyons into the Esplanade, are sometimes several kilometres across, so that our little plane, in its low-level flight, one minute skims the surface with its rare green bushes, and the next leaps the open air above a deep and narrow cleft, or niche, or amphitheatre, as it approaches another near-brush with the following red mesa. Jack (understandably in the circumstances) is now in sole control of the aeroplane; his daughter is glued to the window, just like Chuck and me. We take some pictures, naturally, but above all we are looking, looking, looking . . .

For 300 kilometres we fly through the Grand Canyon – and then back again, higher up, to give a totally different perspective. How can that be expressed? Words? Music? A painting perhaps?

I met people who were utterly under the spell of the canyon, like

John, an old ranger in the Thuweep valley, whom I have now visited
so often. The last time I saw him he winked at me and said, 'He got
you too, the canyon!' Since then I have climbed down to the bottom
and to little-known places which Steffi told me were 'summits' of the
sunken mountain range, and later shared the adventure again with
Chuck and my blonde daughter Karen. I have listened to the frogs
in the crevices of the Esplanade, and more than once frozen with
sudden shock at the sound of a rattlesnake. I remember the night
when a strange supple animal came several times to our camp – a soft
ringtail-cat. He was after the foodbag, which of course I did not deny
to such a rare visitor. And one day, with the help of Tom and Bonnie,
I hope to succeed at last in performing a full 'Eskimo Roll' in a kayak
– so far I have only managed to get halfway, leaving me head under
water. It must be a great thing to achieve, and especially because a
great dream of mine is to descend the whole canyon in a kayak.

. . . A volcanic landscape! Black lava flows slide now below the
wings of our plane, flows that issued from conical dark mountains
millions of years ago, and still cleave to the walls of the canyon.
'That's Vulcan's Throne.' Jack points out a perfect cone of grey
and rust colour. Scientists have worked out that this volcano was
last active 1.2 million years ago, when its lava cascaded into the
canyon. Compared to the age of the canyon, which the Colorado
River slowly carved over a period of six million years in the wide
plateau of what is today Arizona, that is only 'yesterday'. The rocks
of the canyon walls, exposed to the light of day by continuous
erosion, contain the whole history of our earth's crust in their
multiple forms and unusual colours. The 'Vishnu-layer' inside
the 'inner granite gorge' of the canyon (about the deepest spot,
almost 2000 metres below the upper rim) is amongst the oldest
rocks known anywhere on the planet – 2000 million years old.
When, 'yesterday', the volcano erupted, no humans saw it. There
were no humans. But what a spectacle it would have been: the
shiny red, glowing lava flow tumbling for more than 1000 metres
to the river, eventually creating a natural dam to stem the flow
of waters, while on the other side the liquid lava ran on a further
fifty kilometres down the dry gorge. How many more stories does
this canyon hold?

. . . Snow! Everything gleams white over there! A whole forest,
extending for miles along the upper rim of the canyon – trees

under snow. We are still in the plane, and seem to have emerged into winter now . . .

Later on, Steffi would explain to me how the climate is so different at different levels in the canyon. There may be burning heat at the bottom, while a cold wind whistles around the upper rim. I discovered woods on the north rim, with deer, fir trees and mountain meadows . . . just like Bavaria, it was, or Austria. But 1000 metres lower we had just hiked and climbed through a desert landscape with metre-high cactuses.

In front of us now, the wide plains of the Painted Desert have appeared, home of the Navajo Indians, the former masters of this land . . . Jack swings the nose of the plane into an upward curve and we start back. Inside my head, as I write, I still see walls and terraces, moving plains, castles and gorges in swift succession. I feel as if I was allowed a glimpse into the inner structure of a gigantic crystalline lattice. One hour later, from high above, I take a last look at the volcanic landscape we passed earlier in the day, unaware that this would one day become my favourite place in the whole canyon. Toroweap.

Hardly anybody knows it. Only John, the ranger, lives there. Occasionally a visitor will come by, having made the bumpy, hundred-kilometre detour up a dirt road. But to arrive at the edge of the canyon makes the long journey worth while. Carefully, on all fours, you approach the edge of the drop. Then you lie there and look down, down and down 1000 metres to the bottom.

Atlanta – the holy city

'And what wonders of nature do you intend photographing this time?'
Teresa asked, her eyes flashing.

'Only a town in America,' I protested wearily. 'Really, just a town with skyscrapers.' For some while now I had been avoiding all talk of natural wonders – ever since the fine morning Teresa found my box of slides of the giant trees in California. To accentuate their unbelievable scale, I had inserted red-haired Steffi between their trunks . . . more than once . . . so much more graphic, I thought, than flat wooden signposts with prosaic explanations. But try explaining the principles of living photography to a judge! Especially a would-be judge from Italy, who happens to be your wife . . .

In any case, the States are a good deal more than just California
. . . more than Los Angeles − 'that town of the angels', as my wife
would insist on calling it, with a certain edge to her voice. Having
the most honest of all intentions (sorry, the most honest intentions of
all), I took a plane to Georgia . . .

Atlanta − the holy city . . .

Odd title, isn't it? Most good Christian people (like this Austrian
Catholic) know that the Holy City can only be Rome. Even so, I have
to say, nowhere have I met so many ardent 'believers' as in Atlanta
− they believe in progress, in religion, are convinced they have
found the positive solution to race problems, and they are sworn to
extraordinarily bold building concepts. If that were not enough, the
United States had Atlanta to thank for a positive-minded President.
For that alone, I feel hesitant in starting this story.

'Bring me back some compelling shots of Atlanta's famous
megastructures when you are next in America,' my publisher had
asked me − referring to the unusual skyscrapers for which the town
is famous, superlatives of modern architecture . . . That explains
why I was there now. With the best intentions of all, and only
two days to go before my return ticket to Europe expired (I had
stayed too long in Colorado and at the Grand Canyon!) Buoyed with
optimism, I stepped on to the Atlanta plane at Kennedy Airport in
bright sunshine . . . Now it was raining, and almost impossible to
see anything. As we touched down, I could only dimly make out the
grass at the edge of the runway.

How are you even going to find the right skyscrapers in this? I
growled to myself as I boarded the bus at the terminal. They all
looked alike. Some sort of concrete Dolomites in horrible weather.
Still, I made a plan: today, explore the situation, tomorrow take the
pictures − if the sun comes out! But would it? The situation was desperate. And equally desperate must have been the forlorn expression
I directed towards a charming young lady, sitting opposite. She was
surrounded by parcels and the only passenger on the bus besides
me. She answered my look with one of compassion. Clearly, she
was possessed of a heart full of understanding for the predicaments
of others . . .

All very innocent. Nothing more . . . I swear by the Saints of
Atlanta − and by Holy Saint Rupert of Salzburg, too − that this is
not going to be a frivolous story, even if it threatens to start out that

way. So, here I was, caught by surprise at such a sympathetic gaze. One is always pleased to be understood.

'Are you from Atlanta?' I asked the friendly being.

'Sure – you here for a vacation?' She beamed at me, an angel under this desolate, shrouded sky. And a native of this town! A sensation of relief ran through me, as if she would be able to blow away these heavyweight clouds in an instant . . . Immediately, the day was less grey. And I lost no time letting her know that I was by no means on holiday, as she supposed, rather . . . (what should I say? Something impressive! A little white lie?) . . . rather on an important assignment for an Austrian university . . . which . . . er, which needed photographic documentation of famous Atlanta! (To tell the truth, my publisher was Italian, and Saint Rupert – well, hopefully he was still back in Salzburg and didn't hear that!) Bemoaning my bad luck with the weather, I told her how lost I felt in this enormous town. That at least was true. With an expert eye, I had assessed the weight of her luggage: it looked as if there was the possibility of lending a hand here – I had been a Boy Scout when young, and none of my Scouting virtues (nor skills) has gone to waste since. Moreover, it was clear to me that, as a local, she could scout out my options and possibilities better than I!

If she had a mind to.

Pearlstrings of lights were strewn through the branches of trees in an avenue between mighty skyscrapers, whose walls reared into the fog above us. Just before they vanished from view, high up, I could make out cross-connections between them, floating tunnels from one building to another. And, on the sidewalk, a multitude of colourful reflections shone from the wet asphalt. A dynamic mosaic, like the ever-renewing patterns of stained glass chips in a shaken kaleidoscope. Such beautiful pictures. Only my 'megas' – the tall ones – eluded me in this weather! 'Tomorrow, perhaps,' comforted Barbara (that was her name). But I no longer needed consoling: I was in high spirits . . . it's always a thrill to drop in somewhere from the sky and continue living as if you had always been there! Whenever it happens, you feel as if the earth is welcoming you . . .

Two hours I have been in Atlanta, and before that knew nothing about the place, never met anyone who lived there – yet here I am, choosing gifts with this blithe spirit for a feast-day that exists for me, too, somewhere else in the world – for Christmas! I carry parcels, advise on whether we should take this or that . . . She smiles, nods. True, I find myself wondering occasionally what I am up to, my bewilderment emerging now and then – but, on the other hand, it is as if I had always been here; that's how it is. I am at home.

Turning a corner, I notice a sign: bright red writing, letters as big as houses, dazzling out of the murk: COCA-COLA! Mega-Cola. It's no surprise to find it dominating everything, here: Atlanta is the headquarters of the multinational company. This is where the brown, foaming fluid started its victorious course . . .

Blacks, and more blacks: my companion guide Barbara tells me that about a third of the inhabitants of this town are black; there is even a black mayor. A black couple under a brightly coloured umbrella – presenting a composition of yellow, blue, red and green triangles – flirt happily, leaning on the railing of a bridge as we pass. Black consciousness here appears to me quite different from in New York, freer, more relaxed – am I right? Barbara replies that much is happening here, and the ghettos are disappearing.

So, what about 'Underground Atlanta'? I had already heard about that. Oh, that is just for the tourists, with souvenir shops, cheap entertainment, cafés, bars . . . not worth your while at all to go there! says Barbara, almost primly. Okay, okay, I feel tempted to soothe, but decide to keep quiet. She seems rather high-principled, which is a pity, really. Being so nice, otherwise. Then I think back, to how on the bus she said, 'Of course, you could always come with me. I'll do my Christmas shopping and show you all the important places.' What a lucky strike, I thought – such a delightful lady, and so helpful and understanding right away. Maybe I even radiated triumph – glorying in how easy it was to get by as an Austrian in the States!

While we continue to walk down the street a whirl of ideas spins through my brain: how exciting, to help such a person to do her shopping, how useful that she is willing to show me all the important . . . Ah! but not Underground Atlanta! Alas, she seems really serious about that . . . might one change her mind? Bend it a bit? ('Kurt,' an inner voice warns me, 'you are not in California, here. Behave yourself!') The parcels and string bags begin to weigh heavy: a good deed every day – sure, that's what I am already accomplishing, brave Boy Scout that I am . . . But what about a second one? At this critical moment, with goatee beard and broad-brimmed hat, Baden-Powell floats before me – he raises three fingers, in international salute . . . I take it as a sign: it doesn't have to be just one!

Frowning, the apparition vanishes back into spiritual fog: apparently that wasn't quite what he meant. (I have since found out that B-P's three fingers stand for duty to God, Country and helping one's Fellow Man – or Woman. So I was not totally wrong! But some days are full of misunderstandings . . . which would soon be confirmed.)

My good deed is getting more and more ponderous: now I am carrying five string bags and cardboard boxes. However, I don't blame my good fairy, and think of Baden-Powell. If destiny provides you with a strapping mountaineer from Austria for Christmas . . . She only hangs on to the full black shopping bag she was already carrying on the bus, 'Christmas tree balls – watch out, they're glass!' she explains with a dismissive gesture when I attempt to take it. 'And peaches,' she adds with a sweet smile, 'peaches from Georgia are the best in the United States!' From her clear eyes shines deep conviction. Really, the best? What can be the secret of those convincing peaches from Georgia? But I don't rack my brain over it for long. Atlanta is altogether a convincing town, I think to myself – and cannot foresee that next morning it will appear to me holier than Rome. At present, that is not in question. Barbara speaks of Georgia's peanuts. Their popularity has diminished. For political reasons? Perhaps. Nobody, however, could say that of Coca-Cola; on the contrary . . . Triumphantly red, another giant neon sign glows out between the grey-blue silhouettes of the mega-buildings. Is it the same one I noticed before? I turn around on my heels . . . Could be. I am a bit confused in this glittering, glistening metropolis . . . What if Barbara were to lose her way? No, she would never go astray . . . I feel pretty sure one could never lead her from her strict path.

Coca-Cola. I have personal experience of that. A sort of passion. I was almost addicted to it. But then I kicked the habit. Does that happen to Americans, too? How come today I keep noticing advertisements for it everywhere, to which normally I would not pay any attention? But this is an unusual day anyway. Even the gentle rain tickles pleasantly on the skin. Another laughing Cola poster!

At the same time I notice a vending machine. Barbara has seen it too. We could have a Coke, she suggests. Oh, tempting Atlanta! Why not? And, though I do not really want one, I draw two from the machine. It tickles pleasantly in the throat, and we smile at one another. How could we otherwise, with all that publicity; but is Barbara's smile merely dutiful? Cheers, I say to myself, glancing at my companion: no, it is genuine! Cheers – for this brimming city, Atlanta, bubbling over with surprises . . . Cheers (and I steal another look) for this sweet girl's great Coca Cola town . . . By the way, I could use another one! Am I going to become addicted all over again?

I pull Barbara into a bar – she does not object. Before we enter, I peer up at the sky and think that it still looks like the thumbs down for my photo-mission. Still, is it my fault these damned megastructures are lost in the clouds? In any case, there are some pretty enthralling compositions down at this level, some very shapely images . . . and so close to hand! Sneaking another look at my companion, I feel tempted to say something. We sit down. The waiter arrives and, hissing, a fresh Coca-Cola shoots into the glass – my third today! (I had already been given one by the stewardess, shortly before landing in Atlanta.) I really should stop now, otherwise it all starts again – Barbara is on her second glass. She looks delightful.

What a craving! Can I help it if Coca-Cola makes me high? It is a dangerous drink for me. I have heard it can dissolve one's teeth – a whole set of false teeth – within two weeks, but such stories are of course fairy tales. I, for one, can still boast a wolf's full dental pride as my own! What would my Little Red Riding Hood say to that? Does Barbara know her Brothers Grimm? ('Kurt!' I am warned again. My patron saint, Rupert himself this time? Too late! Under the effects of the brown elixir, my fantasies are working overtime. Everything appears highly positive to me. And Barbara?) She now casts a wide-eyed, almost innocent glance at me, and smiles – encouraging, no, inciting, 'You don't speak much . . .'

True – it is quite a while since I have said a word! Oh, good Little Red Riding Hood. 'Sorry,' I answer pensively, sucking air through my wolf's teeth, 'I am a person who thinks a lot,' and while she nods, admiringly: 'I was still worrying about the megastructures.' She is wearing a claret-coloured dress, flatteringly cut, front and back. All is mega! I become absorbed in the image. 'Really, nature is responsible for the best work,' I add, 'think what an eternal structure the Grand Canyon is!' Her wide, deep eyes, are enlightened, and profound as the skies of Utah.

All of a sudden, a chance movement yanks me abruptly back to Georgia. The black shopping bag tips over. Those peaches! I jump up to help, but am rejected: 'It's all right. Take it easy!' And bending forward, Barbara sets the bag upright again. A short, insignificant gesture, but offering such a delicious and confusing view! Oh, Georgia – the Peach State! She smiles at me as if nothing had happened. And of course, it hadn't. Thoughtfully, I regard the claret-coloured dress. Wine or Coca-Cola? That is now the question.

'By the way, where do we have to go with all these parcels?' I ask quietly. (Oh, good Saint Rupertus, I feel your warning gaze! But am I not allowed to discover Georgia with heart and soul? Please stay in Austria's apple orchards tonight and turn a blind eye to my reconnaissance. Aren't you supposed to be a vegetarian?)

Barbara throws me a long glance, and for an instant seems confused by my question. With full reason: it is already evening. 'Well, actually, yes . . .' she replies, rather shyly, and smiles. 'The best thing will be if we go to my home.'

(Holy Saint Rupert, don't blame me!)

That was my last Coca-Cola today, I tell myself, as we glide through the thousand vibrating, flickering lights of Atlanta. Now for the wine.

(Saint Rupert remained hidden.)

*

We enter the house. Does she live alone? I am apprehensive that our promising acquaintance might be disturbed by outsiders. I remember a similar situation, where there was a wild and jealous dog . . . but that is a different story.

As she opens her apartment door, there is neither a stern-faced, six-foot fiancé, nor a slavering wolfhound – instead, a voice, clear as a little bell, rings out, 'Hello-o-o!' . . . and two friendly blue eyes under neatly coiffured, red-blonde hair scrutinise me frankly.

Barbara introduces me, 'This is an Austrian photographer, Wendy,'
I am treated to a magic smile. Heavens above! Almost too much of
a good thing! Another ethereal being! I feel myself wavering: should
I be happy or sad? On balance, I was sad. What a complicated
situation . . .

Still, I had not the slightest inkling of the series of body blows
which were heading in my direction.

At least I had found a home, I thought, and looking around,
wondered: where will they put me? But that was not important.
Not yet. 'It is wonderful for a stranger to find friends and assistance
when he arrives in a big town for the first time,' I said, and meant
it truly, as I stretched out my legs. They were feeling the strain of
Atlanta's long avenues, and my arms were stiff from the weight of
my pretty companion's parcels. We were sitting in the kitchen.

The answer caught me totally unprepared . . .

'We are a religious household, and one of our aims is always to
help people,' the red-blonde smiled warmly; both of them nodded.
Barbara offered me one of her peaches – all orderly, on a plate.

My face must have spoken volumes, and my spiritual flag dipped
immediately to half mast. What a blow! The pretty young lady,
whom I had accompanied all afternoon, from shop to shop, who
had been so charming and brought me to her house, had not done
so, as I supposed, in reponse to my irresistible appearance, but out
of 'love for one's fellow man' – Christian charity!

I fancied the insipid taste of watered wine on my lips – I needed
a Coca-Cola, urgently. I got it. 'Wine or Coke . . .' I remembered,
upset, and stared at the ceiling. But the bubbling elixir coaxed
me from my sad considerations. Everything could be rationalised:
hadn't I seen far worse matters through? In my mind, in this hour of
disappointment, suddenly appears my father . . . Fathers will always
help their sons. Didn't Father graduate in Theology during the time
he was studying Biology before becoming a high school teacher?
There is a proverb: 'Nothing you learn is ever wasted.' Even if only
your sons apply it.

Barbara unpacked the other mega-peaches from her shopping
bag and put them on the table. I sighed: everything had entered
a different phase, somehow. Yet: hope dies slow. Following the
principle 'Father will sort it out,' I entered the field of Theology
myself, telling them how he was an expert on different religions, had
graduated twice – and how, even with so many flawed interpretations

of the Christian doctrine which exist today, he could still see through them perfectly well.

The girls smile and nod politely – they say, Atlanta too is a religious town. I then start talking about Saint Rupert: I scrape together all my Catholic knowledge, feel like a participant in some religious quiz, who despite diabolic buffets of fate, is finally making headway again, and growing optimistic once more. Even so, by and by I get the feeling that something is wrong. Difficulties of comprehension? The red-blonde girl looks at me with almost a touch of challenge . . . Then she says, still amicably, but somewhat reservedly: 'We are a Baptist community.'

There is a great silence. I gasp for breath, in deep desperation.

'You are an Austrian, therefore Catholic, and it is not your fault,' says my pretty young lady consolingly, Barbara, my Little Red Riding Hood from the bar where the Cola-revelation took place. At this moment, I feel like a scorched and toothless old wolf.

Even so, at the same time, I recognise the clear need to prove myself a valuable member of human society. While I am brooding over how to rebuild my damaged status in this house, a young man – another Baptist – blows through the door and announces that he has been discussing metaphysical questions with his friend upstairs. I grasp the opportunity with both hands and escape to the first floor, to converse with the Baptists. I expect to return in a short while.

In our discussions we even reached an acceptable compromise! Meanwhile, however, down on the floor below, all discussion centred round where the Catholic should sleep. And before I could explain that he was happy with little comfort, they had booked me into a hotel. That's how it goes, if you don't, like a devil, keep your hoof in the door . . . *Himmelkreuzdonnerwetter!* *Himmelkreuzbirnbaum!* *Zum Teufel nochmal!* . . .

*

How did the story go on from this point? As a matter of fact it went surprisingly well (looked at with a cleansed mind). A photographer appeared: Oliver. Not only did he take me to a simple motel, but wanted to accompany me the following day . . . 'to all the important places'.

There was to be a Baptist meeting, too, late in the morning – which I was invited to attend. Barbara and Wendy were working in a hospital, and Oliver had free time only after noon – before that I would scout around on my own.

And my patron saint from Salzburg, who had disappeared so abruptly during my chat with Barbara? I have to confess, I saw him again. The night after, I had a terrible dream: Coca-Cola, Barbara, and Saint Rupertus – it was a nightmare, a revolting mixture, bubbling in my brain! But by and by, things cleared up, purified: the face of the saint rose above the sin. And I called out to him from the depths: 'Saint Rupert! You should have told me right away . . .!'

Then I woke up. I don't know whether saints take malicious pleasure in others' discomfiture. Surely not. But before he disappeared, I swear my Saint Rupert was grinning . . .

*

I rose early, grabbed my cameras – but it was raining. After a while, it stopped, though the sky remained covered with low-moving clouds, damp fog and streaks of mist reaching down . . . Oliver, the photographer, had given me some tips where to go for my 'megas'. For want of time, I turned down a visit to the Cyclorama. This is a circular painting, with a circumference of 122 metres, a height of 15 metres and – wait for it! – weighing 8164 kilos. It is, I confess, the only picture whose weight I know. To be serious, it is one of the three biggest paintings in the world, a breathtaking depiction of the Battle of Atlanta in 1864, during the Civil War, when the town was almost totally destroyed. Rebuilt, Atlanta today is the only real metropolis between Washington and New Orleans, situated at 300 metres above sea level in softly undulating countryside below the southern Appalachians. It is the economic and cultural focus of the American south-east. Practically every big enterprise in this area has its head offices in the town with its near two million inhabitants. A friendly lifestyle, pulsating vigour and futuristic buildings characterise the capital of Georgia.

Besides their architecture, the mega-buildings were interesting to me, above all, for what they offered to the people living inside – and their effects upon them. That is why I was on my way this morning to the Colony Square complex. Oliver had recommended one particular 'monster' of interconnected skyscrapers! I found it contrasted sharply with surrounding low villas, set in gardens, and some old houses tucked in front of it. A friendly man in the porter's lodge of one of the skyscrapers explained the layout to me, by means of a model in the entrance hall: 'Here is our hotel, this is the bank, these two buildings are apartment blocks, this one too – in part, at least – but inside there is also the library, the post office and the hair salon; our swimming pool is right here, ice rink there, and over this side are all the stores: food, clothes, and a drug store . . .' He pointed first to this, then to that building – incredible: nothing, absolutely nothing had been forgotten! I looked at him with wide eyes – then asked, where hereabouts I could find a Coke machine. 'Just back there!' – he gestured.

I fetched a can, and sat down on a bench in front of the post office, in order to reflect upon all I had seen. It was my sixth can this morning – already I was well on my way. I put it down to the multitude of home-made chapatis I have consumed throughout much of my life in the Hindu Kush, the Himalaya, the Karakoram: their effect has been to make my stomach elastic – like that of a boa constrictor – and for days I can stay without food . . . but then I have to eat a lot. It works the other way round, too! And applies to drinking as well. I am familiar with it from other periods in my life when I was into peanuts besides Coca-Cola. It becomes a big effort to stop. The Americans, I notice, drink the brown elixir like their daily water, not needing even to burp. Admirable.

After a visit to the library, a look at a skating class, I take the high-speed elevator to a rooftop restaurant which the porter had recommended. What a hurly-burly! Cooks in high hats, elegantly dressed guests – an exclusive high society meeting? A feast? A marriage? Some binge evidently, judging from the giant cakes! Am I allowed to take pictures? I tell them I am on a commission for (how did it go?) – an Austro-Italian university . . . 'No problem!' A piece of cake and a Coca-Cola – that makes the seventh today. As I go down from the seventeenth floor with the flashing special express lift, I cannot restrain a loud and extended burp when the cabin brakes sharply and comes to a halt at the tenth floor. I am still at it when the door opens – and the gentleman who joins me, apparently calibrated by steady consumption of the local brew, looks in my direction, astonished: 'You come from abroad, don't you?'

Embarrassed, I have to admit that is so, just as the fast lift sets off, squashing my intestines once more, 'I am from A-a-u-u-stria' – and once more I can hardly contain the rising fizz as I aspirate the name of my home country. We are down now, thank God! No more Coke today, I swear an oath. My over-expanded chapati stomach is – after seven cans – obviously at loggerheads with it.

Altogether, though, I am very impressed by this fine complex. What scale! What mind-blowing variety! Here, you really can find everything on one and the same spot.

Back at the porter's lodge, I thank the man for his tips. Suddenly, he says, drily, 'We are going bankrupt.' Bankrupt? Yes, bankrupt, he nods. I cannot help feeling sorry for him.

Forgetting my resolution, I say, 'Let's have a Coca-Cola together?'

'No, I hate it!' He shudders with disgust. I stare at him as if he were the First American in person . . .

What the man in the porter's lodge revealed was – as I found out later – typical of the financial situation of other mega-complexes, too. Is that absurd? How many people want to live in a place where they can find everything, absolutely everything within easy reach of their home? Whether or not the constructions might be true superlatives of mega and modernity. On the flight back to New York, I would read in a newspaper about the economic problems of the megastructures: some were used to no more than 25 per cent of their capacity. That could be a proof of the psychological problems which arise from living in a concrete mega-world.

Almost with a bad conscience, now, I felt thirsty once more for the elixir. I found a machine at the next corner. The last can! Really, the very last today, I told myself.

Kurt, it is raining again! Have you still not come to terms with your Saint?

An hour later I arrive at the Baptist community. A religious ceremony in a small plain church. Many people. A man in the pulpit with a large golden book open in front of him speaks, tells, reads. The building is very simple. I sit down on one of the benches, stay till the end. Oliver, the photographer, is not in here. As the people pour out into the open, one of them asks, 'Are you the Austrian?' Yes, I say. 'Oliver is at the Hyatt Regency. We'll take you over,' and he points to a small group of devout Baptists. That's fine – the famous luxury hotel is one of my objectives anyway.

Suddenly, an elderly Baptist lady asks me: 'Have you already thanked Jesus for this day?'

I catch my breath abruptly. Dear Lady, I am tempted to reply, that's quite something to ask of an Austrian Catholic. But the truth was I hadn't, yet. Instead, waking up to rain this morning, I had already, quite early in the day, combined several Austrian pear trees with the heavens, bringing in crosses and thunderstorms in good measure (our native swearwords are famous for their adaptability!). On the other hand, while I wrangled with the holy weather-maker, Saint Petrus, the farmers of Georgia must have been thanking God for the water on their fields.

There was no need for me to do that. 'I haven't yet found time for it,' I answer the white-haired lady.

Everyone was staring at me now, as the woman said, 'Well, you are a Catholic . . . but we will pray for your soul,' and, turning to the others, in a loud voice enjoined them: 'Let us pray for Kurt!' They began right away, all of them praying for my soul. Such a thing had never happened to me before, neither in Rome nor Salzburg – I was moved to the bottom of my profound Austrian heart. Now they began to sing a psalm, and with all this conviction around me, I timidly wiped away a tear. The sky had cleared a bit, a sun ray beamed . . . in front of my mind's eye my publisher at once appeared! My pictures . . . as fast as possible, get to the Hyatt Regency! Carefully, I plucked at the sleeve of the singing lady: 'Can we go now?' It was not very tactful to disturb her. The sunbeam went out . . .

*

Off to the Hyatt Regency, Kurt! Oliver was there already. Who knows how long he had been waiting but he seemed not to be impatient, merely said; 'Hurry up, we must get to the next intersection! The fog has lifted and we don't know for how long! The Peachtree Plaza is over there. Maybe you will get to see it in its full glory. We can come back to the Hyatt Regency later, and have a look at the inside.' That sounded reasonable, it wasn't quite as high. Off we went, and despite our hurry, I noticed how the reflections of several high buildings were curving in strange distortions in the mirror-walls of others; in the sky above us light and dark grey clouds intermingled.

'Here we are – step over and don't look up till then,' said Oliver, taking my hand; I followed him to a certain spot on the sidewalk. Then I raised my eyes.

A gigantic tube of metallic shimmering glass stood an unbelievable seventy floors high . . .

The Peachtree Plaza Hotel

The Peachtree Plaza Hotel. One of the most impressive buildings I ever saw. An awe-inspiring architectural masterpiece, it is the highest hotel in the world – but even if under today's obsession for records another, higher one were put up somewhere else, such harmony and elegance could hardly be surpassed. I am standing at the base of the metal and glass cylinder, the summit of which is still in the clouds, though faintly visible now and then – and I am awestruck. I tilt back my head, as if standing at the bottom of the Guglia di Brenta, wanting to look to its very top – exactly so! The Guglia, that beautiful column of rock in the Brenta Dolomites, is close to 300 metres high – the Peachtree Plaza is almost the same size . . . perhaps one rope's length less.

Amongst the rock towers on earth it is one of the most outstanding, in every sense of the term, with a shape of magic regularity, a harmony in outline – an elegance that enthrals not only climbers. To my mind, amongst man-made structures, the Peachtree Plaza most closely approaches it. Oliver, standing at my side, explains that there is not much point in reaching the top of the giant cylinder, since we would then simply find ourselves in the grey of fog, in the clouds. The word 'skyscraper' has become very hackneyed nowadays, no longer evoking emotion – but anyone standing with us on the pavement that day below this mega-building, would have seen and felt how, in the true sense of the word, it was truly 'scraping' the sky.

Later, I learned some more interesting details: the dance hall of the hotel can hold 3500 people and there are 1100 rooms! The Hyatt Regency also has 1100 rooms, but is built in a different way; it has a revolving restaurant on top, but its main attraction is its enormous lobby . . . which we entered soon afterwards. Usually, when you go into a hotel, you see a reception lobby of medium height, with more or less furniture, according to the category of establishment – here, however, after I had passed the hall porter, I was rendered breathless. This was a lobby eighteen floors high!

What a welcome – what a 'reception' – I thought. Then, I started counting the floors which surrounded it, like a giant court, but did not come to an end before my attention was drawn to the gigantic, shimmering illumination in the middle of the hall, easily twenty metres high: a column of bundled strip lights, opening out higher up into a sort of circular fan – like the spokes of an inverted, half-open giant umbrella, stuck into a spindle. In between, there was a glimmering, like reflections of water – perhaps a fountain – you could hear its gentle sound coming from somewhere in this big space. In the soft light of this enormous fitting, I discovered a circular café in the background, which was apparently hanging on a rope – but then, while Oliver, a photographer like myself, had gone for a walk in response to my 'I have to stay here for a while', my wandering eyes focused on something else: a dark, multi-angled column protruding from the wall to my right. It was not only its enormous dimensions, but more particularly what was happening on it, that captured my whole attention and made a slight shudder go down my spine . . .

Attached to the column were three elevators, incredibly exposed . . . the whole thing was such a bold structure that it seemed more a device of science-fiction, or belonging to a spaceship of the distant future. Somewhere up around the eighteenth floor of the lobby a lift-cabin, made of glass, and spangled with lights, appeared glued to the dark column. It looked terrifying! Just as I marvelled at the lack of vertigo exhibited by the riders of these cabins, two of the odd, longish shapes began to move like 'glow-woodlice' up the trunk of a big tree (I apologise for the comparison – of course no sort of louse at all is thinkable inside the Hyatt Regency!). One might perhaps call them 'glow-worms', since part of their bodies did indeed emit light, but these strange contraptions, sliding up and down at considerable speed, had nothing romantic about them: I thought them programmed and weird. Gigantic woodworms from another world, ovoid and shining, crawling along the edges of the column, their legs hidden. One of the three shining 'insects' had stopped now at the fourteenth floor, another was just coming down, the third disappeared through a hole in the ceiling . . . to the floors higher up. To regain my equilibrium, I needed a Coca-Cola – but this is one place, strangely, where there was not a can to be had; from the suspended café, I heard the pop of a champagne cork . . .

Throwing a last glance at the glittering spindle with its neon umbrella spokes, I went outside. This time I did not look for the receptionist.

*

The same day, I saw the Omni-Sport Arena, the Atlanta Memorial Arts Center and still more structures that all borrowed from the world of fantasy. I, for one, think that in no other town have architects realised futuristic buildings with such imagination and flair. It needs much conviction to do that. And religion? Perhaps, that too. At any rate a great conviction. To an artist, creation is also his religion.

Oliver got me to the airport early next morning. He and the two girls, Wendy and Barbara, along with the other members of the Baptist community, had been so friendly to this curious being from another part of the world – this Catholic Austrian! To whom, on the other hand, their world appeared strange and full of surprises. Hopefully, my friends will one day come to Salzburg!

What will I show them? Our own megastructures of course: Hohensalzburg, our big castle, then the domed cathedral, followed by the Franciscan Church, and the Church of Saint Peter, then . . . good heavens, I realise now, we have no church for holy Saint Rupert, our patron, whom I have called on so often in this story . . .

But before that, by the way, we will have a feast in Saint Peter's Cellar. With wine from mega-wine-siphons and . . . Peach Melba!

Will I succeed in cracking the secret of the giant peaches of Georgia – next time round?

The lake

'All space is but a nut-shell.' I found that written on a piece of paper in my pocket, thought it sounded like *Hamlet*, though I cannot remember putting it there. I used to do that – on a climb, sometimes, or a walk, even in a bus . . . the ideas were not always legible, not always right, but better than not being captured at all. What you are told by a moment – its truth – can be unique. Later, you may only be able to find a shadow.

*

Star space . . . Milky Ways . . . Oceans . . .

My 'ocean' is to be found in the Bavarian foothills. It is only a little lake. And I do not propose betraying its name.

It changes its face as the year progresses: covered with ice in winter, and in spring by a dusting of pollen from the fir trees. During summer thunderstorms a hundred thousand little spheres of water dance on its surface, and afterwards, the sun lights up its ripples again, or the moon rocks on its swaying surface, or the lake holds a whole skyful of stars.

On certain days in autumn, when the air is so still you think you could touch it, when fresh snow in the mountains lies without melting, and when in the moorlands the sedge and mosses have changed their colour to yellows and russets – then something peculiar happens to the lake: it becomes a flawless mirror, absolutely calm. So immobile is it then, so smooth its surface, that you don't see it any more . . . If you approach gently, planting your steps lightly, so as not to set up a tremble in the swaying bog, then it seems that the trees at the rim grow towards a sky in the depths, and their lowest branches, reaching out towards the invisible water, are granted entry into this magical space which has opened at your feet, reach on down in an endeavour to touch the echoed branches stretching up vainly from below.

As you watch, no longer can you be sure which branches are real; there seems only to be a tree growing into the sky above and below . . . and you must take care not to overbalance into eternity if you lose your footing.

Because on such a day, the whole world is in a nut-shell.

*

What my little lake told me was right, in essence, even if – as I later learned – my Shakespeare 'quote' was flawed*. For a mere in a bog, as well as for the North Sea around the British coast with its thundering white horses . . . words are only the shell around a core of feelings and facts . . . What is inside could well be the same . . . whether it is a simple man who speaks, or a great poet.

In the plane

When I hang in the skies somewhere, travelling from continent to continent, and it is night, I am happy with the beautiful jewels that

---

* 'I have checked your *Hamlet* quotation. It is from Act II, Scene 2, and should read: *O God, I could be bounded in a nutshell and count myself a King of infinite space* . . . So you just turned it around a bit. Just.' (From a Letter written to me by Julie.)

are granted me from the deep. They are like greetings from the earth, after the black of the oceans. And what glittering treasures have been mine, for moments only . . . The juxtaposition of the hundreds of lights in a village, or the many thousands in a town, under the starry vault are never repeated. And as the plane moves onwards, these ever-changing patterns have just enough in common to remind you of earlier delights. And that too makes you happy.

It is like with the crystals of Mont Blanc: since finding my very first as a boy, they all are mine, even though I don't hold them in my hands. I know they are there.

The same with the desert floor at night under the invisible rays of Rick's 'blacklight' – an ultra-violet prospector's lamp which created a dazzling fluorescence from certain minerals: when you walked through the dark, suddenly a feast of 'emeralds' would light up the black night, and enormous 'rubies', and gems with no name . . . You held your breath and plucked beaming stars from the ground.

A fairy tale come true: that was this walk with Rick through the midnight desert. And later, at Klaus's house, we spread the seemingly insignificant collection of stones over the carpet, and with the aid of Rick's magic lantern, transformed ourselves for a few minutes into proprietors of shining treasures, of unimaginable wealth. Klaus himself is an engineer, sober-minded you might think, but no! Otherwise he would not have said: 'There must be poets, too!'

Swathes of light from Los Angeles: down there, too, I am at home, where the desert begins. And I have to go again . . . even if Rick has now stashed his prospector's lamp somewhere in a corner. (Having married Marcia, a real-estate agent, he finally struck a lucky vein.)

I will go back, nevertheless.

Thoughts in an aeroplane, lights in the night, towns – they are no different from the desert floor.

Isis

Mojave Desert. Brown hills, pale silhouettes – still dark; day is only just breaking. Renata and I have driven through the night from Los Angeles. We are bound for Death Valley . . . which is said to be one of the most bewitching places on earth. Only later did I learn the story of its ominous name . . .

It was in the winter of 1849–50, at the time of the Great Trek to the American west, when two families with their ox carts decided to take a short cut across the wilderness of the Great American Desert in order to get to Los Angeles, from where they wanted to head north to the Californian goldfields. As the season was already well advanced, they believed it would be impossible to cross the Sierra Nevada on account of the snow.

The fabulous gold strike of James Marshall at Sutter's Mill on the American River on 24 January 1848 had set in process a mass migration, unique in history. Up to 1849 15,000 people had travelled the Oregon Trail to northern California, and another 4600, mostly Mormons, had arrived in the Salt Lake valley, where they decided to stop and found their new Zion. But in 1849, the first year of the Gold Rush, no fewer than 25,000 overlanders reached California. They came for a variety of reasons: some to find new land to settle, others hoped to get rich quickly and without difficulty, and still others sought adventure and new horizons.

Thus, by the late autumn of that year, a colourful mix of peoples* with more than a hundred ox waggons had started from Hobble Creek, some hundred kilometres south of the Great Salt Lake. They knew almost nothing of the Southern Route (the old Spanish trail to Pueblo de los Angeles) and so its dangers – namely, lack of water and of forage for the draught animals – were of lesser significance when weighed against the notorious blizzards which threatened a late Sierra Nevada crossing.

After a hard month, travelling through Utah, controversy divided the party: a sketch map was produced which promised a much shorter way to the west, whereas another described this area as 'unexplored'. The group separated. Almost all the waggons headed westwards, but upon encountering a bluff, difficult for the oxen to negotiate, seventy-five of them, the majority, returned to the Southern Route. Only four family groups, led by William Lewis Manly, pressed on to reach the Amargosa Desert, to the east of Death Valley. By this time they had very little food left and, between finding one spring and the next, were almost dying of thirst. Wearily, they entered the immense and nameless valley only to find a high mountain ridge blocked all

---

* 'A truly American composite,' Leroy Johnson told me when I joined him during his search for the historical escape route of the people stranded in Death Valley. For his book on this story see the Bibliography.

forward progress. While Manly and his friend Rogers set off on foot in search of a way over the mountains, hoping to be able to return with food and horses for their women and children imprisoned in the desert, those left behind were obliged to slaughter their scrawny cattle to stay alive.

When the two men finally returned, having covered more than 700 kilometres – with a single mule and the knowledge of a way out – it must have seemed a miracle to their waiting families.

From a point which today is still called 'Manly Lookout', and which Manly and Rogers reached with one of the survivors three days after they began their escape, they saw the snow-covered peaks of the Sierra Nevada ahead of them, and the deep valley and desert behind, which they had just crossed. The three men took off their hats.

'Goodbye, Death Valley,' one of them said.

Since then, the valley has borne this name.

Less than a century and a half has passed since then . . . and almost everything has changed. The Indians, who tried with their bows and arrows to kill some of the oxen of the stranded trekkers, have long disappeared. An asphalt road now leads down and across the desert. Nobody today can imagine the indescribable fatigue and desperation of the involuntary discoverers of Death Valley – unless he, too, has left the road, lost all sense of direction and finished his water.

Because of its natural beauty, the valley was declared a national monument. For some visitors it is one of the most beautiful places on earth.

*

We have been driving for many hours now, through the night. I peer out ahead, at the pale sky in the east. Faint, glimmering desert shapes pass by outside. Renata sits beside me, her white-blonde hair glimmering too in this dawn light, long, smooth strands hanging beyond her shoulders. I can hardly make out her blue-green eyes with their dreamy expression, which can give way so suddenly to determination. She is special and contradictory. Her ancestors came from Russia . . . but not only from there. In some way, it seems to me, her personality embodies all the contrasts of the world. Yet she can be so clear and straightforward.

We two want to get to know this strange place we have only

heard about, Death Valley. Renata, like most people who live in Los Angeles, has never been there. 'You won't find it dead at all, this valley. It's alive,' insisted our friend, good old Campy, a real desert fox, one of the Vagmarken. 'If you go there in springtime,' he said, 'you'll see flowers sprouting everywhere from the sand, splendid flowering cactuses, a real place of wonder . . .' and he smiled all over his leathery, sun-tanned face, adding with a warning twinkle, 'You may even fall under its spell.' And he gave us a long look.

Well, then, this is spring! A time for snap decisions and doing things straightforwardly. Like visiting Disneyland (the Los Angeles Kindergarten, as I so disrespectfully called it). We did that yesterday, on a whim of Renata's, and I must confess we were like children at a fair. All at once I realised the enormous art that had gone into the intricate working models, and the so-skilfully produced puppets – three times we went underground on the Caribbean pirate ship. I would never have expected it of myself! Now we are on our way to discover another place.

The desert shapes pass, pale as the ash-blonde strands-of my companion's hair. She is serious now, contrary Renata, yet I remember how she can be playful as a child. Her presence envelops me, even in silence, and I do not know how I could ever escape her strange wiles.

The road leads us directly towards the long ranges which hide Death Valley. Behind their black silhouettes the whole sky starts to burn with orange flames. Everything shines, glowing around us. Any minute now the sun must come up. We brake the car, drive into a clump of Cat's-claw bushes dotted with yellow blossoms. Quick! Quick! We throw the doors open, jump out.

There it is! The sun! Sliding above the mountain rim, flaming, flaring, with cosmic might! We are mesmerised, transformed by the trembling, incandescent sphere floating above the desert . . . a force to ensnare the soul . . . and, suddenly, something is born from this power that touches the core, that creates dreams and reality.

Isis.

A goddess of nature.

Since that day, that is the name I have given my companion. Something, somehow, had changed. It lasted for a long time. We carried the sun inside ourselves.

And I returned there time and again.

*

A soft haze over the salt flats. A strange, mellow, intangible spell emanates from the landscape of death. Almost hypnotic . . . We are on the mountain ridge about 2000 metres above the valley floor, looking down, and it is as if something is reaching up to us. What can it be? The spirits of the desert? Perhaps it is the essence of Death Valley that is touching us and which is in all these things here around. Tall yellow flowers, like marguerites. Tender rose-coloured blooms that have opened on the cactuses. Yellow-red, and even green soft rocks and soil, just like the colours on a giant artist's palette. Eroded ochre mushrooms of rock between, as large as houses. Strange weird tufts of grass, a foot and a half high, like corn-stooks . . . 'the Devil's Cornfield'. Waves of sand dunes behind . . . imperceptibly wandering shapes. Bushes, once engulfed by the moving crests, have emerged years later on the opposite slope as wooden skeletons, spreading stiff branches – like fingers in hopeless defence. Tracks of the little animals that have scampered across the surface, and giant curls of rocks, like spellbound snakes, high across a mountain face. Desert lizards, lightning quick, and placid island peaks protruding from enormous fans of gravel. Black and orange gorges, and small volcanoes that once, eons ago, filled the valley with their thunderous roar. Barren salt flats . . . looking as if they have been violently hoed. Some old carts, relics from when borax used to be extracted here; people also searched for gold and silver. One old-time swindler, a plausible rogue remembered as 'Death Valley Scotty', even built a castle in a side canyon – with money he charmed from the banks on the strength of gold-strikes he never made.

Oh yes, if Death Valley could speak . . .

About 200 kilometres long, the valley is, and very wide – during the Ice Age it was a big lake, which has almost evaporated now. A couple of fish still live in it – more precisely, a certain species of fish has survived all that time; they have multiplied and adapted . . . over many thousands of years, thanks to a little spring. At the deepest point of the salt basin, eighty-four metres below sea level, there is still a bit of water left, not potable of course, which is why it is called Bad Water today. Almost unbelievable that it survives, considering the valley is the hottest place in the western hemisphere.

But the glaring heat of the summer has not yet started . . . the red tufts of flowers of the Indian Paint Brush are nodding their heads, whenever the warm, gentle breeze caresses them. Springtime . . .

We approach the dunes. From far away they had seemed just an insignificant flaxen patch in the blue-grey expanse of valley – bare of outline. Only as we get closer do crests and shadows appear, a rippled pattern of yellow waves, like loess, expands before our eyes between the high dark mountain ridges that bound the valley on either side.

Cautiously we enter this landscape of sand, curious to know what we might find. With a mounting prickle of anticipation, we enter the maze . . . Waves of an unknown ocean under the desert's smile – below dark blue mountain silhouettes. What will we discover? At every step the contours of the maze subtly shift, a new furrow opens, a basin, a new billow rising in front of us. A butterfly sails through on the breeze: 'I want to know,' it seems to say. The same wish has burned in us all day long. What waits behind the next sandhill? As if an old, teasing question would release its secret . . .

Another furrow, another ridge, another view from higher up: shimmering dark forms in the vibrating air . . . plants, bushes, an immense, seemingly infinite plain, tiny dots in the distance, melting in the haze.

We learn nothing else but to be in the valley. Yet this answer fills our hearts with joy, and still more longing. We go on.

Soft, yielding sand under our steps, and the late afternoon sun is projecting our shadows onto the waves of our ocean, growing, stretching, jumping, merging . . . What is it that makes us so happy? Just the sense of being?

There is more, we know there is more . . . It pushes us onwards. And the desert voices promise: yes, yes, be sure you will find more . . .

And then it happens, strong as a scream yet totally silent, with that suddenness peculiar to Death Valley: somewhere colours start to bloom, bizarre lines emerge, where nothing but brown or grey existed before – fantasy shapes materialise in a moment, stand there, shining, woken by the sun, by the light, still and secretive.

The Wizard in California.

A magic landscape at 8000 metres – high wind patterns on the South Col of Everest, with Makalu shining in the background.

Spring is coming to Death Valley and a desert plant unfolds on the Grand Canyon's Esplanade.

Death Valley . . .

A hundred times you may pass a place and nothing is there – nothing of significance to move you – and you go on. Then, all at once, it is exactly on that spot the desert flower opens so astonishingly – and you stand, entranced, unable to believe it was there all the time . . . You may come again and again, it will never be the same, and you can never know whether or where it will happen again.

Will it, where will it happen again?

Dusk is approaching, twilight stalking over the hills. We stop. I take Isis by the hand. We will go no further today.

As we leave, we carry the certainty with us that we will come back: we have consorted with the spirits of the desert.

Will it happen again?

One thing is true: you may return, and return, and return . . . never will the valley appear the same to you. Yet it is. You just feel it. But never can you foresee which reality you will encounter, and whether magic – just for a moment – will call from the sand, from the rocks.

The Wizard – climbing the Needles of Sierra Nevada

A young lad appears from the dark of the conifer forest and enters the bright green of the manzanita, the infamous scrub which covers the ground here so densely that sometimes you have a real fight to get through it. He is tall, athletically built, but he moves slowly towards us, and he stops again and again. He has a dark expression on his face. Something must be wrong.

'What's the matter, Joe?' Herb asks him. (My companion was the rock climbing 'King' of the Vagmarken, a dedicated Needles climber.)

With no change of expression, the other muttered, 'Mike took a screamer. He's coming now,' and he nodded glumly behind him. There was his friend moving painfully round a bend in the path, step by slow step, his clothes torn to pieces down one side – the skin, too, probably, for he was all bandaged up.

There was not much we could do for him; it had happened, and now they were on the way back to their car, their weekend at the Needles over. We wished them luck.

While we moved on, Herb pointed over the trees to one of the monstrous granite spires that make up the Needles. 'That's what Mike was leading when he came off,' he told me, 'Fell fifteen metres.'

Giant slabs soared through the branches, bright in the sunshine, some of them completely yellow with a rough and abrasive lichen. I could picture how it would be to come off on one of these. Your clothes would be eroded off first, then your skin, then more. 'I'm not surprised it is called a screamer – you wouldn't stop screaming.'

'That's about the size of it,' Herb nodded. 'But it only happens to the leader.'

Obviously the second man never falls far enough. Looking at the compact granite slabs my thoughts wandered back to the steep ice faces of the Alps – those were what I understood . . . 'Herb,' I said, 'these are your mountains, you are the Needles expert, you lead today . . .'

He smiled, then said he had no taste for screamers either, and why didn't we do a little bouldering . . . And immediately he shot off, up on some knife-edge, performing a solo ballade, jumping across to another boulder, doing several pull-ups. 'Don't you want a go?' he asked.

'No, Herb,' I replied, 'I think I'd better save my energy for the Wizard. I don't want to wear myself out before that.'

He understood. And I have to confess that delivering all those lectures in the preceding months had left me in no great shape, really. Several times that day, attached to some tiny feldspar crystal or other on these impressive granite slabs, I would find my mind wandering back to the screamer Mike took in the morning.

First of all, we climbed the Witch. She is another of the granite personalities here, about ninety metres tall and with a strange bonnet on her head. Her normal route is only Grade IV. No problem there, I thought, as I felt my way cautiously up towards the bonnet, even for an Austrian ice-specialist . . . Nature used all her magic when shaping these Sierran Needles over endless time for us to enjoy today. There is a Hermit, a Warlock, the Witch, even a White Lady, who really does proffer the profile of an elegant woman. Last, not least, there is the Wizard. He is the most uncanny of the whole eerie crew. Really sinister, like a giant gorilla in a hat, his tongue lolling from an open mouth. He is tall, perhaps ninety metres. When I first saw him, I was seized with a desire to stand right on top of his hat – so wonderful that must be, I thought, really wonderful. Oh, I did so want to do it! 'Where does the route go?' I asked Herb.

He was delighted at my interest, grinning. 'You see the waistcoat? See the thin fissure? Up that! There's a chimney to get there' – he shrugged disparagingly – 'but it's no problem at all.'

The crack running up the waistcoat was a thin, straight line, thirty metres or more with no interruption at all. 'Is there a good belay up there?' I tried to sound jocular, light-hearted.

'Nope.' Herb went on drily, 'None. You have to go right up through to the collar without stopping. And then there is the gorilla's face . . .' He smiled now, 'The eyebrow is quite interesting!' At this his expression melted into ecstasy.

'How difficult?' I wanted to know. '5.8.'

The Californians are a precise people. In my earlier days I had climbed European Grade VI. Here free climbers had arrived at 5.11, even 5.12! Of course, they put in plenty of practice – weekend after weekend in one of the desert Klettergartens, or on boulders just on the outskirts of Los Angeles, even within the town itself. And San Francisco, too – Yosemite is only a drive away.

You need special soft boots to be able to jam your feet into the cracks, and you need to jam your hands or fists in as well, otherwise your feet could slide out. You turn your foot as much as ninety degrees in a crack to hold it in there. It hurts sometimes, of course, and by evening, unless you are one of the really hard men, everything hurts: feet, fingers, hands, arms! But when the sun sinks behind the mountains in the Mojave Desert – or wherever – the 'American Lake District' empties and during the long drive home, one climber will work on another – massaging feet, neck muscles, arms – a wonderful thing is this Californian buddy system!

Steffi is a dab hand at it, superb; everyone agrees she is surpassed only by Chuck. If he works on your toes, he does it with a vibrating high frequency that no one else can match. Your legs, your feet are soon as good as new, and you are ready for more cracks in Californian granite.

Back to Herb. He is sitting on a granite boulder, sorting out the gear we shall need. Free climbing means climbing without artificial aid, but it does not mean going naked up the rock, like a squirrel. Herb creates a pile of slings, karabiners, and an assortment of aluminum cubes or 'nuts' – some small, some larger. An appropriate one of these in a crack will provide a belay so secure that the second climber, whose job is to take it out, may find the want of a special hooked tool for the job. Just as the old-style burglar needed his big bunch of keys, the rock climber cannot go anywhere without arming himself with an enormous bundle of slings and nuts in all shapes and sizes (less if he uses Friends).

Meanwhile, I almost forgot, Steffi has appeared on the scene; a helpful angel, she will sit patiently at the bottom, guarding our things and taking pictures of the climb.

Herb is ready. We leave the trees and crawl down through a gorge. After a fight with some bushes, a few easy rock passages, we approach the Wizard. He looks down at us – I can feel it – his great tongue lolling, an enigmatic look on his face. (The expression is always changing, according to the sun's position and the shadows moving across the rock.) We arrive at a niche at the bottom, and off Herb goes, swinging, with incredible lightness, around an edge. Belaying him, I think: It won't look the same when I do it. I'm up to ninety-two kilos again, though I will certainly lose some today.

Herb scuttles up the chimney, Grade IV only, and there he is, on a little ledge, selecting a nut from his bundle. Soon he calls down for me to follow. Ligh-footed, I twinkle round the edge in a dance of pure joy – or, should I say, I pressed myself into a crack and groped blindly round, trying to find some hold or other on the other side. Then comes the chimney, vertical as all chimneys are, but with good handholds. Right! Here I am, Herb! I fix a good anchor, Herb augments it with two additional nuts in separate fissures, quelling my surprise with a dry, 'You can't be too careful with Europeans! You still climb with pitons there!' I sighed. At least I was firmly attached, like a statue of Abraham Lincoln.

'Now, be sure and belay me damned well!' Herb says. 'If you want to take a picture, do it now, not later. If I fall off up there on the waistcoat, then it's no joke. You really have to hold me!' He smiles, but I know it is serious.

Herb starts off up the rock gorilla's waistcoat which is splashed here and there with patches of intense yellow, the lichen. I wonder it wasn't called King Kong, rather than the Wizard. He moves up sound rock directly above my head, on tiny, but good holds . . . but then they run out. I see how he has just his fingertips in the long fine fissure we had spotted earlier. He tries to get some grip with the rubber soles of his rock boots on the vertical slab to his right. There are no holds anywhere, but the sole grips by pure pressure. It's a technique which of course he knows well, but this vertical dièdre – the narrow groove in the enormous slab – is impressive. He is a very good climber . . . sometimes I see his face, his tensed muscles, hear the chink of his climbing gear. Otherwise, it is quiet, still, but for the whisper of a light breeze now and then out there in the trees of the Sierra – or is that just my imagination? I try to memorise the moves Herb makes, the contortions and steps, remembering I have to get up there, too, and on my own! I have also got to take out all the mini-nuts on their thin wire slings, jammed deeply in the waistcoat's crease. Herb has inserted them as he climbs, as quickly as he could, but very accurately. He is now twenty-five metres above my head on a vertical slab, and for the first time calls down to me: this is where the fissure runs out, he will have to turn a corner to find the next crease in the garment. I can see the soles of his boots carefully edge round high above me. I hold my breath. A fast move now, fluid, elastic, he is round, disappears. Soon he calls from somewhere up there. It is my turn now. I start on up.

The sky seems full of nuts to me – and none of them wants to come out! Keep the legs wide, stay in balance, pull, fumble, fiddle with the 'fire hook', streams of sweat running down my face. I swear, then pull again . . . some of the nuts are held absolutely fast. 'Don't you dare leave any nuts behind,' comes faintly from above. 'It's a matter of honour here, to get them all out!' Can't have that, I think. The next guy up finding one of Herb Laeger's nuts! He would never hear the end of it. Sweating, I strive to maintain our climbing honour. Finally, I am two-thirds of the way up the dièdre, spread uncomfortably between two granite walls which meet at a wide angle, when, suddenly, I have to grab hold of a nut to save myself slipping: it holds well, but that is probably why afterwards it absolutely refuses to come out. I work and work away at it, streams of sweat pouring from my whole body – it is a hot country, this, it really is – and then (I hardly dare commit it to paper) I say, 'To hell with it!' and leave the nut where it sticks. Herb has so far not realised this.

When I reach him, I am decorated with slings like a Christmas tree; he sits happily on a little ledge, whistling a melody. He has taken off his shirt, which is hanging on a sling with a nut in a crack. Three more nuts go in for me – the old business, Herb having regard for my bulkier outline – and thus, secured, we both sit on this beautiful ledge, looking over the fantastic granite spires to the woods beyond. What a wonderful range, this Sierra Nevada . . .

The Wizard's eyebrow! Everyone knows what beetling brows gorillas have – this one has a real overhang – 5.8, no less! Herb leans backwards horizontally, feet in a niche below, then suddenly pulls out one leg and sets the foot carefully on to the edge of the eyebrow! For a second he almost does the splits, but immediately pulls up his body, to attach himself completely to the eyebrow. Soon he is disappearing beyond the overhang.

The rope runs in short jerks through my hands, through the karabiners in the nutted slings, then I hear his shout from above, while Steffi yells from below: the summit! Herb is standing on top of the gorilla's hat – right on top of the Wizard of stone! It takes me somewhat longer to heave my ninety-two kilos over the eyebrow, and as I do so I vow to lose more weight in future – but a wide crack in the hat makes the end of this pitch a dance. I put in a special *Variante* of my own, drawing a grin and a shake of the head from Herb. Two worlds – old and new – so happy together on this day. I hope one day to exchange the hospitality and show him 'my' Mont Blanc! '*Berg Heil!*' says Herb, with an American accent, and we shake hands on it.

Two men on top of the Wizard.

On the Gulf

A day between Europe and Asia . . . a boat in the far distance, almost lost in the hazy grey glitter of the Gulf of California, off Mexico.

*

Lines in the sand around us – lots of lines with gaps between.
'What are you doing?' Isis asks.
'I draw seconds.'
'Seconds?'
'That's right. Every line is time, that passes; and where I don't draw a line, time passes, too, but somewhere else for someone else . . . I shall come back here and make some more seconds for you to see. Think of these lines sometimes, when I'm gone . . .' I answer.
A whole pattern of lines covers the sand, straight ones, curved ones, semicircles, braids and cables, but never a circle.

As we walked on towards the water, suddenly I saw the design again. The sea had made it! We were crossing a flat open stretch of beach covered by an incalculable number of ripple marks, straight and curved, some in parallel, small elevations and depressions in the fine sand left by the retreating waves . . . we were walking across hundreds of seconds, which the sea had drawn. Before we reached the water, the shoreline behind us had become a thin, narrow band in the distance.

The closer we approached to the water, the more distinctly could be heard a peculiar rushing, a sound composed of a million individual sounds, a tone that approached and retreated, went off to the side, that gradually enshrouded and inundated us. There was no understanding its pattern for hundreds of smaller and bigger waves and currents were running and lapping across each other . . . it was a mysterious sound, enticing beyond words. A hypnotic spell.

Further and further we venture into it, this vault of sound. We enter the water, the sand strangely hard and smooth underfoot – quite different from before. Holding each other's hands, we cling together as the many currents gently buffet our bodies, and all the while we are engulfed in this spellbinding rushing, are touched by the countless ripples, dancing around us like a pattern of small, sharp peaks, and the thousandfold dazzle of light flashing in our eyes, many, many suns. No more coast, no more sky, only the rush, rush, rush in a space of dancing suns, in which the seconds close into circles. We are in a space without gravity, no longer aware that our feet touch the ground anywhere.

We remain wrapped in each other's arms.

PART SEVEN

Makalu (8481 m) – the turning point

'But why that, Kurt? Why does it have to be that?' The question came from my old friend and expedition companion Markus Schmuck, whom I had just bumped into navigating through the crowds of tourists in Salzburg's famous Getreidegasse. He had evidently heard of my proposed trip to Makalu, or he would not have been treating me to such long and earnest scrutiny. Of course he meant well and only wanted to be sure I did not embark on anything foolish. I knew that.

It had been twenty years since Markus and I made the first ascent of Broad Peak with Hermann Buhl and Fritz Wintersteller, the first of the eight-thousanders to be climbed alpine-style. The climb was judged by many at the time to be a crazy enterprise – no oxygen, no porters, just the four of us.

Well, we had succeeded. But that was then. No one can deny that twenty years is a long time: you only get older.

So here was Markus trying to talk me out of going to Makalu. And he was not the only one. Helmut Wihan, the best pulmonary specialist in Salzburg, who was treating me for a bronchitic allergy I had almost certainly picked up from staying too long in town, was adamant that I should not venture an inch higher than Base Camp. Another doctor friend simply said, 'Kurt, you can't expect to go on for ever. It's time to call it a day.' But I wanted to do it! Wanted to have a go! I needed to know what it would be like – this beautiful Makalu – could not bear the thought of life without it. I had seen it from Shartse when I was with Hermann Warth and Nawang Tenzing. They would both be coming on this expedition, too, and there would also be Karli Landvogt, our doctor from Greenland in 1974; Hans von Känel, an ebullient Bernese climber; Dietlinde, Hermann's wife, and two other Sherpas, Ang Chappal and Nga Temba.

'You should think it over,' Markus repeated anxiously as we said goodbye, and he hung on to my hand as he shook it, giving me another of his long and concerned looks – as if he did not expect to see me again.

Yang Lhe – the enchanted forest

Between the trunks of the Himalayan firs, rhododendrons are a riot of bloom. As far as the eye can see, splashes of every colour from white, through rose to a deep deep red, and all mingled with yellow and mauve . . . a living Impressionist painting. It is spring, a perfect dream-like spring. The whole forest seems to be under a magic spell. Wafting gently from the fir branches long fronds of green lichen weave a mobile and intricate web of three-dimensional lace. Caught in the web are the crystal notes of birdsong from many, many birds. A waterfall, like white satin ribbon, hangs from a granite wall, so high that the water is transformed to a fine spray long before reaching the ground. A small log hut in a clearing amongst the trees is surrounded by prayer flags on long wands of bamboo; they stir gently in the breeze. Om, mani padme hum, om mani padme hum . . .

It is a sacred place.

Between the prayer flags I come upon a rock bearing the traces of a carved outline. Buddha, perhaps? I cannot tell, but instinctively feel that this precious place with its fabulous trees is enchanted, the enchanted forest of an unknown deity. There seems no other way to explain my remarkable recovery . . .

I arrived down here racked by such terrible coughing spasms I thought they would never leave me. I had already abandoned all hope of going high on the mountain, and had left Base Camp, on my own, to drop down to around 3500 metres. That was three days ago – or was it four? I have lost all sense of time. Few people ever come here. Two or three times a year, perhaps, the inhabitants of Shedua on the other side of the Kongma La Pass make the journey to celebrate a religious feast, and during the monsoon you occasionally meet a herdsman with a small flock of sheep or goats, or a couple of cows roaming along the Barun valley from pasture to pasture. Otherwise, the place is deserted. Dangerous gorges separate it from the villages of the great Arun valley. So, I am quite alone here.

High altitude cough is a pernicious disability which has struck down many a Himalayan climber. The French, when they made the first ascent of Makalu in 1955, suffered badly from it during the early stages of the expedition. If you have never experienced it, it is hard to imagine what a convulsive cough it is: a few days ago Dietlinde fractured one of her ribs in a coughing fit and Karli had to strap her up with a huge sticking-plaster bandage. Nawang Tenzing was another victim, but he managed to shake it off. Not me! I saw my only chance in getting down to a lower level, into the rhododendron jungle. I felt so dejected, desperate. When you have spent all your life in mountains, and suddenly, on such a beautiful peak as Makalu, you are forced to give up, it takes some adjustment. Had I really grown too old, or was it just this accursed cough? Was Markus right after all when he warned me the time had come to pack it in? How do you accept you may never climb again on the great heights of the world? How can you come to terms with that? I endeavoured to calm my mounting panic, persuade myself it would not be too bad: Kurt, I said, I know it's hard, but even without big mountains, life can be worth living.

There are plenty of secrets beyond the mountains, not only on the top? Everywhere there are thousands of secrets, wherever you go in the world.

But that doesn't stop it being heart-rending to accept you will be excluded from the one deepest experience of all, for all the time that is left to you.

Then I felt the forest around me, this magic forest with all its beauty. And only then did I begin to experience solace. It was as if love was streaming towards me from all sides. I can find no other way of describing it. I do not consider myself superstitious, but there is so much in this world which nobody can explain. The conviction began to grow in my mind that the forest of Yang Lhe must be sacred. I wondered if a clue might be found in the very name Makalu, the origins of which are uncertain although there are a number of theories about it; but then I thought that forest perhaps has nothing to do with Makalu at all. It is simply here.

Yet, there is something in the branches.

Is it the Isis of another world?

Am I meeting something I have encountered somewhere before? In my mind everything seems connected.

Even today, I do not know what happened to me during those days in the magic forest of Yang Lhe. I cannot explain it. But when I started back up the mountain, I was a different person. What is more, I was completely restored to health. It was not long before I could tackle Makalu in such good form that my friends could only shake their heads in disbelief.

I was grateful to the unknown goddess. A little bell, which I had brought with me from Mont Blanc, may still hang there among the tree branches near the prayer flags.

Through East Nepal

The drizzle started on the way up yesterday. Every so often, one or other of our heavily laden porters would lose his footing on the slippery red clay and slither back down the path to the laughter of the others and yelps of Yahoo! Thanks to the high-profile tread on our boots, Hermann, Hans and I were instantly delegated to be 'protecting fathers' (as some of the women porters called us). We did not spare ourselves, struggling up the steep slopes with a Sherpani or two under our wings.

So, despite the pouring rain, we arrived at our day's destination in the high spirits that characterise this country, Nepal. Khandbari, at about 800 metres in the foothills of the Himalaya, was the first village on the long and rugged approach to Makalu. Our joy at having arrived there had a deeper reason. Only those familiar with the standard expedition scrimmage in Kathmandu, the 'Zermatt' of the Himalaya, can appreciate what competition there is each year for the few available charter planes. The team leaders who come off worst arrive at their mountains too late in the season, running the risk of being overtaken by the monsoon just as they are about to make their summit bids.

Humid monsoon winds, sweeping in across the Bay of Bengal, bring welcome rains for the farmers of India and Nepal. But to the mountaineer, they spell thunderstorms, excessive new snow, avalanches – in short, an end to the expedition! There is only a brief weather window for mountaineering activities between the end of winter in the Himalaya, and the onset of the monsoon –

from mid-March until late in May. The post-monsoon season is even shorter.

Hermann Warth, who for three years had headed the German Development Service in Nepal with his wife Dietlinde, shared joint leadership of this Makalu venture with me. Our first expedition boxes had arrived into the care of Nepalese friends in Khandbari two years ago, before ever we obtained permission for our climb. But as a mountaineer you must be an optimist, otherwise you could never keep rekindling summit dreams from one venture to the next, especially when you know that an objective like this is one of the most dangerous you could undertake. We received our permit for Makalu from the government of Nepal against payment of an official peak fee of 14,000 rupees (about £1000; today it would cost more than six times as much). The previous November Dietlinde had set out on foot for Khandbari in east Nepal with forty Sherpas and Sherpanis and a total of 1100 kilos of baggage left over from a previous expedition, which had been stored in Namche Bazar near Everest. It took twelve days to get there and, ever since, all seventeen members of the Shresta family have been obliged to live their lives around our Makalu boxes and sacks, which took over a large part of their house, our base in Khandbari. They endured it with their usual unshakeable cheerfulness.

Hermann, meanwhile, as a half-Nepali himself, was fully aware of the battle for charter planes that took place each March in Kathmandu, and – while three 'Europeans' of our international team (namely Karl Landvogt from Germany, Hans von Känel from Switzerland and myself from Austria) handled the organisation at our end – he booked a cargo flight for us on a Twin-Otter to Tumlingtar for 10 March; in other words, the day before yesterday. Still, alpinists all have to be aware of the proverb which says that in Asia, nothing happens as you expect it to. It applies especially to charter flights from Kathmandu in March.

Although mountaineering fellowship is said to span the world, any leader of an expedition in Kathmandu at that time would prefer to be the only one there – until his plane has taken off. So when Hermann passed on to me greetings from Wolfi Nairz who had been in town a few days before, I had only one question. 'How many planes does he need?' 'Three Twin-Otters,' Hermann replied, 'but don't worry. Ours is already booked.' I think of the mountaineer's proverb and cross my fingers. March 10 comes and we load all our baggage on to a Land-Rover: glorious weather, perfect for flying. The phone shrills. Hermann's face drops as he picks up the receiver: our flight is cancelled – some damage to the aeroplane.

Hell! Anything can happen in Asia! But then again, *really* anything can happen in Asia, and instead of waiting for a week, which we could have expected, we find ourselves taking off the very next morning, even though it is raining and you can hardly see any mountains for the grey haze. By the time we are in the air, I have the uncomfortable feeling that it won't be long before we turn back. Pilots here navigate entirely on visibility, and ahead of us nothing can be seen but grey entangled in grey, carpets of cloud amongst mountains. I take out my small plastic compass – a freebie from an earlier flight – seeking to know at least in what direction we are heading. Lieutenant Deepak Kumar Gurung, the liaison officer appointed to us by the government, has noticed my expression of concern and smiles encouragingly. 'The pilot is a cousin of mine,' he says.

So I put my compass away. Hermann winks at me. 'If there is any chance at all of getting there, we will. The pilot won't want to make a fool of himself before his relatives.' I'm sure that's right. It is presumably why we are flying at all.

We seem to be heading south, towards India. Ah, I think, he is going to sneak in the back door, from the Nepalese lowlands, the Terai, which so seamlessly share a frontier with India.

Large streams of rubble, like winding snakes, glimmer up from a hill country almost obscured by mists – the Siwaliks. We are flying at lower level now, groping our way from one rubble stream to the next. To our left, in the distance, are long ridges, greyish-blue whalebacks leading east, waymarkers which constantly disappear then re-emerge. The plane now makes a turn above a boa constrictor of debris of a pale and glowing yellow. A wide ribbon of water comes into view. Can it be the Arun, the large river which flows through the mountains of eastern Nepal?

Hermann Warth and I travelled along the Arun in 1974 on our way to Shartse, beyond Makalu. That was when we first set eyes on the mountain we are going to now, and where we got to know each other and the inimitable Nawa Tenzing, our 'Sherpa' friend from the other side of Everest – not really a Nepali at all, but a full-blooded Tibetan. Indestructible, resolutely good-humoured, he would crack jokes even throughout the terrible tempests on the corniced ridge of Shartse. He is a member of this Makalu expedition, but under the flag of Nepal, together with two true Sherpas, Nga Temba and Ang Chappal, our Sirdar, both of whom had impressed Hermann with their skill and fellowship in 1977 on Lhotse.

These two are with us on the plane, sitting together and looking intently through the windows at the river below. Nawang Tenzing has been waiting in Tumlingtar for a week now, guarding our Makalu boxes at the edge of the airstrip. He will be surprised to see us arriving in this weather! The pilot is turning the machine to the north – then this must indeed be the Arun! Already we are floating along steeper mountain flanks with outcropping rocky ribs. Gorges are opening up, valleys . . .

Below us appears a wide valley with a longish oval of green, framed in a bend of the river . . . the meadow which is used as a runway. We spiral down towards it. Houses of the hill-people slide under the wings, terraced fields, one above the other, single trees . . . There follows a thunderous rumbling, such a juddering and jolting, a thrust and a moaning of wheels . . . we are rattled and jounced, but . . . we are on the ground . . . jogging over grass and dirt . . . we have arrived!

That was some Nepalese navigation – a zero-visibility flight, following an experienced nose! We break out into cheers for the pilot, clapping till our palms hurt, while the machine slows to a final halt. All out! We are in high spirits under the overcast sky. We made it! A major hurdle on the way to Makalu is passed.

Now, a day later, the rain is pummelling wildly on the tin roof above us and a reddish silt-heavy brook sluices down the village street . . . This is no Salzburg drizzle: this looks like the monsoon.

Seeing such torrents emptying on to Khandbari awakens our worst misgivings: will the way to Makalu be open, or will snowdrifts prevent our porters getting over the mountain barrier in to the Barun Sanctuary? This lot will mean a metre of new snow at least on the Kongma La, a pass of more than 4000 metres over which we have to coax more than a hundred porters and our three tonnes of gear. The outcome of our expedition could be determined up there before ever reaching Makalu with its 8481 metres.

But you need a cool head as a Himalayan climber, or you might as

well stay at home. You know things never turn out as you expect –
so best keep smiling! Be sure that when the sun comes out, it will
melt the snow, so we carry on gaining height with our singing band of
porters. Loaded with duffel bags, boxes, a ladder and plastic drums,
they mount the terraced hillsides towards a rounded ridge that will
bring us to nearly 2000 metres. From there it will be downhill on
the other side all the way to the Arun River, 1000 metres below.

Just as we are putting up our tents that evening on the pass,
on a grassy patch among some bushes, hailstones rattle down on
us from fast-moving black clouds. Within moments everything is
white. The porters scuttle into one of the hastily pitched large
tents, abandoning their loads in pools of melted hailstones . . .
Quick! Quick! Get everything off the ground! Stand stuff on the
ladder, or on stones, or hitch it up in the branches! Only then, in all
this confused ant-like activity does it become apparent that not all
the loads are here. Hell and damnation! Ang Chappal and Nawang
Tenzing scamper back along the wet, skiddy path as fast as they can,
darkness closing in around them. What can have happened? It turns
out that some porters simply dumped their loads by the wayside and
trotted off to stay in the surrounding villages. Finally, very late, we
have everything back together and the campfires burning. The storm
passes, stars come out . . . and familiar faces smile out of the glowing
firelight, as one suddenly recognises this or that lad again from when
he was with us four years ago on the way to Lhotse and Shartse.

The morning of a long day dawns clear and wonderful; a day in which
we shall press on relentlessly, following the jungle-covered ridges
high above the valley of the Arun. The mountain range opposite
begins to quiver in the first pale light – five six-thousanders and
the 7000-metre Chamlang. Behind them rears a gigantic, regular
pyramid, its summit already rosy with sunlight. It is Makalu.

Strikes – Left with nine out of a hundred

Nowadays, to speak of the 'battle' for peaks is no longer fashionable.
But if the game is to get three tonnes of expedition equipment on
the backs of a hundred porters through storm and tempest, over
snowed-in mountain passes, one may justly speak of struggling with
elemental forces – and as far as the inhabitants of the villages of
Shedua and Num could remember, there had never been such

quantities of snow as fell last winter. Add to that all the fresh snow that has come down in the last few weeks . . .

The gap in the mountains we want to negotiate, the Kongma La, is 4200 metres high – and, strictly speaking, it comprises two passes. At the beginning of summer, wonderful rhododendrons bloom up there, and there is a little lake with prayer flags . . . but at present everything is buried under several metres of deep snow.

Having left the Arun behind us and dismissed our porters who came from the hill country beyond the river, we hire a hundred mountain men and women at the last jungle clearing below the pass, people from Shedua, Tashigang and Bungim. Then, together with two Naikes (porter chiefs), we set off again. The first day's climb passes uneventfully, apart from a few early season leeches in the jungle trying to suck our life-juices and invading our tents at night. We notice them in time, and snip them in half with scissors. More humane treatment only brings its own revenge: toss them out of doors and the creatures merely cling to the tent wall to come visiting again in the higher camps when you least expect them. (When we return after the expedition there will be countless numbers of them lurking in wait for us in the trees and bushes by the wayside.)

On the second day of ascent we meet the first snow in the rhododendron forest – old, rotten snow in great heaps. The men and women from Shedua, carrying as much as twenty-seven kilos each, have to battle through it continually, often up to their waists – it is the most toilsome labour, torture you could say, for a mere twenty-eight rupees a day (about £1.20). You can understand how they would prefer to go home. We have distributed gym shoes, blankets, snow goggles, and just pray they will stay with us. The crossing, they keep telling us, has never been so bad. For us, everything is at stake. Up near the Kongma rock, the second leg of this stage, where expeditions usually wander over wonderful meadows, the snow is almost two metres deep in places. We decide to pitch all the tents we have to get our shivering army of workers out of the cold.

I man the modest field kitchen with our expedition cook, and we work till 2 a.m., seeing that everyone gets warm tea inside him (or her).

In vain. The next morning more than fifty porters desert us. We struggle on with the rest. Hans and I break trail almost to the top of the pass. The men behind us are still up to their waists in snow, but seem cheerful, laughing and joking about it (we truly do have the crème de la crème of these hill people now). But just before the pass they fling down their loads, and start back, most of them saying they will return in the morning: they are only going as far as the forest. We have no idea if we will see any of them again. Hermann prudently opens the trail to the top of the pass while Dietlinde – still down at the Kongma rock – guards the abandoned boxes and sacks, half of the total loads. It can be imagined how grateful we are the next morning to see black dots slowly pulling out of the grey layers of cloud below us, and moving along the white, undulating edge of the mountain . . . we count them. Yes! Nearly all are back!

Hot tea is handed round – then comes another half-hour of racking suspense. Will they stay, or go down after all? Our Sirdar, together with the liaison officer, implores the men and women to continue with us, pointing out that the trail is already broken as far as the pass. It is a very steep slope, but Hermann's tracks are clearly visible. They decide they will come on. Thank heavens!

That same evening, the first fifty loads arrive at a small pine forest on the Barun side of the Kongma La. There is nothing to be seen of the little lake and its rhododendrons but a dark watery patch in the snow desert. This is where the prayer flags stand, but only the highest of them peep out of the snow now.

Just as I am taking a photograph, a Sherpani passes by with her load. '*Tulo pani*,' I say, Big water! And I point at the sorry little puddle. She laughs, sets down her load and rummages in a little bag which she draws from the folds of her clothes. Then, murmuring a prayer, she tosses a coin into the water.

I grope in my own pockets, but I have no money on me. I find the beautiful stripey, silver and blue crystal of cyanite, which I picked up a few days ago in a field, wanting to take it home because it was so unusual. 'Makalu,' I say, and throw that into the water as well.

The next day, while the remaining fifty porters trudge back over the pass to fetch the other half of the loads, I cannot resist the temptation to wing down these slopes, which have cost us so much agony and effort. I carry my skis on up to 4000 metres, then whizz, deliciously, downhill.

In the Barun valley, nearly all the porters leave us, and we spend many days with the nine faithful who remain of our hundred, ferrying loads from there to Base Camp. That is after it has snowed for sixty hours without stopping. At least this gives me the chance of more skiing every time I go down to pick up my daily load from the Barun forest. After three weeks of approach, finally the mountain stands before us.

Chance and mischance with the oxygen – my friends' summit

A weird droning emanates from the blue sky above us like a distant express train, a monotonous, eerie sound . . . incessant. No less strange is the reflected light which bounces off Makalu's rust-coloured granite, from a shining shield that rears in front of us, tilting into the sky. There is a difference of more than 3000 metres in height between here and the shield's upper rim; it is gigantic, unimaginably huge, and yet seems almost close on this clear day. The storm batters the edges of the giant shield, high, high up, while here in Base Camp the air remains calm and still. Banners of snow are sometimes flung from that gleaming rim; they circle a while then disappear . . . Only the sound, the unearthly droning of the high-altitude storm, the Makalu Express, rumbles on.

The top edge of the giant shield has a deep notch – the Makalu La, a saddle at about 7400 metres. To the left of it rises Kangchungtse (7678 m), which is known also as 'Little Makalu'; and to the right, rising in several steep and vaulting upthrusts, another 1000 metres of height to the summit of Makalu itself (8481 m).

Twenty-three years before our visit, French climbers found a way up this side to the summit – the first ascent. Since then, despite a number of attempts, nobody else has been able to repeat it, partly in view of the mountain's enormous height, but also because of the constant rearrangement of its snow and rock features under the battering of fierce storms, effectively renewing its virginity.

A New Zealander, Peter Mulgrew, who had suffered amputations to his legs after sustaining serious frostbite on Makalu, called this eight-thousander (in his book of the same name), No Place For Men. Nevertheless, men have gradually solved one problem after another on this difficult mountain: the French Ridge, the South Face, the Czech Buttress, the South-East Ridge are all great, immense routes. But they have claimed their victims.

No traverse of Makalu has yet been done, but, having lost so much time in the terrible snowstorms on the Kongma La and afterwards, and realising the bad conditions on the south-east side of the mountain, we have almost stopped speaking of such a possibility. But perhaps, if we get up the north-west side quickly and the monsoon holds off until late . . .?

Our Northern Base Camp was established on 4 April on top of a sandy shoulder at 5400 metres, and the little party remaining after the porters' departure has been working day after day on Makalu's steep flank, in an attempt to reach the aforementioned saddle, the Makalu La. Starting from our High Base, we can leapfrog campsites of earlier expeditions, and have already (on 8 April) put in our Camp 1 800 metres higher between the crevasses of a glacier plateau. Feverishly, we press on. It was Hans and I set up Camp 1, and Hermann with Ang Chappal who install Camp 2 on 13 April at 7000 metres.

To approach this camp is a steep and exposed climb, on which we have fixed 200 metres of rope. Anyone coming up heavily loaded must take special care since a false slip here could send you plunging into the void.

Time and again the Makalu Express roars . . . gusts are so fierce that it would be impossible to reach or leave this Camp 2 without our safety line. Sleepless nights in rattling tents erode our nerves, but one day, finally, and again caught by a storm, Hermann, Chappal and I, after a steep climb on granite slabs and snow, anchor two tiny tents with ice-screws into the sheer mirror of ice that covers the saddle at 7400 metres. Camp 3 on the Makalu La is standing and it is only 24 April. Does that mean we are still in with a chance for the traverse?

We hug one another, buffeted by the gusts: a first victory! Only 1000 metres from here to the summit; we can scarcely believe it!

Things continue more speedily than we expected. First, we must fix a line for belaying the access to this saddle, then Hans pushes the route onwards with Temba, then I with Nawang: at 7700 metres we cache five bottles of oxygen for our first summit team, Hermann and Ang Chappal. They are the fittest of us all.

And what next? The traverse? Not without some preparation on the south-east side of the mountain. I can't help asking myself during these days: Is Makalu asleep? Is this mountain really going to allow us tiny ants to crawl from bottom to top in less than a month? The prospect seems incredible, but our luck holds out.

Nawang gives Hermann and Chappal a hand establishing Camp 4 at 7950 metres, breaking most of the trail and carrying an enormous pack without using any of the oxygen. Then he returns to Camp 3.

Both of us are knackered, suffering from terrible high-altitude coughs and from our strenuous exertions up there. We descend, while Hans comes up with Karl (our indefatigable doctor, who has ferried loads like everyone else), and Hermann and Ang Chappal gain the pointed summit of Makalu – happy, on top of the world, for all of us. It is May Day, 2.45 in the afternoon. Hermann, as planned, used oxygen above Camp 4. The Sherpa went without.

On 10 May, in the evening, I am sitting in our Southern Base Camp, at 4800 metres, beside a crackling campfire with some porters who have brought up wood for us. The flames enliven the twilight, giving out a wonderful warmth. The last rays of the sun have set Makalu's summit pyramid aglow, high, high above our heads. Soon, the icy cold will rule up there. Spellbound, I watch as swathes of cloud play gently below the tipmost ruby rocks. It is a calm beautiful evening, and the light so beguiling that it makes you long to be on top at this minute but to hurry away with the last ray before the night can bind you in its terrible space-cold. It calls to mind that similar evening, twenty-one years ago, when Hermann Buhl and I stood at sunset on top of Broad Peak, 8047 metres, bathed in ethereal light, indescribably happy . . .

I have no idea as I gaze up at Makalu's rosy summit that Hans, Karl and Temba are standing up there . . . and that their view and mine and our thoughts meet in these last sun's rays.

But the cruel night lies in wait.

They are late, too late, not intentionally so, no more than Hermann Buhl and I intended to be on our summit at that hour. Afterwards, one is bound to ask how it came about, what one could have done differently, but meanwhile nothing can change the course of events.

Pensively Karl regards his black fingertips and swollen toes. In the two days since he came down, we have tried our best with injections and everything possible to help him. Hans, after days of snow blindness, sees the blue toes on his left foot for the first time . . . yet despite the excruciating pain which wells over him from time to time, he does not question that the summit of Makalu was worth the price.

We were lucky, he says. It could have been much worse. And we all know that is true . . . After an open bivouac at 8250 metres, if all you lose are the tips of one or two fingers or toes, you have been lucky!

They might so easily never have resurfaced from the death-like sleep which overtook them when they finally arrived back in Camp 4; they could have gradually slid from semi-consciousness into eternity. Instead, they are here! And the first jokes come from their lips.

What actually happened? When I was on 'sick leave' down in the magic forest, trying to shake off my racking altitude cough, the second summit party ventured their luck: Hans, Karl and Nga Temba. With back-up from the others, everything at first appeared to go well. However, shortly before setting off for the top, all the evil spirits went on the rampage! One oxygen set after the other broke down. Attempts to repair them only led to loss of energy and time. Finally, all three, with Hans in the lead, moved off determinedly for the summit without artificial oxygen. At 6 p.m., they were on top, convinced they could still get down to Camp 4 before dark. But as night came, they realised that the cold had drained their headlamp batteries. The result was an ice-cold bivouac in a narrow alcove at the bottom of the final couloir, at 8250 metres, just below the steep face which rises beneath the summit ridge . . . Only Sherpa Nga Temba came through without frostbite – and as early as possible next day, he descended from Camp 4, helped down by Ang Chappal. Hans and Karl radioed that they, too, would be descending from there that day, but instead, they fell asleep as soon as they reached the tent. The bivouac had exhausted them terribly.

At the end of their strength, they staggered in to Camp 3 (7400 m) the following day where Hermann and Nawang did their utmost to persuade them to continue, finally physically conducting them down, despite protestations that all they wanted was to continue their sleep.

They may never have woken again.

Makalu . . . with a monkey wrench

'Tea's ready!' sings out Ang Rita, our kitchen boy, in a voice loud enough to be heard all over the little tent city that is our Northern Base Camp in a sandy hollow at 5400 metres. With no sense of hurry, the small crew gathers in the spacious tent we call 'Alex'. Its fabric, once white, is now a venerable grey from several expeditions' service. Approaching, I catch the sound of laughter and joking. Even Karl, our doctor, hobbling in beside me on his two sticks, has lost none of his sense of humour. He comes from Bavaria, after all! And Hans, who we call 'the Bernese Lightning-streak', reflects wryly that so long as his toes hurt, they must still be alive.

I am the only one who is a bit subdued. The day after tomorrow, I shall set off with Hermann and Nawang Tenzing to attempt the highest peak of my career. It is eighteen years since I climbed one of the Himalayan giants – Dhaulagiri (8222 m) – and almost twenty-one since I stood on the top of Broad Peak in the sunset with Hermann Buhl. A third of my life has passed since then, a life of climbing, adventure and discovery. Will my luck hold over the next few days? That is why I am so quiet and preoccupied. The others too, of course, are well aware of the unpredictability which attends this, as any summit attack.

Everything worked like clockwork when the first two went to the top, Hermann Warth and Sirdar Ang Chappal. Hermann had no trouble with his oxygen set and Ang Chappal, by choice, climbed without. But the second attempt was disastrous – and since coming back from the forest, I am only now getting more details. Of the five oxygen sets we had brought, three failed to work at all, and the reserve would not function properly, notwithstanding that all the equipment – which had already performed successfully on a Kangchenjunga expedition in 1976, and on Lhotse the following year – had been put through stringent scientific testing in Switzerland before we set out. Obviously the apparatus preferred a neutral Swiss atmosphere to the thin icy air about 8000 metres. Luckily, Hans is something of a Mr Fixit, and has been able to locate one of the faults at least and cure it, miraculously, with a simple spanner. But for how long? He himself is not optimistic it will last. Hans reinforced his reputation as a technical genius on Lhotse last year; finding his oxygen flow blocked suddenly above 8000 metres by a build-up of ice crystals inside the apparatus, he calmly stopped and urinated through the tube and mask, instantly clearing the trouble!

Repairing oxygen sets at high altitudes is not usually accomplished so simply, however, and as a precaution we shall take two spanners with us in our rucksacks.

Nawang Tenzing, the good-natured Tibetan who now lives in Nepal, the one who struggled along the cornices on Shartse with

Hermann and me in the storms, is also giving cause for concern. He cannot decide whether he really wants to go to the summit or not. He says he hates the cold, is reluctant to disturb the mountain gods, does not want to set himself up as an object of envy among his neighbours back home, yet we know he longs so much for another glimpse of his lost homeland – and how fantastic it must look from up there! I know how much it means to him: I saw how he danced in the snow below Camp 2, when he first got high enough to see into Tibet.

It was Nawang's indecision that finally resolved Hermann to join us, even though he had been up once already. 'It would be marvellous if you could make it, too, Kurt,' he told me, adding that if he did make it again, he could bring back the stone from the top that he had promised his wife and forgotten to pick up the first time round!

Ever since shaking off my altitude cough a week ago, I have felt in tremendous form. I suggest to the other two that we make a lightning dash, bypassing Camp 2, and getting to the top and back in just a few days, like we did on Broad Peak twenty-one years ago. We would use oxygen from 7950 metres – although if it should fail again, I'd be quite prepared to try without, alone if necessary. None of us is interested in haemo-dilution. On the expedition, only the doctor, Karl, has tried thinning his own blood and that of Sherpa Nga Temba before their summit climb, but it is questionable whether it had any appreciable effect. For my part, I absolutely refuse to manipulate my body to enable me to reach the top. If my own blood is not good enough to get me up there, well then, I don't go.

And oxygen? It is true I climbed Dhaulagiri and Broad Peak without it, but now on the world's fifth highest mountain I will take the apparatus, and use it if I must; with or without it, I do not intend to push beyond my limits. I can see no sense in reaching the summit of a mountain at *any* price and by *whatever* means. No summit can ever be worth the lives of your companions, or yourself, or your ability to think and feel clearly in future. To sacrifice even part of that ability for success, makes of that success a failure.

Will you get closer to an understanding of the Why by climbing without oxygen to the greatest heights of the Himalaya? Or is the comprehension of why we are always drawn back to these mountains anyway beyond our intellectual grasp? Himalayan expert Elizabeth

Hawley in Kathmandu told me an interesting thing. When Reinhold Messner listened to the tape recording he made of himself after struggling to the summit of Everest, he had to confess, 'It made no kind of sense at all.' He may have hoped, I guess, to have captured the sensations of another world. In vain. But this is one of the reasons why we mountaineers have to return. One thing I don't believe is that people who reach these high places feel nothing beyond the basic satisfaction of having made it. Even if some say that's all there was to it. Perhaps they have forgotten or don't know how to speak about an emotion that goes beyond words.

Certainly everybody has had the experience of their most wonderful dreams vanishing the very moment you want to keep hold of them for ever.

On 17 May, we set off: Hermann, Nawang and I, supported by Nga Temba and Ang Chappal who will accompany us as far as Camp 4, and Ang Rita who is to stay behind in Camp 1.

To start with, everything runs according to plan. And on our second day we manage the whole steep climb to the Makalu La, where our Camp 3 stands. The weather is splendid. But then, on the third day, a terrible storm blows up out of a blue sky, and continuing on to Camp 4 is out of the question. With horror, we realise that the high winds of the last few days have completely polished away all the snow from the slopes and surfaces below Camp 4. There is nothing but gleaming blue ice all the way to 7900 metres. This will make it extremely dangerous coming back from the summit unless we can fix some ropes for our protection. We are not prepared for anything like that. In the thick of the storm, I go out and cut what rope I can from the easier sections below the Makalu La, to help us higher up. The next day, 20 May, we luckily succeed in reaching Camp 4 – during the early afternoon.

The sight which greets us there is one of devastation: the tentpoles of a crushed three-man tunnel tent protrude from masses of blown snow like broken ribs. Nobody has been here for eleven days. The small igloo tent has fared better, but is not big enough to house all three of us.

I will not accept that this is the end to all our hopes! With the Sherpas, we extract the remnants of the buried tent, splint its ribs and patch it up as best we can. It should make an emergency shelter for Hermann and me. Nawang can have the red igloo. Ang Chappal and Nga Temba wish us luck and disappear round the corner of our little camping niche to head off down the fixed ropes on the steep blank ice.

It is a long night, very long. At the first glimmer of day we start our preparations for leaving, an irksome business in the makeshift tent. We can only move one at a time, and even putting on boots involves lying down and wriggling in a complicated sequence of acrobatics. Nawang prepares breakfast as we sort out the oxygen gear. As I am to be the trail-blazer, I set off ahead of the others at 6 o'clock, with just one bottle of oxygen. Hermann and Nawang will follow shortly, bringing two bottles each. After I have gone, however, their apparatus gives them some problems and they do not get away until 7 o'clock. Meanwhile I stamp laboriously up into the white solitude. Sporadic eddies of air spatter me with cold powder snow. On the steeper slopes, the surface has been compacted by storms and shatters into angular flakes at every step. It is Herculean toil. I feel like an elephant who has taken the notion to walk up a slope, only to find himself too heavy for the ground.

Zigzagging makes no difference, and I decide to keep stomping straight up, the polygonous flakes often reaching to my knees. I puff like a locomotive, but have the feeling that I am making good progress despite the steep gradient. I know that at any moment my apparatus could cut out, but put my trust in luck and don't worry about it. Already I am over 8000 metres. My snow goggles gave me some trouble at the beginning. The glass kept misting over. Our face masks had all been individually adjusted for a tight fit, yet mine was still allowing a small amount of damp air to escape into the inside of my goggles. I tried going without them, keeping my eyelids half closed, but the dazzling glare off the snow would not permit this for long. Now I wear them propped slightly off my nose to allow air in at the sides, and this seems to work. I have also discovered breathing becomes easier if I incline my head forward, but I have to remember to look up from time to time to keep on the right course.

The furrowed, rust-bright final wall of Makalu is directly above me now, bordered on each side by ridges, and crowned with two small summits, quite close to each other and joined by a rim of snow. Meanwhile, I continue up the slabby wind-pressed slopes, working in the direction of a distinct and steep couloir. I only stop when I reach a kind of shelf, probably masking a hidden crevasse, at about 8200 or 8150 metres. Then I turn round and gaze out beyond the white summits of Little Makalu and Chomo Lönzo to the blue-brown plateau of the Tibetan Highlands, mountain chains and flatlands fading to infinity. To my left rises the mighty pyramid of Everest, proffering its beautiful East Face, and the audacious bulk of Lhotse. Two tiny dots have appeared now, little coloured figures, Hermann and Nawang, following my winding footsteps. I take off my mask and set the rucksack down on the sparkling ledge. Only now do I remember to take some pictures.

Looking up again, I am surprised to see a series of strange stumps sticking out of the snow ahead, one behind the other: this is where, ten days earlier, Hans, Karl and Temba left their tracks deeply impressed in the snow. Subsequent storms must have blown away all the softer snow around each step, leaving these little columns, fossil footprints, some thirty centimetres high or even more. Between them and indeed everywhere the storm could reach, the upper layer of snow has been scoured away to leave a hard, steep, crystalline surface, which only the tips of my crampons will penetrate.

I am pleasantly surprised that the abrupt removal of my oxygen mask, and breathing the thin air has little effect on me. Of course, I am sitting down, resting. Still, I intend to keep an eye on myself on this my first, and probably only oxygen climb. (I could not foresee then that only eight years later I would reach the summit of K2 with Julie Tullis without using supplementary oxygen.)

By and by my two friends catch up . . . their sets clearly working all right now. After a short rest, I lead off again, up the steep slope to the start of the couloir, but then, when I look back, I see Hermann suddenly stop and rip off his mask. The wretched thing has packed up! He decides to keep going without it, but very soon starts to slow down, his movements growing clumsy. It is easy to see the effect the oxygen starvation is having on him, but he does not want to give up: he knows he is in the best shape of any of us. It is obviously time I got the rope out from my rucksack. So I traverse across to a big rock at the left of the couloir, where we can stop and rope up.

Hermann says, when the two men join me, that perhaps he had better turn back after all. His feet are starting to get cold. Nawang and I should have no trouble reaching the summit from here with just one bottle each. In his opinion that ought to be plenty of oxygen.

Here, we are at 8250 metres, standing in the shadows cast by the prominent rocks of the headwall. It is very cold. Unfortunately, something now seems to have gone wrong with Nawang's set as well; a faint whistling indicates that the precious gas is leaking away somewhere. Hermann tries to mend it with one of our spanners, tightening up two of the fittings. The alarming sound stops and we sigh with relief. Then he uses the second spanner to adjust my regulator, which from the state of it, must have been battered at some time by a desperate mountaineer with his ice axe. The head of the arresting-screw had been broken clean off. It means that you need a monkey wrench to fit an oxygen bottle to it. No problem, so long as you don't lose your wrench! Curiously, this was the set that gave us the least trouble of all.

'Lucky old sod!' Hermann smiles at me, as he changes the bottle. Then, 'Have a good day, the pair of you!'

Just then I notice, below some rocks, an oxygen bottle sticking out of the snow – complete with its regulator – presumably left behind during the epic retreat of our second party. I retrieve the precious fitting and slide it down the rope to Hermann, for him to take back. He sets off down: now it is just Nawang and me. It will be our job to bring back the stone for Dietlinde!

Nawang and I work our way up the steep couloir, over rock and snow, only one of us moving at a time as the other belays. Brilliant sunshine outside this gully. Indeed the weather looks beautiful, with just the occasional little gust twirling wisps of spindrift around, but there's no time to waste admiring the view. Up! Up! Every moment could be precious. We cannot know how long our oxygen sets will last, and the higher we are if they do pack up, the greater our chances. We won't need them coming down, that's something . . .

As I belay, I ponder again the pros and cons of climbing 'by fair means', and it is easy to convince myself not to use oxygen another time when heavy equipment proves little more than a talisman!

At a vertical rock step where a dangling rope remains from the first summit attempt Nawang signals urgently that he is again experiencing difficulty with his oxygen. I yank my mask away from my mouth and shout to him. Does he want to try this steep pitch without it? He shakes his head. So we struggle our way up around the right-hand side, like two proboscideans. The fixed rope is clearly just for the descent. Suddenly I notice something wrong with my own breathing, and rip the mask off again. Far from coming as a shock to my system, the thin, cold air outside is a blessed relief! I swallow deep draughts of it, like a thirsty man gulping water – pure, clear . . . and it is only a couple of pitches further on that

I realise part of the reason I feel so light-headed is the paucity of oxygen. Nawang joins me on a little ledge – he, too, is climbing without his mask now – and we sit down to take stock. What are we going to do? It cannot be far up to the ridge – why don't we dump all the superfluous weight here and climb on without it? And as we deliberate and fiddle, we find ourselves striking the offending masks and tubes with our fists. To our amazement, in so doing, we obviously loosen some of the ice that has built up inside, for when we shake them, small fragments tumble out. To my surprised relief I find I am able to breathe through my mask as well as before. The rough treatment has also helped Nawang's set, although whether he sets it to deliver one or four litres a minute, he gets the same amount – or rather, not quite enough. All the same, he prefers to go on with it, than without. We leave a thermos flask and an ice hammer behind, and set off again, up between some rocky blocks towards the summit ridge. This at least I feel sure that we will reach. Perhaps the summit, too, but I dare not let myself believe that yet, even though reason tells me there is not much in the way to stop us. Still, at this height every single step you make is a gift – you have no right to it.

We reach the summit ridge! So that's 8400 metres! A gentle, almost horizontal ridge it is, along which we can easily walk side by side, as if on a sloping roofhang, but we know that above the ridgepole to our left, the ground must certainly fall away to nothingness.

In front of us now rises – no, floats above the 3000-metre chasm of the Barun – a magical creation, to which we come closer by the minute. It is a true castle of the gods – the highest, final pinnacle of Makalu! My companion lets out a startled shriek – or was it a cry of astonishment? – some muffled words of Tibetan under his mask.

'Nawang,' I seek to reassure him with a calming gesture, 'we can do it!' My words belie the fact that I, too, am deeply moved at the sight of this fierce, lonely, beautiful ice-covered structure, rising nakedly into the clear blue sky and wrapped around by the intermittent sparkle of thousands of tiny, floating ice crystals. It might not have been the right response to Nawang's call, but our masks hide every expression on our faces, make words unintelligible.

We take the last steps along the flat ridge. Then stop. The summit! There it is, right before us!

The final seventy metres are incredibly exposed. Steep flutings of snow rear up like surf from the blue depths, to connect, as a thin hanging bridge, the first, lower, summit with the second, which towers a full fifty metres higher. The rusty-brown rocks beneath are clad in a tracery of shimmering ice. The snow has been blown up by storms from the giant walls of the mountain, extending them skywards, so that the two sides now meet in a piped seam, so fine that in places you could pinch it between your fingers. I cast a glance back at Nawang – and he nods, silently.

Up we go!

The first summit is safely behind us: in the steep crystalline surface below the white piping I hack out a place large enough for Nawang and me to stand in. It is quite exposed: I cannot resist the temptation to look over the other side. Through a tiny gap, I see clouds, and beyond them, directly below me, the characteristic outline of P 8010, a pinnacle on Makalu's South-East Ridge, first climbed by two Czechoslovaks in 1976. There, too, is the steep final wall of Makalu, scene of a tragic Czech–Spanish ascent and the way by which a strong Japanese party earlier reached the top. This is momentary. My main concern is Nawang: now that he is close to this unearthly summit, this abode of the gods which so affected him lower down on the ridge, will he revert to his earlier confusion . . . and not want to climb it?

With this in mind, I had not stopped on the first summit, but run out the rope to its end. I need not have worried: on reaching the fore-summit, he regards the airy ridge, this Jacob's Ladder of snow leading across deep immeasurable space to the loftier summit, warily and with unconcealed amazement, but he does not falter for a moment. And as he comes across it, balancing his every step by thrusting his ice axe firmly in the snow, I am struck by how quickly and confidently he moves.

Two days ago, Nawang had told me: 'If we get to the summit, you will be very happy – and I some.' Now, to my astonishment, he exuberantly flings his arms around me on the narrow stance, exclaiming how happy he is! It gives me more pleasure than I can say.

Very slowly, every nerve in me tight, step by cautious step, hold by hard-won hold, I carve us out a passage with my axe up along the white rim, to reach a small rocky patch. With a sound belay, I carefully watch Nawang across, then go on . . . Suddenly, I am aware of an apex of snow against the blue sky only five metres above my head, a perfectly regular form out of which, to right and left, stick thin wands of bamboo.

My surprise lasts a moment only. Like a flash it hits me: this is the summit!

I inch towards it. The intangible gift of sky and earth has become reality. MAKALU! Here, in front of me. I sink to my knees, and clutch the highest tip of the snow with both hands. This point where all the ridges of the mountain come together, this Makalu is mine!

A wave of unbelievable joy washes over me, and I am strangely excited before this unique summit, this icy point in the sky.

I make room for Nawang, I have to move to the other side of the summit. There, beside a yellow oxygen bottle which was probably left by the Czech–Spanish expedition, I thrust in my axe and belay my companion. Up he comes! Just a couple of metres apart, we stand facing each other, the white summit of Makalu between us, and below us the ridges of the mountain, and clouds and peaks, and the silhouette of Everest in the distance. More clouds are moving in from the west . . .

We should not stay up here too long. I want to embrace Nawang, to shake hands with him and say '*Berg Heil!*' but he is ignorant of summit rites, and has in any case already conveyed his joy to me, lower down. Now he takes off his oxygen mask and stands mutely regarding the scene, eyes filled with wonder. Finally, he unscrews the regulator before ramming his near-empty cylinder into the summit snow; I follow suit, except that first I must rummage in my sack for the monkey wrench. Neither of us thinks to look at the gauges: regardless of how much gas we have left, we don't intend to use any going down. Then, as if in silent understanding, we press each other's hand, and I take a few photographs – close-ups, for you could not step back.

Perhaps it was the racing clouds, fear that a storm might catch us out up here; or maybe it was the euphoria of reaching the summit – impossible as that had seemed only a few days ago when I was coughing my heart out down below – I don't know why, but I forgot all about the flags I was carrying in my pocket and which I meant to photograph up here. So much had happened . . . since I fled to the jungle in such desperation, convinced beyond all doubt that my dreams could no longer come true . . . now, to be standing here, above the world, not just in my thoughts, but in flesh and blood, body and soul . . . this was like the wingbeats of destiny, a magical floating feeling, against which the everyday world had no place.

Not until we are below the lower summit again do I realise my omission. Oh, Lordy! What will they say back home when there are no pictures of the Austrian flag, or the Alpenverein flag, or any of the others, on the summit? Hastily, I press my camera into Nawang's hands so that at least we shall get a picture of the flags on the summit ridge! One thing we did not forget: the stone from the top for Dietlinde! From the last rocks under the snow summit, we have brought several samples: granite, quartz and a kind of dark slate. But now we must hurry off the ridge as fast as we can, for the storm, heralded by the wild clouds, is already upon us. We urgently need to get into the shelter of the couloir. We reached the top at 1.30 p.m., and have every hope of making it all the way down to our camp on the Makalu La this evening.

We manage it: at around 5 p.m. our Sherpa friends Ang Chappal and Nga Temba embrace us in the ruins of Camp 4, and at around 8 o'clock, after an exhausting descent to the saddle, a beaming Hermann welcomes us into Camp 3. The first 1000 metres lie behind us. But the night is a calamitous one for me: I am awakened by the tormenting pains of snow blindness, my penalty for taking off my goggles several times when climbing the rocks of the couloir. I treat myself right away with a variety of eye drops, and Hermann concocts some special goggles for me using sticking plaster, with narrow slits to see through. Wearing these, I stumble off next morning, with him belaying me. The cold air seems to help the pain – I can see slightly better – and after a few hours, following first the fixed ropes then retracing the familiar route across the glacier, we reach Camp 1, 1200 metres lower. I sleep there for a couple of hours, the sleep of the dead, lying in the snow outside the tents – and then we put another 800 metres behind us to arrive in Base Camp. Now, as I peer up through the thickening dusk with my least-affected eye, it seems like a dream that only yesterday afternoon I was standing up there on top with Nawang Tenzing.

A few days later, on 25 May, our porters having come from

Spirits of the air in the Western Cwm of Mount Everest. *Below*, Ang Chappal, Kurt and Nga Temba have a glass of chang in Solu Khumbu.

The full moon disappears behind a peak above the Barun valley. *Below and facing*, the magic forest of Yang Lhe, where I retreated in desperation to nurse my high-altitude Makalu cough. Here I recovered my health.

Our porters from Tashigang in the snows of the Kongma La. *Below*, Makalu (8481 m) rises high above the Barun forests.

Tashigang for us, we set off on the return march. No longer is this a journey through deep snow, but one taking us through rhododendron forests in bloom . . .

In Yang Lhe the birds are singing. I feel so happy and thankful. For everything. An inexpressible energy will accompany me from now on. What it is, I don't know. We all leave here changed. We were in the palace of the gods – and that, perhaps, is what alters our lives.

*

It was surprising, with how much courage and humour Hans and Karl managed their painful return across the mountain passes. They knew that was the price for the top. To the rest of us, it meant a lot to see that for them, too, the blossoming trees were a splendour, and the chang-parties put on for us by the locals, a pleasure. We had every reason to feel happy. Even if we had not achieved the traverse we desired, each of us had fulfilled a life's wish: to stand on top of Makalu. And Didi, Dietlinde, smiled too, hugging her summit stone; she had never envisaged going to the top herself.

Even if it does not appear so at first glance, this had been quite a special enterprise: between the first party reaching the summit and the last, three full weeks elapsed. We had all helped each other, and in that way everybody had his chance.

Moreover, Hermann had put into practice, for the first time on an expedition to an eight-thousander, his idea of including Sherpas as totally equal partners in the venture, with their own claims to the summit and the load-ferrying being the business of everyone, with no exceptions.

It may seem remarkable, too, that our food provisions came almost entirely from Nepal. And oxygen? Today, I think that with such a team, we would have been much better off without it, particularly considering our good acclimatisation.

For myself, Makalu proved an unexpected turning point: within the space of fifteen months I was to stand on the summits of three eight-thousanders.

Depot Kurt

This was the name given to me by Pierre – Pierre Mazeaud, the
one-time Sports Minister of France who led the 1978 French Everest
Expedition, on which I took part as mountaineer and cameraman.
We were sitting having breakfast one radiant morning in the Valley
of Silence, in the spacious communal tent of Camp 2 at about 6500
metres. Suddenly, the Sports Minister wrinkled his nose. *'Dieu,
quelle odeur de fromage!'* he exclaimed. 'My God, Kurt, what is
that terrible cheesy smell?' He sniffed the air around him. *'Ça ne
vient pas de la France.* It's certainly not a French one!' And he
threw a sharp glance in my direction. *'Impossible!* It seems to be
coming from these boxes. Kurt . . .?'

I retreated into deep silence, for he did have a point: the cheese
in question was mine.

By rights, it ought not to have been up here at all: these boxes
were supposed to contain only my official film equipment. One,
however, was highly unofficial, and anything but FRAGILE, as it
boldly maintained. Even back in Base Camp the French had been
funny about the Nepalese yak-milk cheese (as big as a waggonwheel)
which I had bought at the Takshindu dairy, refusing to allow it to
enter the Valley of Silence. 'We can't waste Sherpa power carrying
it. If you want it you can roll it up the glacier!' Jean Afanassieff had
been quite sarcastic, and the whole expedition was quick to point
out, 'We have our own cheese, Kurt – French cheese!' at which
they all nodded emphatically. But these dainty French cheeses were
such minuscule mouthfuls that you could easily juggle several in one
hand: nothing like enough for an Austrian appetite! (Otherwise, I

Internationale Makalu Expedition   **JME**
अन्तराष्ट्रीय मकालु रक्सपेडिसन
International Makalu Expedition 1978/2034-34

Good relations with Himalyan spirits continued beyond this mountain.

had no complaints about their excellent food. Only in the upper camps were you aware of the relentless modern tendency towards 'ever lighter, ever faster' . . . An excess of superlight freeze-dried packets certainly kept you running, converting the slogan into drastic reality . . . by way of tummy ache . . . 'ever lighter, ever faster!') As I am a champion of genuine, natural provisions on the mountain, I agonised long over my gigantic cheese wheel. Eureka! Wasn't I entitled to a film Sherpa? A film box was emptied out . . . and half the waggonwheel stowed inside; a second film box accommodated the second half of the nutritious round . . . then the Sherpa marched towards Camp 2. He carried the valuable load with the utmost care (valuable, that is, to me, even if not as fragile as he was led to believe). I couldn't prevent Mazeaud's nephew, our doctor (anxious to declare his goodwill for the film) from carrying the other box up into the Valley of Silence, but I hoped he would never discover what he had done. All these thoughts passed through my mind, while Pierre Mazeaud, head down like a bloodhound, snuffled his way round the tent, remarking as he did so, 'That smells (*sniff, sniff*) like Nepalese cheese. Kurt, what do you know about this?'

I remain mum. To crown it all, he's a lawyer, I thought. What will I say? Because one thing was clear: the moment of truth was very close now . . .

'*Halte-là!* It's coming from this box!' Pierre was triumphant. 'One of your film boxes, Kurt!' And he skewered me to the tent wall with a glance, as only a lawyer can who has just driven his victim into a blind corner. I made a clean breast of it, opened the box, cut off a slice of yak cheese for Pierre, saw with satisfaction how he munched into it, even with a short laugh – so then, it was not that bad an idea . . . was it?

But suddenly his expression is back as it was. He pontificates: 'Kurt, you have more gear than anyone else on this expedition. Look around you! Boxes everywhere. Wherever we sit, wherever we stand: everywhere, it says KURT DIEMBERGER – FRAGILE . . . *ou pas!*' And he pointed to the clearly far from delicate cheese.

'Oh, come, steady on,' I tried to calm my explosive Gallic friend. 'You know I have to make the film.' But I knew that bringing in the film was only part of the story; really, I did have a lot of things.

Unfortunately, here in Camp 2, this was becoming so evident

because my well-proven 'depot system' had not had a real chance to get going. (I can't tell you if I invented it, but the idea is always and everywhere to have personal depots – on Everest that means a box in Camp 1, another in Camp 2, a bag in Camp 3 . . . so that wherever you arrive, your gear is waiting; but, as I said, for the moment it had all bottlenecked in Camp 2.) Pierre Mazeaud – with a wide move of his hand, as if delivering a great speech to parliament – affected not to have heard my justification. 'Kurt,' he said, 'you cannot deny that it is true . . . You need the Place de la Concorde for all your paraphernalia . . . and even that wouldn't be big enough.' He took a deep breath (no wonder, for such a tirade at 6500 metres of altitude). 'I mean,' he continued, 'that besides my logistics for this expedition, which is to put France on the summit of Everest, I need a separate logistical plan for the depots of Kurt Diemberger . . .'

I was contrite. It is true that I like to have a down jacket waiting for me in Camp 3 and, let us say, another one in Camp 1 or 2, and – of course – one in Base Camp as well; moreover, if possible, a sleeping – no, *two* sleeping-bags in Base Camp, a further one in Camp 1 and then one that stays in Camp 4 – because I hate to be running uphill and downhill all the time, overloaded with gear, sleeping-bags, mattresses! Anybody can see that mine is a good system! Let me just add, for all those who might be saying, 'We never would have thought that Diemberger is so lazy,' that when you're making a mountain film, you are already quite loaded – simply having to carry the movie camera – and, far more than any other expedition member, you are obliged to keep clambering up and down, to and fro.

So, please excuse my depot habits . . . (apparently, I have not fully digested Pierre's parliamentary preaching). But I also want to toss another positive aspect on to the balance. I had already initiated this system of depots long before I ever dared to dream of getting to the Himalaya. I was even using it back when I was a crystal hunter and needed to shoulder the weight of hammers and chisels and of course the heavy burden of rock samples and crystals which I found high up on the mountain.

To save always having to carry the heavy tools up to the same parts of the massif, I told myself the best thing would be to simply squirrel them away up there. Thus was my system born on Mont Blanc. (There are several good crystal sites and almost all of them high up; between guiding trips or when the weather was too bad for a big climb, I used to like going up there. Crystal-hunting is something marvellous!)

But we are only at the beginning: enter the marmots! (Or, more precisely, their burrows.) Because there is no better place to hide a hammer than a marmot hole – safe from avalanches, out of sight, and moreover no effort involved. Hammer and chisel into one burrow, the stove into the next, a bottle of whisky into a third and . . . no problem, there are enough of these holes! The first time I went back, not long afterwards, I ran into a problem: I found the right place easily enough, but then I had to search like a dachshund – there were almost a hundred holes in the slope, and everything, everywhere looked very similar. Remedy: I carved a mark into a rock above the hammer hole when I eventually found it, and bore in mind that the whisky hole was five steps to the left, and the stove was stuffed into the tube of another dwelling eight steps to the right, while obliquely below . . . It is clear that every system must first be developed, it doesn't simply fall from the sky.

Ever since then the depot system has worked brilliantly. I was so convinced of it (and still am) that eventually I applied it to my everyday life as well. However, as this became more extensive and complicated, the more years that passed, I have to confess that the system also had its drawbacks: either you are lucky enough to find a wife who is *au fait* with everything, or you conscientiously feed every move into a computer – otherwise it can happen that you don't always know where is what or what is where.

For example, I am still searching – two years on – for one of my Leica cameras. No small thing, really, but it has been two years already . . . And it is not the only thing I'm after. Such a search can be full of emotions – and the pleasure, if you strike the motherlode, is great. I enter now into the 'thoughtful' part of this chapter – it reveals all the pros and cons of the depot method, which I still favour – even if I haven't yet located the Leica. I recommend it to the reader who wants to follow me in my search for something lost, to rope up with me – we will range worldwide . . .

To begin with, I think: Now where is it likely to be (whatever it is)?

But it doesn't come to mind. Which, as we all know, is destined to step up the pulse rate.

So again, more heatedly, the age-old question, such as was demanded no doubt by a Stone Age ancestor hunting for his flint axe: Where on earth can the bally thing be? (Variations like 'In heaven's name . . .', or 'Where the bloody hell is it . . .' may be of more recent vintage, but are nevertheless equally ineffective.)

Now, there is only one remedy: to calm down, and think.

So, I make a start and work through the most probable places where the thing could be. That is – at home, naturally, which means in Salzburg, or Bologna, or Portomaggiore.

In Salzburg is my father.
In Bologna is my wife.
In Portomaggiore is my mother-in-law.

As the year passes, all these places are in turn my home. Therefore, if I'm searching for something, I know that books and slides and mountaineering equipment are most probably in Salzburg. In Bologna, where my wife lives, things do not usually go astray. And in Portomaggiore, at Mother-in-law's place, I have to look around if it's a case of missing garments or things to be mended. (My wife loves decentralisation of work; basically, her own depot system, in a wider sense.)

If I don't find what I'm looking for in any of these three places, then it gets more complicated. The thing may then lie anywhere in the world between Kathmandu and Hawaii. And if I want to dig it out of my subconscious memory, I must take to a couch (psychologists work to the same method), and ponder for some hours . . .

This business of order, or should I say, the instinct for order, is inherent to our family. My father and I are fanatics for order. This may be the very reason we mislay so much. It is why my father passes hours engineering new systems for locating items more easily. I, for one, think he's a genius – he is always dreaming up some new and logical system, but mostly in my absence. When I return home, he proudly shows off his latest scheme – and I groan, for I couldn't find things before. My father knows that – and therefore he attempts somehow to work universal principles into the programme: last time I came home I found the contents of two wardrobes carefully distributed according to the specific gravity of each item! What have I been looking for since then? Everything. But that's by the way.

While I am floating on my couch across countries and continents, I visit many friends; and thus can now introduce the reader to the surprises in store for a depot-being.

The system, as I've already hinted, does have its weak points: when, after two years of exploring the recesses of my mind, I went to fetch my suit from Herbert Tichy's house in Vienna, he said to me: 'I've given it to the postman.' How come? 'I racked my brains for quite a while about this mysterious suit. It didn't fit me. But the postman looks brilliant in it.'

You do have to be careful with writers: they are always so lost in their own stories . . .

Vienna, one way or another, has not proved the most satisfactory location for me: recently some mountaineering gear, a couple of books, and other personal items arrived from there in a cardboard box. Inge had got married. Yes – time doesn't stand still! (Everybody will understand the practicality of keeping a climbing rope elsewhere – not always having to fetch it from Italy.) Oh yes, another rope is sitting at José Manuel Anglada's pad in Barcelona, my Spanish depot. By the way, recently I brought him a key, a very big key, two feet long! I bought it at a flea market in Bologna because I knew that José collects keys. However, after a short glance at the antique piece, he said to me, it was a beautiful key, very fine craftsmanship, but, well . . . from Italy . . . not genuine; even so, he was pleased to have it. I wonder perhaps when I brought him the fake artefact, whether I put the real Leica in the bottom of his wardrobe? Perhaps it sleeps snugly there, as if in a marmot's tunnel? You see, in Barcelona, you hide everything. It is like a Spanish Naples. The fact that Anglada still has his valuable key collection is certainly due to the three special locks on his door. What lies there, lies safely; so if that's where my Leica is, it will be all right.

By the way: you can also get pleasant surprises with this system.

Not long ago, I was 'presented' with a pair of skis out of the blue; Orazio and Annie from the Squirrel Albergo in Courmayeur had dug them out of their cellar, and discovered 'KURT' written on them. Now I remember: those were the skis with which I descended the Tirich Glacier in the Hindu Kush thirteen years ago . . . My God, where things end up!

Another reliable place is the Black Forest. Even if I don't know precisely what I have deposited there. That is where Trudy lives; she is sixty-nine and comes from Berlin . . . she always transforms my loose-knit Austrian soul into military shape . . . for days I sit there framing and cleaning my slides. Moreover, she knows everything as far as the natural sciences are concerned; I can listen to her for hours. Thirty years ago we stood on top of the Gross Venediger in the Austrian Alps . . . It is true, when you stay at her place you have to get up as early as at the Kürsinger mountain hut – every day an alpine start!

But let us get closer to home: Munich . . . a traffic-node in all my journeyings. There, at Uli's, resides my film gear, thus saving me from fastidiously declaring it to our brave Austrian Customs officials every time I make a frontier crossing. (Perhaps the big business conglomerates with their multinational branches have also learned from the marmots?) Yes, and a projector and God knows what else is stashed near a Bavarian lake with Gerda and Volkmar. There I was recently shown the 'yellow card' because their lobby door could hardly be made to close any more – so a part of my gear is lying now over the road with my artist friend Herbert Finster. In the near future, I shall carry some miniature paintings up Everest for him (as a sort of a 'pennant' for art) – so that he can know his is the highest art of all, even if the exhibition attracts the least number of visitors.

Further to the north, into the Pfalz: there in Kaiserslautern in Klaus and Brigitte's cellar I have, besides a trunk of amethysts and agates from the nearby volcanic area, a whole row of boxes filled with copies of my book *Summits and Secrets*. From there, it is not far to Luxembourg with its cheap flights to America . . . my next depot is in New Jersey at my cousin Elke's. The depot in London, however, at Ken Wilson's, had to be dispersed. When his wife had their second baby, he needed the space himself.

Back across the ocean – Hawaii! A box of slides, forgotten after a lecture to the former King's family, the Kawananakoas.

Auf Wiedersehen, Carol and Dudie, Phil and Fran, Elelule . . . I need the slides again – and not by post! See you next year . . .

Estes Park, Colorado: a pair of mountain boots – but I'm not quite sure. Are they still with Michael Covington and Steve Komito? (With Steve, who sold and soled boots for all the mountaineers in the west?) Or did I leave them with Gordon-the-millionaire in Nevada? I'll have to write a card.

Canada, Banff: a box of dinosaur bones in Evelyn's bedroom. They'll be all right there a bit longer.

Los Angeles: different things at different places.

Not to forget! Kathmandu: aluminium cases full of Himalayan gear with Miss Hawley and duffel bags at Mr Kalikote's. I can start a small expedition at any time at short notice. Before heading off I would then sit again with the 'living archive', Miss Hawley. This charming lady, who you would be justified in calling a landmark of Kathmandu, and who knows really everything that's happened in the Himalaya, having painstakingly recorded it over many years – such as the 'horse race', as I called the legendary page from her archives which we have discussed from time to time. She keeps a table of all the mountaineers who have climbed 8000-metre peaks. You can see quite clearly how they are proceeding from year to year – this one has two, that in the meantime has three, one has four . . . And then there are two who have five each: Reinhold Messner and myself. We have been running neck and neck for some time . . .

This will certainly have changed again by next year, because at this moment Reinhold is on his way to Mount Everest, and for my part, it's only two weeks till I go as well – I don't know why destiny requires us to be stumbling over each other's legs all the time. It's not intentional, although we have always been on good terms and in the past have enjoyed talking about mountaineering. I even think that for a while I once had a suitcase at his home in Villnöss.

(*from my Diary, 1980*)

But on to other places. In Warsaw, this wonderful, vital town – artists; museums; courageous lovely people, full of ideas – there, sadly, I have no depot. When I was lecturing and travelling around the country, I wanted to leave various bits and pieces behind, but my wife, who was with me, meticulously packed everything away, down to the last sock . . . Now my Leica flashes into my mind again, which I am still hunting for – before this book appears in Italian, I must run through my list of depots carefully, otherwise my wife won't be asking where I left the Leica, but: Why did he leave it there?

Düsseldorf: High Camps 3 and 5 – if you're overweight I recommend the latter, rather than the glorified jogging through the woods adopted by my colleagues – since the brave Amazonian Erica, in her fifth-floor apartment, has no elevator. At Wolfgang's (Camp 3), however, I have been working for two years already on a non-urgent soundtrack. Every time the wind blows me into town. (I've got two boxes there: perhaps the Leica is in Düsseldorf?)

Mon Dieu! How could I forget France in my round-the-world couch trip? I have not yet conjured up the *Petit Bateau*, the little boat in Cazères! Louis Audoubert, Marc Galy, the two Pyrenean specialists, are now more often travelling in the big mountains of the world. Louis, small, compact, blue-eyed, always laughing, a bundle of energy, soloing the Brouillard Ridge to the top of Mont Blanc in six hours; twice up the entire Peuterey Ridge, once even in winter – the 'wildest priest of the Alps'! In the end, he was left with only one crampon on the Peuterey Ridge – and his faith. It is true he had held a mass on the summit of Aiguille Noire just before. Now he is not allowed to do that any more – he got married. He has a lovely wife, and still his faith, this Louis! When he was a priest, I became godfather to his sister's baby son – and left my copy of good old Dyhrenfurth's book *Baltoro* there. It is said to have journeyed into Spain where mountaineers are preparing a new expedition with it. Yes, in the Pyrenees at the time I picked up French and Spanish, and puffed Gauloises for three months – although I was a non-smoker. (But that is a different story.) Altogether, it's incredible how useful this depot system proves to be – fantastically so, despite several flaws. I want to thank all my depot-managers – and manageresses.

Back to Italy: I haven't been in Trieste for a long time, even though I'm a member of the local Club Alpino. Bianca, my agile ropemate on several climbs, is unfortunately now always on the road herself, never there. In Treviso, however, where a kind elderly lady lives, Telene, who makes really outstanding spaghetti, there I stop quite often before I visit Gianni in his shoe factory, who has equipped my expeditions from the very beginning with mountain boots – there are always boots of mine at his place.

And so, I get to Varese once more, to Tona and the children, take a pair of skis and mountain equipment for Mont Blanc because

I've got some tourists to guide; we are having a pizza in the garden, looking through the trees at our dear Monte Rosa. *Arrivederci*, darlings . . .

When the Mont Blanc trip is over, I want to take another look at my marmot holes up there on the mountain, before returning home to Bologna!

To Teresa, my patient wife.

*

A propos Mont Blanc: I was there again recently, back where I learned the crystal hunter's wisdom, the principle of the depots, right at the place of its discovery. By the marmot holes below the Aiguille de Triolet. I found the mark on the rock without difficulty. And the hole with the hammer, too. It had grown quite rusty, but – I mean – two years had passed since the last time. Immediately, I start looking for the stove, the chisel and the whisky bottle . . . Nothing. Have I got it wrong? Impossible. Then it dawns on me: these diligent marmots! The wretches have dug so many new holes in two years. I am wandering over the slope, to and fro, up and down . . . where is the whisky, where is the chisel, where is the stove? How many metres to the left and right have I got to go? Surely the whisky will have matured nicely in the meantime? In vain: I didn't find it. If you come across it, remember to toast me. The stove didn't show up, either. Perhaps a marmot with a flair for invention has incorporated it into the architecture of his larder. So, well, I'm sipping cold water from the stream. At least I found the rusty hammer.

But something else besides I haven't yet found. What was it? Something else in the marmot holes? What was the reason for this voyage down memory lane? Oh yes . . . if anybody knows where my Leica is – I haven't yet given up hope!

PS: I would ask all my friends who read this book, please don't start digging in your wardrobes and cellars and then send me an avalanche of parcels! Already one has told me on the phone he found some old mountain trousers at his place, and might they perhaps be mine? I told him, please, see if they fit the postman first!

PPS: Two weeks before going to press, quite unexpectedly I bumped into Pierre Mazeaud on his way up to Mont Blanc – the ancien ministre des sports et des loisirs carried a mighty rucksack. I was surprised – despite his charming companion. '*Seulement une petite tente* . . . just a high camp,' explains my friend, after greeting me cordially. Then he quickly climbs higher, too fast for me to follow him with my client.

Next day I'm looking everywhere on Mont Blanc for a high camp – I cannot find one: has my friend secretly become a convert to my depot system? 'DEPOT PIERRE'?

(from my Diary)

'Take One' . . . on the summit of Everest

Eight thousand five hundred metres. Rotten rocks, shattered by the extreme temperatures of high altitude, crumble as I lean back against them, breathing deeply, rucksack at my side, camera on my knees. I am not so much sitting as crouching in a wind-sculpted open scoop in the snow. Across its edge, I gaze down the icy roof of the highest mountain on earth, and along the flutes of the East Face. In the depths, some three or four thousand metres below me, lies the Kangshung Glacier. An irregular pattern of mainly snow-covered moraine, it flows eastwards, past the silhouettes of Shartse and Pethangtse, and on towards the last granite spires of Chomo Lönzo. Above them, dominating everything on this side and masking the indigo shadow of the Arun valley, rises the beautiful pyramid of Makalu, the only 'big' mountain till my eyes reach Kangchenjunga, far out on the horizon . . . A beautiful day! The day of the century – a gift from the gods one might be tempted to say – a gift to whoever is climbing to the top of Everest today! For me, it is.

I am alone. Nearby, Lhotse, 8511 metres high, thrusts up like a crystal, the fourth highest mountain on earth, steep, brusque, cold. Silence and no wind at all . . . not here at least, where I am . . .

You must film! The thought tugs me from just quietly allowing my mind to slide from peak to peak, floating through this enormous space below . . . That is bound to happen more often this day, for on the one hand, here I am, climbing to the top of Chomolungma to fulfil a great wish – it seems incredible to me, even up here at 8500 metres, that it can yet come true, but logic says, 'Yes, it will' – and on the other, I am here to record the ascent of my French comrades on film, and even sound on the summit . . . I am cameraman to the French.

Where are the boys, by the way?

Kurt, shoot! Coming up, outlined against the Western Cwm, I can see their orange shapes, and I manoeuvre the figures into the frame of the viewfinder – Jean and Nicolas with, in front of them, a Sherpa. Obliquely above them, closer to me, I capture Pierre – Pierre Mazeaud, my ropemate, though we will not be using the rope until we get higher up, somewhere around the South Summit, certainly for the traverse of the sharp, exposed ridge to the very top. At present, it is every man for himself as we move unbelayed. No fall, not the slightest stumble, is permitted here without sending you irretrievably down into the depths.

To move freely is essential for me anyway. On a rope, I could never traverse off the route, as I have here, in order to film the others when they climb through the horizon's jagged blue line. It is an overwhelming horizon . . . peak following peak, and to the south the shimmering ocean of clouds with, beyond them – India!

A super shot! Despite the difficulty of holding my breath in the thin air so as not to joggle the picture, I feel happy, content, like a fisherman with a great catch! The camera whirrs, and my comrades pass by, heading on further, up towards the deep blue sky . . . Aah, hell – the film magazine is finished! I need to put a new one in . . . from my rucksack, beside me in the niche . . . Panting, I open the lid, albeit too late for another shot. While I am rummaging I remember how, with such high hopes, Pierre Mazeaud and I climbed up to this place yesterday, along with Ang Dawa, the faithful Sherpa, the only one to remain with us in the storm two days ago. It was a tiring struggle, not least because of the filming and getting higher at the same time, a heavy load of nearly twenty kilos on your back. Besides smaller items, the three of us carried two bottles of oxygen each – one for breathing, and the second for . . . at long last, Pierre and I decided to dump our ambitions and the bottles here and to descend to the South Col at about 8000 metres; we had been breathing only two litres a minute – not enough for what we were doing, a truth that dawned on us when it was too late. Thus, the desired summit was out of the question.

Today, we are again at this place, where all previous expeditions established their highest camp – around 8500 metres. We decided against such a shelter and so did the Germans of Dr Karl Herrligkoffer's expedition. Three of them reached the top yesterday – Hans Engl, Hubert Hillmaier and Sepp Maag. In any case, Pierre and I would never have been able to establish a camp here, with only the help of Ang Dawa. That is why we thought to come up this morning on a single bottle each from the South Col, and then continue to the top with the second one from our cache. Hopefully, that would last till we get back here, though that is not so critical: descending you need incredibly less air and effort at high altitude. Meanwhile, we are no longer alone: a couple of Sherpas have decided to join us, with Jean Afanassieff and Nicolas Jaeger, our two 'youngsters'. The Sherpas will accompany our group to about 8600 metres, where the gradient rises steeply to the South Summit, then they will go down.

High time to move, Kurt! Already the figures above you are too small in the viewfinder! I get my things together, deposit the used bottle, connect the full one to the oxygen regulator, go through the awkward process of putting on the mask again, which I had taken off to be able to film better, and continue, step by step, diagonally upwards towards my friends, carefully thrusting the ice axe into the snow at every move . . .

*

There was no way I could foresee, at this moment, that this day was to decide my further career and life – that after it I would continue as 'the cameraman of the eight-thousanders', a title given me by the French. These pages can only be a snatch, a day out of many days on Everest. Five expeditions I have made there, and several other visits to the people of the area. Only once did I reach the top. Which does not matter: 'I go to the mountains for moments like these . . .' Julie Tullis's words might have applied to those minutes spent in the niche on the ridge, looking down over all the peaks and hollows. We thought very much alike, and she was to become my film- and climbing-partner. In her book *Clouds from Both Sides* Julie included our later experiences on Everest.

Since catching my first glimpse of the mountain in 1974, and capturing on celluloid the giant cornices and our icicle-framed faces as Hermann Warth, Nawang Tenzing and I fought our way higher along Shartse's ridge – the East Peak of Everest – I have made six more films about Chomolungma and its people, the most recent in the winter of 1993 with my daughter Hildegard, on Tibetans and their customs to the north-east of the mountain. The twenty years in between have brought many changes in the Himalaya – I have been witness to those now for thirty-five years. There has been true development as well as the odd side-shoots, like speed or competition climbing on big mountains, but you can still find all styles on Everest, mixed like a bouquet of flowers! To enter discussion on them here would lead too far, especially when a brilliant book compiled by Peter Gillman appeared for the fortieth anniversary of the first ascent,* but I think some brief jottings from personal experience and thoughts on the matter might stand well here:

The French enterprise of 1978 was a huge siege-style expedition, with many Sherpas, fixed ropes, and using bottled oxygen. Nearby, Doug Scott was making an attempt on Nuptse in pure alpine style. I take it for granted that a number of readers, spoiled by later speed reports, will smile over our undertaking. But can they ever imagine what a struggle that bloody oxygen load on your back involved? Nowadays, there are still reports about great aided climbs – but their oxygen, which is not usually over-emphasised in the text, weighs so much less than the old 'British air', or even the more modern apparatus of the French that we had. A Russian titanium bottle of the 1990s weighs only 2.2–3.3 kilos! (Against our 7 kilos in the 1970s. That is 36 pounds for two bottles and regulator etc.) This reduction in weight of roughly fifty per cent seems to me an extremely important factor in contemporary 'traditional' ascents. A few more years could pass and hardly anyone will be able to appreciate what an endeavour Edmund Hillary's and Tenzing Norgay's climb had been . . . before their route became a general crowded highway.

*

* Peter Gillman, *Everest, the best writing and pictures of seventy years of human endeavour*, Little Brown, 1993.

In 1981 when Ed came with us to the East Face of Everest as a member of an American expedition (on which my job was that of film director), climbing techniques had already progressed enormously. Without that, we should never have mastered the vertical headwall below the ice monster we called the Helmet. (Two years later, a rocket helped set up a cableway there.) On that first attempt, none of us made it to the summit – however, our film was awarded an Emmy. This was the avalanche-prone face that had so intimidated George Mallory and his companions in 1921, sending them scuttling round to attempt the mountain from the north side. In 1924 George Mallory and Sandy Irvine disappeared in the clouds close to the summit and never returned . . . Three decades later Hillary and Tenzing made their historical climb to the top from the south, but we will never know for sure whether Mallory and Irvine had already reached there before they died.

Another pair of great mountaineers wrote their names into Everest's history for ever: Reinhold Messner and Peter Habeler with the first ascent without supplementary oxygen in the early summer of 1978. Yet another pair, Erhard Loretan and Jean Troillet, in 1986 made the purest modern alpine-style ascent on the mountain, succeeding on the North Face without a tent, but carrying a shovel with which to make snowholes for a bivouac. On the south side any lightweight climbing is handicapped by the big Khumbu Icefall; purists have to suspend their ideology, accept a jolt in their reasoning, and only start their stylistic climbing later. As did Reinhold Messner in 1980, when I was there with the Italians. When his Sherpa left, I 'lent' him Nawang Tenzing, my camera porter, who kindly carried his tent to the site of Camp 3 on the Lhotse Face for an unsuccessful solo attempt. It is altogether impossible for a rope of just two or three people to overcome the permanently collapsing, slowly wandering cascade of ice, which moves at about a metre a day, in an elegant way. Even Doug Scott, before his alpine-style push on Nuptse with Michael Covington and Joe Tasker, brought over two bottles of whisky to the French Base Camp. 'Here is a lightweight contribution,' he said to them, 'for going over your ladders.' His response to the icefall was a human and very welcome one. I think that every hard route decisively interferes with such technique as is possible – or, better, advisable – but of course, it is a matter of respect towards the mountain as well. When filming for the British and Scots on Everest's North-East Ridge in 1985, Julie and I

Hans (*above*) and Karl (*below*) return from their icy bivouac at 8250 metres on Makalu, exhausted and frostbitten, the price of their summit success.

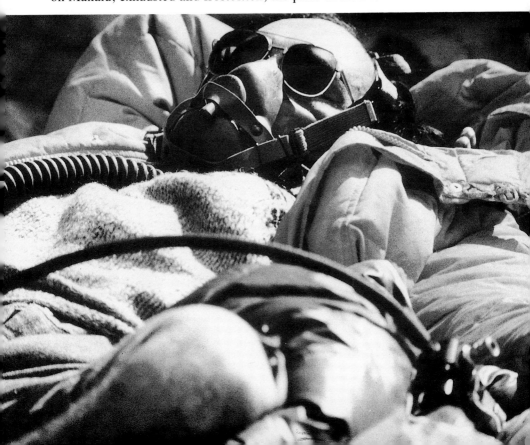

Above left, the razor-sharp summit of Makalu offers no space for photographic manoeuvring, so my picture of Nawang Tenzing has to be a real close-up. The cane behind the oxygen bottle marks the highest point. *Opposite*, climbers can barely be discerned left of centre among the rocks and spindrift at 8000 metres.

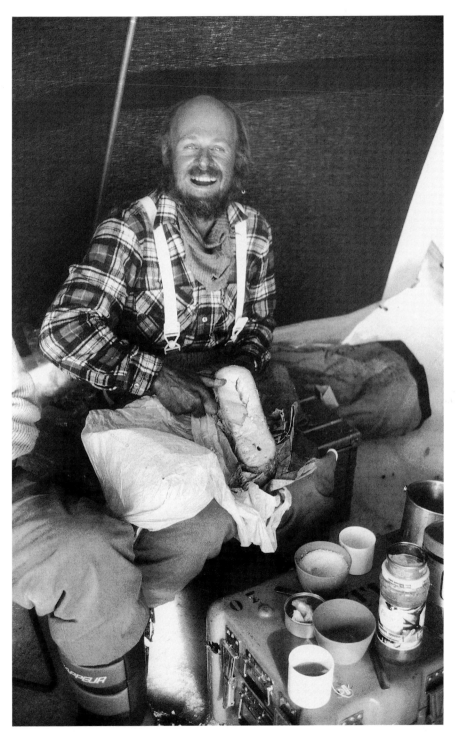

Pierre Mazeaud, above left, makes a grave accusation: 'My God, Kurt, what is that terrible cheesy smell? It certainly isn't a French one!' But I myself thought the smuggled yak cheese was excellent, if unFrench. *Opposite*, yaks grazing at 5000 metres on the pastures below Everest.

Tree ferns on Hawaii.

The highest film team in the world: Kurt and Julie, below right, with Uigur tribesmen and camels on their way via the Shaksgam valley in Sinkiang, China, to big glacier country, to Gasherbrum and to K2.

Thanking the mountain gods on top of Everest.

crawled several times into the snowcaves dug three years before by Chris Bonington, Pete Boardman, Joe Tasker and Dick Renshaw, recognising them as the best protection against the terrible storms which batter that ridge.

I believe a mountain is not there to demonstrate a particular technique at whatever cost, nor to show how good a guy is . . . In my eyes, that is an abuse – a peak is not a measure of skill, but a much bigger thing, an entity, like a big tree standing beside an anthill. You can become the fastest ant and still never understand what a tree really is. On a mountain a human can only try, and sometimes come close to an understanding . . . When we arrive at it, there is no word and no measure.

*

The South Summit! Some 8760 metres (28,750 feet) high. Already higher than anywhere else on earth. My eyes wander across sharp ridges and pointed peaks, into the depths, to the hazy grey-blue of the forests somewhere behind them. An almost tipsy, crazy feeling of height! Everything is removed. Is so far down.

Even Lhotse, reaching up from way below, appears now to be a bit lower. When I worked myself over the snow edge of the South Summit, at first I did not see anybody up here, only the sharp last ridge that continued rising towards the sky in front of me – ever higher! Solitude, unlimited distances in every direction I looked.

Then I discovered Pierre close by, behind a small curved snow formation, sitting on a patch of even ground and pondering on something. He was slowly uncoiling the rope which was to link us from now on. Was he thinking too about the incredible gift of this day? All this space around us? When I look towards Makalu, I believe in the goddess of luck – whichever name you know her by. A strong feeling comes through the air. Yang Lhe? From there her magic blessing reached to the very summit of the big mountain. Does it reach over here, too?

Then Pierre snatches me back from my thoughts. He wants to know if that is really the summit above us, definitely the highest point? I nod in affirmation, for it is as if I had stood up here before: the view is so familiar to me from pictures I had seen. The final ridge, rimmed with cornices above the last rocks and the short, but impressive upthrust of the Hillary Step. Right now, clear against the sky, our two 'youngsters' appear: Jean and Nicolas, who went on ahead, are high on the summit ridge, two tiny figures . . .

Pierre and I rope up. We look at each other. Does he think, as I do, that in the end Everest is actually our 'Mont Blanc'? We have known each other for fifteen years now, so many times planned to climb the White Mountain together and it never worked out. Everest will be our first shared summit . . . We start. Pierre takes the lead. Deep, dark and blue, the sky curves like a dome above the highest point on earth. Out over the immeasurable spaces of Tibet.

Eight thousand eight hundred and forty-eight metres: we are standing on the roof of the world. We are speaking, coughing, embracing each other. We laugh, walk (rather wonkily) from one rim of the summit snows to the other, look down: Tibet, the grey-brown highlands scattered with snow-capped mountains as if they were floating islets of cloud. And at its edge, above long jagged waves of ice rising from blue depths like a swell of surf, Cho Oyu soars in the west, and further still, Shisha Pangma. Makalu, to the south-east, and Kangchenjunga far beyond it at the horizon – thousands of summits in between and hundreds of valleys – yes, it is like the coastline of an ocean.

We look down to earth from the heavens. And we feel in heaven. A day of days!

We have taken off the masks, switched off the oxygen taps; a couple of metres below the highest point, on the southern slope in the wind's shadow, one does not feel the cold. Only on the icy, horizontal crest of the summit, where you can sit as if on a bench, are you hit by a chill, steady draught from the north, blowing off the Tibetan Plateau. The Chinese tripod? Invisible, maybe gone. My French companions are speaking by walkie-talkie to Base Camp, and the radio operators are relaying their words (and our shared happiness) via space to Paris. Pierre, his beard encrusted in frost, excitedly tells his story – complete with gestures, as if he were making a speech in parliament – to all France. Only fractions of a second later his countrymen learn what it is like up here, a 'world first' live transmission from the top of Everest . . . we used a satellite.

A strange 'bridge' then, in 1978.

There was another world-first on top of Everest that day: the first cinematic 'clap', or, as those in the business would say, 'Take One!' Nobody had ever before made a film with people speaking, laughing, telling what they were thinking up there. The means I used were simple: a Mini-Nagra-SN recorder and my 16 mm Bell & Howell magazine camera, which I had to wind up by hand, as it ran by clockwork. At 8600 metres we split some of the weight between us. We took no clapperboard with us to the summit, but did not expect this to present a problem. In an alpine meadow you can just clap your hands to give a signal for synchronising sound to pictures. But now on top of the world, none of the good fellows wants to take off his gloves! Wisely, but an eiderdown 'clap' is imperceptible to the little mike we have. So, I let them keep their gloves on and, instead, yell '*Chac*!' with a single big wave of the arm in front of their faces at the start of a scene on sound. That worked, up to a point . . . but, combined with the jerkiness of the cold camera mechanism, gave the cutting editors in Paris something to get their teeth into. Still, the outcome was great! You can see and hear the joy of those guys, stumbling, beaming, waving and panting their *Chacs*! And Pierre's enthusiastic words . . . Certainly, with delicate art, much of the coughing has been removed from the French sound version, but, I mean, please, that was the first time Frenchmen had stood on rooftop of the world!

Take One! Take Two! Take Three!
    Among the scenes I shot up there is the shadow of my waving hand at the rim of the summit snows, above Tibet. It was a bit of a joke, but great to wave to the world. Perhaps I was influenced by the minister's performance.
    We spent at least an hour on top. For a while I was sitting on the highest – and coldest – park bench in the world, just looking and thinking. It was then that I noticed a lingering expression of disbelief on Pierre's face – but we were here, really here, above the world on a day of days!

It comes hard on you to leave such a fantastic place. I want to carry it with me for ever! Up, Kurt! I say, and turn around on my heels to gather the whole, immense panorama from the top of the world into my lens . . . to Makalu, India, Nepal, Tibet . . . and back to Makalu. Still, I don't want to leave it.

But I must! Soon . . . Something like a frenzy has seized me in an endeavour to retain it all by means of my cameras as the moment of descent draws nearer. Take Six! Take Seven! Take Eight! Take it all with you, every moment. Can you?

Only then, as we leave, the very last minute I find time for it . . . I press my face against the summit-snows and thank the gods.

Om mani padme hum

Death Valley in winter

Pale grass, like white-blonde hair above the salt flats. Snow in the depths. Snow, or salt?

Silky sheen.

It rustles every time the wind passes over, the tufts yield to the pressure of the wave of air then stand up again immediately; only some stalks continue to sway uncertainly to and fro.

The air is cold up here at 2000 metres, here, at the mountain's edge above Death Valley, and in the shade of the rocks there remains even a trace of snow – like a veil, which the diligent Californian sun will soon melt away.

We are sitting, sheltered from the wind, in a niche open to the valley and the sun. Renata is wearing the down jacket. On our faces we feel the thin warmth of the December light. A little bit of warmth up here, existing only where the wandering rays touch briefly.

The desert mountains on the other side of the valley are white with snow – and also the salt flats deep down, deep below the level of the sea, seem to be nothing else but snow.

The gentle, soft haze, which in a summer past shrouded the valley floor – this indefinite something which seemed to reach out to us, has disappeared. It has given way to a clarity, hard to comprehend. This landscape under the invading blue of the sky is full of precision, engraved, every rib of rock, every mountain, every ray in the wide fans of gravel is picked out, as if in pen and ink.

Have I come here from Europe for this?

Convincing clarity. Still impressive, yet – 'It has turned into a landscape of almost German exactness,' I say.

Renata gives a light laugh, but says nothing.

I step out on to a projecting rock to take a panoramic sequence of photographs – it is the first time I've done that in Death Valley. Somehow I want to keep hold of the valley, not let it go. Is it ours still? Are we losing it?

'Let's go down there.'

I sense that the valley we know still exists somewhere, hidden.

A few burros, wild donkeys – fairly tame they seem to be – look at us as we drive through a barren canyon towards the valley floor. Are they 'ours' . . . those of Aguereberry Point? As we stop, one of the animals comes to the window. Yes, we've got something for you! While the creature chomps contentedly – Renata is offering it biscuits – I think of the braying we heard last night, over there in the Panamint valley where we had stopped during the long approach near the old gold-digger's hut. There, the snow-covered silhouettes of the highest ridges of Telescope Peak looked dreamy in the moonlight, and the dark valley below only revealed its width and depth through the distant calls of the burros.

We have reached the floor of Death Valley, pass northwards along the sea of dunes.

To the source.

It is the last place we have come to see. The only one, where I still hope now, in December, to rediscover my old Death Valley. Our Death Valley . . .

Whenever I think of the source, then that means for me not only water which appears from the earth in the middle of a side canyon of the desert. It means both the water and the tree. Even if there are a couple of other trees not far away, doubtless over a hidden waterway – they are nothing unusual.

But this tree . . .

It surrounds the source.

At first glance you think it's many different trees – then you realise: none of them is coming out of the ground, but – like mighty branches, like great shoots from a recumbent trunk – they rear up, all coming from one and the same, almost metre-thick, tree body, which lies on the ground, or sometimes free above it, in many coils, like a sleeping reptile, around the place of the spring. A strange being – the roof of leaves seems to belong to a forest when you look up, and yet it is that of a single tree.

The ground is covered with a thick layer of dry leaves into which you sink with every step. They swish loudly with every movement, rushing almost like a wave when you cross them. It is true it could as well be a sinister place – but it isn't. To me, it means absolute concord, a little universe – in the centre of which there is the spring. Sometimes a bird appears, touches down at the edge of the water, which seeps almost imperceptibly out of a dark patch of ground from between the leathery brown leaves; it only takes a short way to reach close to the tree body, then it disappears again into the layer of dried leaves. This little water is very special, absolutely silent – it comes out of the ground like the elixir of life; totally clear. And that's what it is.

The grey-green leaves of this strange tree beat against each other with their hard edges – yes, the wind from the wintry-blue heights has arrived down here too: but it is not cold. Another wave of air – and I hear the pummelling of the leaves like a slow rainshower that moves from branch to branch, stem to stem of the tree-being, which flows and ebbs – sometimes surrounding us here, then approaching again, rustling, from another direction, sometimes shaking the whole tree in a cascade of sound.

We dip our hands into the water, look down on to the black bottom, only a couple of inches deep. 'In winter, Death Valley is not the same,' says Renata, wiping a damp hand across her face. It is completely still now. Silently, the water oozes from the floor.

'Nothing has changed here, but we have been away so long,' I say, and look up; slowly the leaves in the deep blue sky start to move

again, a shower runs through the tree. I myself have been long and far away – I think of the Himalaya.

'Perhaps it's we who've changed.'

The leaves play their clapper-game. How many days? When they fall, there are new ones. As long as the water comes out of the ground. The tree must be ages old – and has always been in this spot.

Do you still want to tell me something?

Have you nothing else to say?

. . .

Be still, don't you hear it? The leaves!

Don't say a word. Listen.

In this sound is love. And it rises, every moment, beyond the rustling leaves out into the infinite blue.

Death Valley, in winter. Valley of Death?

The valley of – Always.

*

PART EIGHT

Hildegard Peak (6189 m) – Island Peak

Many years ago I stood with Tona on the summit of a nameless six-thousander in the Hindu Kush. It was a first ascent and we wanted to call it Hildegard Peak after our little daughter. But unfortunately that was not possible. Today, tall, blonde Hildegard climbs her own summits, and asserts that a mountain's name is not so relevant. The mountain is yours for the moment you stand on its top. For her, the people who live at its foot are much more important. But I remember on her first six-thousander she was really keen. Island Peak, which stands like an icy cliff in the airspace above the wide valley of the Imja Khola, is surrounded by mountain giants, which completely dominate it in size but cannot compete with its location, plumb in the centre of this valley of glaciers, moraine ribbons and meadows.

It is almost sunset when Pasang and I arrive beneath Island Peak. Hildegard comes running up to me enthusiastically, her tall figure distinguishable from way off by her long yellow hair and the faded blue down jacket, an honoured relic from Hermann Buhl's last expedition. She tells me all sorts of stories about what she has seen, and the new words she has learned from Gyaltsen, Nga Temba and the three Sherpanis; and she is so much looking forward to the summit; I can see it in her eyes, feel it from her questions. For a moment I am reminded of setting off with Tona for her first six-thousander . . .

Both Hans Englert and Erhard Spiller are in good form, the two Hessian mountaineer-clients with whom I will try the summit the day after tomorrow as a guided rope of three. I know that I can trust my

daughter to Pasang Phutar's care on the other rope. Gyaltsen and
Nga Temba, along with our three Sherpanis, will accompany us to
a higher camp tomorrow, which only Pasang knows: he has been to
the summit of Island Peak twice already. The men will wait there
till the rest of us come back from the climb with Pasang.

A little fire of gleaned twigs crackles as twilight fades and the
moon rises, and the Sherpa voices pipe up, telling each other stories
and jokes. Suddenly my daughter remarks that it is so wonderful
here, so perfect, she cannot begin to contemplate that it will all
be over in just three days when we need to start back. She has
learned so much from and about the Sherpas, and of their life,
that she quite emphatically has to come back again; and she gives
me that entreating, conspiratorial look daughters reserve for their
fathers when they want to win them round to something (. . . she
became an ethnologist later!).

Kantschi, one of the three Sherpanis, combs her long black hair.
Tomorrow she will be carrying twenty kilos up the mountainside,
as will her two female companions. I think back to my Makalu
expedition and the approach to Shartse; on both occasions the
Sherpas and Sherpanis carried the same weight loads. They were
from a village far from here. But in the Everest region much has
changed under the influence of so many expeditions. The Sherpa
can work his way up from porter, to high-altitude porter and finally,
if he has the spirit for it and an aptitude for organisation, to Sirdar.
But Sherpanis do not have access to the same career structure; they
continue to be porters and they hardly learn any English. It would
certainly be very little use to them since the foreigner prefers Sherpa
men for the higher work and is happy to relegate the organisation to
them. And so Pasang, who carries the heaviest loads up to the South
Col of Everest, is here blithely climbing through the steep rocks with
a light day pack and an easy conscience while his sister follows, bent
under her weighty burden. She is a porter after all . . .

We have arrived at an airy shoulder at 5600 metres, close to the
edge of a hanging glacier. Gyaltsen and Nga Temba put up two tents
and Pasang goes for a basketful of ice from the glacier. It is not easy
to get, but no problem for him. Finally, we have water, tea, soup!
Hildegard and the handsome young Gyaltsen have prepared it. It is
delightful, I think, how interested she is in the lives of the Sherpa
people. She has already told me the family background of some
of them. The tea runs easily down the throat, cosy, warm, while

we stretch out our legs comfortably on the foam mats, admiring the wonderful mountains beyond our toes and the rubble-strewn glaciers extending from beneath their mighty walls. Brown, green and blue glacial lakes glint up in the last sunshine. We can go for the top tomorrow – everybody is fine! The Sherpanis go down in the fading light, and soon Erhard's usual snoring is slicing the nocturnal silence.

'Put on your crampons. Here is a good place,' I call to my companions. We have arrived at the last crags of the boulder crest on Island Peak. It takes time, but finally we set foot on the glacial surface in two ropes. Pasang with Hildegard, and I leading Erhard and Hans.

Six thousand metres! Hildegard has glowing cheeks and her eyes shine – I know that her heart is leaping! We arrive at the last slope. It looks steep. A forty-five-degree gradient for about 150 metres. Island Peak is not as easy as it is often made out to be, not at all! Of course, the leader could string a fixed rope from the bottom to the top of the face and make it safe . . . but to climb a steep snowfield just in crampons requires some skill. I do not employ a fixed rope to the top, and we move slowly uphill. I am able to belay securely, first with an ice-screw, then with a snow piton and, finally, another snow piton.

Pasang and Hilde do their job well. Erhard, who is quite heavy, puffs a bit, but will make it. Hans, of lighter build, has less trouble. Then just below the ridge comes a very steep powder snow section, of uncertain but considerable depth. Poor Erhard is at a disadvantage with his weight, but I have secured a fine belay on the crest and, heeeeave-ho! hoist the protesting solicitor's clerk swiftly up the last few metres. There is enough space on the ridge for us to take a breather. The last ten minutes are then a real pleasure, there being no further difficulties and stunning views into the valley on either side of this rounded edge, and out far away to Ama Dablam and Makalu. Above us, blonde Hilde and little Pasang arrive on the summit. They wave down at us and hug one another. Then they hug one another again . . . and again! That's enough, Hildegard! Or you'll ram poor Pasang into the summit!

We know you are on top! Eighty-nine metres higher than your mama once climbed on her Peak Dertona. But what don't I know? Why does my daughter continue embracing Pasang? Secrets of the summits . . . yes, only the Spirits of the Air know who you will go hand in hand with beyond the mountains!

A few steps more and we are all on top. It is ours, this Pasang Peak, Hildegard Peak, Hans Peak, Erhard Peak and my peak, too, of course . . . our Island Peak.

Even a small summit can bring great happiness.

The green flash

It is close to sundown, and the wide Pacific burns before me in the evening light. Through shining palm leaves and orchids flushed orange in the soft glow, I gaze down over an immeasurable expanse of ocean. Here I am only a few hundred metres above the water but, close by, the gentle slopes of Mauna Loa rise to over 4000 metres.

I stood on that summit a few days ago, on that 'Long Wide Mountain' of Hawaii, after making what seemed an interminably lonely walk across a lunar landscape, climbing solidified lava flows, bare of any vegetation, in a primeval world of volcanic shapes, a frozen-to-the-spot army of petrified figures. The icy night I spent crouched in a pockmark of rock close to its top was one of the coldest bivouacs I have made anywhere. Unimaginably for Hawaii, ice crystals sprouted from narrow cracks – as I discovered to my amazement on emerging next morning from my night in the 'honeycomb' of the most enormous volcano in the world, dressed only in windcheater and shorts (and carrying an umbrella!). This mountain, if measured from its roots beneath the sea, would outstrip even Everest with a height of more than 10,000 metres. The brown lava streams, pitted with hundreds of cavities, over which I walked with such caution, listening to the echo of my steps (for hidden 'bubbles' as big as a room are not unusual here), gave way at last to the black surface of a petrified lava lake within the immense crater. I stayed over-long, forgot the time. Everything was lonely beyond words, impressive in its scale and monotony, its perpetual repetition, its silence. Later, when I groped my way back, down towards the big saddle linking Mauna Loa with Mauna Kea, in the scorching heat of a new day, the air quivering between the lava figures, I stumbled over a palette of stones: violet, green, red, bluish-green, even the glint and sparkle of silver and gold! Lost in astonishment and excitement, I picked up a nugget as large as a man's head, only to find it weighed

*– next to nothing at all! Pumice . . . With a sigh, I let it go again –
I wouldn't be making my million that day.*

*I think of all those colours now, as the sun slides into the Pacific, and
I stand on the slopes of the huge mountain which here at sea level
boasts a diameter of a hundred kilometres, but down on the sea bed
is 400 kilometres across. And no longer am I alone.*

*'Maybe in a minute you will see the green lightning flash,' whispers
Elelule, a native of these islands. She lives in Oahu, is spending a
few days on the main island, but her heart – she confesses – belongs
to Kauai, an island of absolute green, the wettest place in all the
archipelago. Many bays, it has, and luxuriant vegetation covering
every inch of rock. Elelule has never been to the top of Mauna Loa:
that is another world, up there! Not her world . . . she smiles. I can
believe it: her tall figure, her flowing, unhurried gestures, the generous
mouth in that sweet, dark face, everything about her cries contrast to
the abstract ferocity of that eviscerated landscape with its enigmatic
frozen lava figures. She knows so much about Hawaii . . .*

*So what is this green lightning? I only learnt about it a couple of
minutes ago: on rare days when the sky above the ocean is cloudless
as far as the eye can see, split seconds after the last blazing fragment
of sun slips below the horizon, a single beam of light pierces the ocean
with a brilliant green flash. Just for an instant, if it happens at all.*

*'I think you are going to be lucky,' Elelule says suddenly in a low
voice. Her dark hair seems to glow in the radiant atmosphere – only
the black eyes remain motionless and unchanged, looking out to sea.
She has only seen the green flash once herself.*

*The sun! Its last rim is drowning in the waters. Will it happen?
Impossible to tell if there is a small cloud far, far out there to interrupt
the endless line of sight.*

*The great orb is gone – only the after-image glimmers before
my eyes. Then, suddenly! I see it! The flash! Green as green,
emerald green!*

*Like a laser, it penetrates the brain, enters the very soul . . . for a
moment . . . it clutches . . . binds you . . . to everything.*

I feel the breath at my side.

A secret . . . The sea and the sun unite.

Spirits of the Air

Gasherbrum, 'the beautiful shining wall' . . . that's what the name means. It derives from the fantastic face of golden crystalline limestone which mirrors the rays of the late afternoon sun when you look at it from the Baltoro Glacier. Gasherbrum IV is not the highest peak of this group, but has given its name to all of them.

My fifth eight-thousander belongs here, in this family of peaks, which comprise four summits around the magic 8000-metre mark, as well as a band of 'kids', several seven-thousanders.

Gasherbrum II is 8035 metres . . . a beautiful pyramid of perfect symmetry. I still find it hard to believe that I have now been up there, my third eight-thousander in fifteen months after Makalu last spring and Everest in the autumn. A magic run of luck . . .

Only a few days ago I stood on top, together with my companions from Austria, Bavaria and 'that other part of Germany' (as my neighbours insist on calling Germany beyond Bavaria). Well, that 'other part' had contributed no less than Reinhard Karl to the enterprise, an expedition organised by dyed-in-the-wool Himalayan hand, my friend Hanns Schell. Reinhard was obsessed with the idea of a Baltoro Marathon (an idea nobody else shared) and he was dreaming of a solo ascent of Hidden Peak, which rises right next to our mountain. Reinhard was a man full of ideas ahead of his time . . . It made for a lot of discussion! We also made the acquaintance of many other people, for the solitude which characterised the fifties was over. Almost as a symbol for the new epoch Jean-Marc Boivin floated under his hang-glider high in the sky above the Baltoro Glacier . . . much to the amazement of hundreds of Balti porters.

However, we did not tackle our mountain very differently from the way our party climbed Broad Peak twenty-two years ago – without the boost of oxygen or the help of high-altitude porters. Luckily, our walkie-talkies did not weigh eleven kilos, as they had then, and also the double-boot had been invented. Nevertheless, the Karakoram weather was as unpredictable as ever and we had quite a struggle, being beaten back more than once by storms.

'But now all fatigue is forgotten. Gasherbrum II is ours, and when I think back to Broad Peak, it seems to me that a whole lifetime has passed since then . . .' I write in my diary.

When will I stand again below a big mountain and demand

of the clouds whether I should climb it, as I did that time on Makalu?

Today is the last day here, the last morning – and a strange thing happens: suddenly in the clear blue of the sky above the big mountains delicate loops, skeins and ribbons appear – then disappear – in a slow flowing movement, a surge. The beautiful pyramid of Gasherbrum is shrouded in a fairy veil of fantastic shape which continues to change as if bewitched. Now, Hidden Peak too wears a curved hat comprised of countless shimmering fibres, which slowly flow beyond its bounds and dissolve away.

Perhaps there's a storm coming?

Now, above Sia Kangri, it starts to shine in all colours . . . green, violet, orange . . .

I gaze at the dance of the veils, deeply moved . . .

Spirits of the Air. Greeting me.

A new horizon

The view from the summit of Gasherbrum into the mountain desert on the Chinese side of the peak, with its deserted valleys and the big ice floes with thousands of pointed towers, changed my world. A new longing was born: I must get down into that place!

How did that happen . . .?

Götterdämmerung in the Karakoram – that is what I wrote in 1979 in my diary of climbing this eight-thousander:

Never in my life have I arrived on a summit in such gloom. We struggle higher, full of fatigue, stopping time and again – this Gasherbrum II is after all an eight-thousander! Really, we should be ascending one of the most enthralling peaks on earth. But today? Clear view into the distance, but with a strange twilight above overlaying everything, like a burden . . . I cannot help thinking of the fantastic sunset display Hermann Buhl and I experienced over there on the summit we shared, an unearthly play of light that seemed to penetrate our very souls. The gods were close to us then. Not now. Did they flee from the many people into the distant spaces of Sinkiang, this immense mountain world stretching to the horizon, empty of people as at the beginning of creation . . .

Behind me, on the Pakistani side, I knew of a dozen expeditions on this Baltoro Glacier where Hermann and I had enjoyed total solitude. The place I came to know when I was twenty-five no longer existed. And I was searching for a new horizon. I found it up there, at the age of forty-seven, gazing out into Sinkiang with the Shaksgam valley at my feet, a deep furrow in a field of hundreds and hundreds of peaks . . .

That same year my life changed course, quite subtly. I met Julie again, who I had known briefly over a number of years, and this time we became rope-partners, not to be separated any more: in the same way as Wolfi Stefan and Kurt Diemberger 'conquered' the Alps as a recognised team in the fifties, so it was now with Julie Tullis from England and me, except that we went to the Himalaya and Karakoram. And instead of the old student lifestyle of my great years in the Alps, there was now a different impetus – our film-making. Soon we would be the highest film team in the world. I did the camerawork, Julie the sound recording, and as for ideas – we found them together. When we made our first joint documentary on Nanga Parbat in 1982 (it earned three international awards) we were, in the eyes of many, no spring chickens: I was just fifty and Julie forty-three. But that did not matter to us. The horizons were open . . .

Under the spell of the Shaksgam

A low, dull sound reverberates in the air. It is weird in its steadiness and enigmatic, here in the total isolation of the enormous valley with its steep walls, which to me are like something from the Dolomites. So unusual is this sound above the wide spills of gravel in the river bed that both of us stop almost simultaneously, just as we round the corner of the embankment of dirty ice, sand and mud which marks the end of the Northern Gasherbrum Glacier. This mighty bulwark along the foot of which we walk lies at about 4200 metres above sea level and is more than two kilometres wide. The considerable force of the masses of ice behind it (the glacier is about twenty kilometres long) has pushed the front almost to the mountain wall opposite. Through the narrow passage the Shaksgam River meanders like a snake, sometimes forking into several branches. Some days ago, when we passed here early in the morning, we could only hear the gentle murmur of the waters. But now? This strange, hollow sound. . .

'What is it?' Julie asks and looks at me with a puzzled expression in her dark eyes.

'Never heard it before,' I reply. Is it something to do with the river? Now, late in the afternoon, the murmur has given way to an intense rushing. Or maybe the wind is trapped somewhere, high above us on these walls?

Slowly we go on, passing the sometimes vertical front of the glacier at a respectful distance for there is danger of sudden rock and icefall. The dull sound increases, until it dominates every other voice in the valley . . .

'Look!' Julie says suddenly, pointing ahead: behind a rampart of scree, a strange 'plant' has appeared, a tumbling, foaming mushroom, a mighty, stocky fountain which hurls stones and sand into the air . . . filling the space with its sinister voice, like a being from another world. It is so bizarre, so unreal, that for some seconds we simply freeze from nervousness and alarm, something indeed akin to awe, as if we had crept in unnoticed to a place where water and glacier spirits meet, a place far from humans where they still appear.

'Come on, let's get closer to it,' I say, when finally I manage to speak, and softly we approach the apparition, as carefully as we can on the loose scree, while the low sound which seems to penetrate everything, increasingly enshrouds us, making the whole air vibrate. The countless hurled pebbles drum loudly back down on to the river bed, a swarm of shiny black dots, as the glacier water fountain clears a path for itself. Amazed, we watch the birth of a new branch of the mysterious Shaksgam River!

For some while we remain spellbound in front of the tumbling, roaring, stone-spitting monster and the relentlessly advancing waters, which soon join another foaming flood that has burst from a dark vault in the steep icy façade – water everywhere! I feel rising doubts whether we will be able to make it through here to our camp with all that water, even if it is only half an hour further downriver. What other surprises are in store for us? A bivouac?

Soon afterwards we spot Pierangelo, our friend from Bergamo, who is as strong as a bear; he carries a rope in his hands and signals to us from the opposite bank of the swollen tributary, which now separates us from the glacier edge. Well done that man! Pierangelo wants to help us; he has come up to meet us from our little base camp. Who knows how long he has been waiting already? He knots a longish stone into one end of the rope and hurls it across to us. We anchor it as best we can, and then I hold it – as Pierangelo does from the other side – while Julie steps into the rushing water and begins to cross, hand over hand. (We are also linked by our ordinary rope.) After a few steps, however, she returns, panting and spluttering – it is impossible! The current all but pulled her legs from beneath her. So then, I indicate first upstream and again at the glacier, yelling to Pierangelo, 'See you later!'

And, that's how we did it: went back to the 'water-mushroom', and beyond until we came to a spot where we could climb the icy ramp on to the glacier, then on, up and down, up and down, in the last light of day over moraine hills and bumps in the glacier . . .

Breathless, wet and tired, we finally reached our small base camp. We had gone a long, long way. After many hours between the ice towers, we had still climbed a fine rock cliff high above the glacier. 'It was a good day,' smiled Julie, while our companions took care of us with mugs of tea, with biscuits and Bresaola. A fantastic group was our little exploratory party. The big Italian K2 expedition, to which we belonged, was five days' march away and somewhere to the west of us, establishing an Advanced Base Camp.

While the chilly night drives us into our sleeping-bags, in the distance there is an indistinct shimmer from the mighty Gasherbrum Wall. Nobody has ever climbed it. It stretches from Hidden Peak to Gasherbrums II and III and on towards Broad Peak . . . All mountains around the 8000-metre mark. Also K2 can be seen, pale, and soaring between the intricate dark silhouettes of closer six-thousanders. Unmistakable, the shape of the giant crystal in the night sky . . .

This is our last night, the end of our time on this glacier. During our five days here we penetrated right up under the North Face of Gasherbrum II – and further, in another direction. It was a great experience to be the first humans to set foot into such a hidden corner, even to find a spot where we might later – perhaps years later – set up the tents for a big and difficult climb.

When we realised that, owing to the complicated nature of the glacier surface, neither our time nor our food would hold out long enough for us to penetrate the last hidden corner of the glacier, which must be at least twenty kilometres long (oh! how much we would have liked to do that!), we ascended just a bit further towards the 'camel humps', two distinct mountains, probably seven-thousanders. God, yes, we swore to come back to this place by whatever means!

Now we are squatting in our sleeping-bags at the tent entrance, looking out into the night with all its shapes, which in our minds are mingling with the images of our days on the Gasherbrum Glacier. A kaleidoscope of floating summits, of glinting needles of ice, turquoise steeples of ice, rows of roofs, points, teeth and dice, with small lakes in between, entire processions of shining figures . . . and of the seemingly endless, curved ribbons of the moraines, brown and grey and black. Wild onions and flowers are dotted here and there at the edge of the glacier. We discover a massive fossilised whelk, which lived here millions of years ago in an ancient ocean. We found it under a huge tower of rock, and wondered if perhaps that had been a reef . . . no water now . . .

The next night was totally different: wrapped in the bivvy bag, we lay between the rocks of a moraine, close together, uncomfortable, but warm – even if when morning came, crusted ice crumbled off us at every move. My beard looked like that of the mountain sprite Rübezahl in winter, and Julie's hair was so full of frost that she could have been a Christmas angel. But to watch how the sun's rays first lit up K2, while everything else was still dark in icy blue shadow, then to see how the light gently edged further and further down until it touched even us . . . to think about where and how one might force a route up this giant wall of seven- and eight-thousanders in front of us . . .

. . . And that, too: the difficult decision to turn back, the acknowledgment that our time here had come to an end . . . on this occasion . . .

Together came question and certainty: Will we come back? We will certainly come back!

There are places, where you know what 'the Endless Knot' means.

The light and dark ribbons of this glacier landscape have bound us for ever.

We sat a long time at the spot where we turned back, and looked

at wonderful jewels of ice – like transparent amulets, standing on
fine thin stems and twinkling in the sun.

Three years later, when Julie and I climbed to the shoulder of K2 in
fantastic weather, on the day before our planned summit attempt,
the great glacier with its curved ribbons appeared in the distance
behind Broad Peak. We saw it, and from the depths it reached up
to us, hanging in the air: Will we come again? We most certainly
will . . .

*

Six years have gone by since then. And I have returned to the
Shaksgam, the place of our hearts' longing. I am ascending a steep
spur, and below me march out the mile-long lines of ice towers,
the thousands and thousands of tall spikes, one behind the other, a
frozen procession. Above me there is a snow saddle, or rather, the
shoulder of a big white mountain which doesn't have a name and
which soars above rotten, steep flanks of dark rock towards the sky.
From up there, I ought to be able to see K2, quite closely . . . no, it
is still beyond the Sella Pass, the gap in the big mountain wall which
here forms the frontier between Pakistan and China, a possible
crossing place, over 6000 metres high, though never yet reached
from this side by anybody. Nevertheless, I feel the Mountain of
Mountains to be so close . . . . Julie is there, remains there for ever –
that takes away all distance. I hear the sound of my steps in the steep
snow whenever my boots break through its crust. Blue shadows all
around me, and an icy chill.

Diagonally above me a concealed crevasse leads from the flank
towards the rounded spur along which I am ascending . . . a feeble
horizontal depression in the surface disappearing before it reaches
the curve of the spur. By any normal judgment the route should be
safe, but as a soloist one cannot be careful enough.

I keep stopping. My eyes follow the serrated line of mountain
shadows, painting fantastic jags on the glacier way below, dark
mountain-shapes enlarging all the time as if they wanted to merge
with the wild rock formations and gentle snow edges on the
other side; and my gaze wanders far to the prominent furrow
of the Shaksgam valley, and back into our hidden glacier corner,
which nine years ago – as long as that! – had been hidden from

our view behind the soaring silhouettes of the 6000- and almost 7000-metre-high 'Camels', as we christened these nameless peaks in the manner of blithe discoverers. It is the secret valley below Broad Peak, which we had longed so much to see. What a desire we felt as the first humans to look around the corner, to enter this strange sanctuary with all its secrets, where nobody had been before, and into which I could now look down from above . . . how much we burned, Julie and I, with the yen to know what was there. We will come back, we said, as we were forced to turn around . . .

I hear my steps crunch higher. Alone. Ice axe in my hand, space all round me. Here I am. My eyes follow the thin rim of sunlight, outlining the ridge above, then sweep down to the curved moraine ribbons, with their jagged lines of ice between – and something like contentment rises to meet me. The sensation of loneliness, which so often burdens me, is gone. Last spring, in Catalonia, when I revealed the possibility of a route up the unknown face of Broad Peak, I knew well enough that, as the oldest member of an expedition, I was unlikely to be chosen for the summit of the 8000-metre peak, but that was not so important, I just wanted to be here again, in the Shaksgam; simply to return and fulfil our old idea, make it come true, what Julie and I had recognised, realise it for her, too. I stop to take a look at the giant ramp of snow, broken by séracs, which leads up to the high plateau of the Central Peak, across the ice wilderness of the east and north-east walls, a magic route, our route . . . somewhere up there, tiny beyond vision, are my companions: the bearded Jordi, always so spontaneous (whether cordial or abrupt) – Jordi Magriña with whom in 1991 I initiated the first Catalan expedition to this place, during the course of which we reached the Hidden Valley; Oscar Cadiach, generally reflective and calm, friendly . . . a great organiser and mountaineer; Alberto Soncini, our 'ice artist', a colourful Italian; and Lluis Rafols, the youngest, with his laughing eyes, mop of hair, a headful of ideas; last but not least the slim, tough Enric Dalmau, desperately anxious for his first eight-thousander! And Mingma, Dorje, Tenzing – our Sherpas – have they managed to get up? I cannot help taking the walkie-talkie from my rucksack and calling up Broad Peak. No answer. I try Joan Gelabert, our radio technician, far out in the Shaksgam valley, but he doesn't hear me either. So I pack the radio away again. One day soon I want to climb up as far as the plateau at 7000 metres: looking over the ocean of Sinkiang peaks from this vantage point half in the skies must be overwhelming . . . However today I will concentrate on taking pictures, which none of my friends could get: the Hidden Valley and our mountain above it; and perhaps a new perspective on to the unclimbed Gasherbrum Wall? To solve an enigma? No, it isn't that alone which pushes me onwards. It is K2, above the Sella Saddle! Will I see it? And, can you get up to the saddle from this side?

It is late. Some of the dark shadow-summits cast into the valley are already pushing their way up between the glowing peaks, higher and higher. Don't stop, Kurt. Otherwise you will not be able to get up as far as the ridge.

My feet have become icily cold in my lightweight boots, which were more suited to walking on the moraine. I must have climbed nearly 1000 metres up here – when I turn around I can already see over the 'Little Camel', which is a six-thousander. There is not much further to go – the cornice-roll above my head draws closer . . . I must aim for that, dare not go directly out on to the shoulder, for fear of another crevasse across the flank.

Yet very clearly, there is no possibility of getting to the ridge over the cornice . . . it is overhanging and possibly ten metres high, but I might be able to traverse below it – I must get out to the shoulder in order to look over to the other side – that is what I want!

Powder snow, icy powder. Up to my waist. Blue shadows. I grind my teeth. My feet hurt. Can I still feel all my toes? No time to worry about that now. The roll is hanging directly over my head. Carefully, and with great effort, I edge sideways in the steep powder. Slow, prudent moves require several breaths each time, and at every step I must work my foot down a few times before the yielding, insecure white stuff will carry my weight. I plunge the ice axe deeply into the bottomless snow. My heart beats up into my neck: the steep slope beneath me drops abruptly away to nothing – in the blue twilight the couloir winds down into far depths. Take care, Kurt! Only move very slowly. Is there no end to it? Sunlight, suddenly! A dazzling brightness! I emerge from the icy shadows . . .

And K2 appears!

Another step. And one more. The snow is better and not so steep.

I am standing in the warming light, just in front of a crevasse and gasping for air, trembling from effort and emotion . . .

The mighty pyramid . . .

K2, there it is! And close to it, the sun.

You are up there, I think, so far – and so near!

Very much closer, here. Entirely close.

In front of me is the snow surface of the ridge's shoulder, bathed in the bright light. Above it, beyond a tremendous chasm – the whole glacier valley – soars the Sella Saddle. Over 6000 metres high. And behind it, as high as the sky, K2!

A whole cascade of ice blocks in all sizes, jumbled one atop the other, seals the access to a depression, a sort of a basin with steep walls below the saddle. But hey, look! At the very righ-hand end, there is a possibility of getting through. Deep in my heart the temptation rises to try it . . . to cross the saddle. Why? To get closer to K2? To stand just across from it? No, it must be something else. Must be the inexplicable urge to push beyond, to the other side – even if I know what's there. Perhaps because a part of my life remains there. Or maybe K2 is still the reason, that which was once the eternal dream for us?

I don't know. I follow the route up to the saddle with my eyes, in all its details . . . and while I am looking, I feel a contentment in knowing it – I will go there – and if not this time, at least I know now where and how . . .

Before the sun disappears behind K2 and the cold blue of the approaching evening enshrouds me, I take some photographs of this stupendous landscape in the last slanting rays of sunshine. They fill me with deep pleasure. Everything is shining and alive. The lines of shadows are like chiselled artwork, the light is weaving designs into the flanks of the mountains, and while my eyes feast on this plenty, scrutinise new tasks, I say to myself: the delay is irritating, but it will be worth it. Return here for as long as your time lasts.

Almost intoxicated, I find myself dipped suddenly into the icy shadow of K2. And talking of time . . . be quick, now, get down! Down 1000 metres of mountainside as fast as you can!

It is almost dark . . . I race to gain seconds, but still treating the snow spur with extreme caution, taking it step by step in my own tracks. Then nothing can stop me any more! 'Skating' across gravel fields, bounding down the slopes of debris and over rocks in giant leaps, down, down following a steep trough with a small torrent – new land for me, because it is impossible to climb back down the way I got on to the flank this morning, along a rib of friable schisty fragments marking the edge of the ice. The important thing now is to find the quickest way down on to the glacier – and to locate an escape route between the ice towers before it is too late.

However, darkness is swifter. It reaches me at the edge of the glacier, just after I have managed to slide down a wall of debris. Here I am, then: night. Ice towers. Morass. Out of the darkness comes the sound of water – it gurgles, drips, rushes. Blank ice walls, dead ends, chaos all around. Even in daylight it would be a problem to get through here – it took a concerted effort to find a way to approach our Base Camp tents a mile further down the valley, but I cannot reach that route from here. It is like being in a forest of Christmas trees made of ice, in amongst the trunks. Utterly confusing. Will I ever be able to get out? Fantasy knows no bounds, especially at night. Reality, however, is different: hovering between hope and doubt I have already climbed two of the towers by the light of my head-torch only to have to retreat once more, have discovered a lake which bars further passage, and finally bypassed it behind another formation of ice. Now I have landed in a steep basin, which can only be escaped by three steep runnels. Luckily some years ago I acquired one of the most modern ice axes – that is a bright spark at least, even at night: one blow with it and already you have a bombproof hold! If only we'd had something like that in the old days . . . Tense with expectation, I inch my way up the steep, shorter runnel and raise my head over the rim: the cone of light hits water. The whole cleft in front of me houses a pond, from wall to wall. Back down I climb. If I cannot find a way out here, the only thing to do is to wait in my bivvy bag until morning. I squat down, chew some nuts and rest for a while. But I still have not abandoned hope – really the whole crazy situation is at the same time somehow fascinating. So far, at least. Meanwhile, two hours quickly pass. It suddenly strikes me that perhaps Joan, our radio man, might be worrying. But my walkie-talkie call again goes unanswered. Perhaps he is already asleep. What about trying the second ice tube? I direct a beam of light into it. Really, it is quite high!

. . . I reach a crest which leads onwards. Is hope in order? Gingerly, I place my crampons, step after step. On both sides water rushes down to invisible depths. Like a tightrope walker I follow my 'bridge' in the light of the headlamp – it is getting wider . . . heavens! Am I getting out of this labyrinth?

Down again, up, a switchback ridge of ice. In the starry sky I can make out the silhouette of the 'Little Camel' in front of me. Good, I am going in the right direction! And it is no longer that difficult. A dark hogsback appears, indistinctly, behind the last glittering shapes. The central moraine! Out! I am out! Now all I have to do is find the camp.

. . . A gleam of light through tent fabric penetrates the darkness! An illuminated dome. It is close to midnight. I hear my own stumbling among the stones, and the voices of the Sherpas from inside. Tenzing's curly head appears in the tent entrance: 'Papa! You here? We making tea . . .'

*

A month later. The summit! The icy Kafka-castle has been climbed. Four of our team made it: Oscar, Lluis, Alberto, Enric. And did so at the very last moment, when our camels for the return journey had already arrived in Base Camp. At the fourth attempt. They staked everything on one last card, in the end climbing at night, and bivouacking at 8000 metres shortly before reaching the Central Summit. The unpredictable weather was about to break again – shortly after beginning their descent they were caught in another snowstorm. This climb was a milestone in the history of the Shaksgam. Ten years before, when the Japanese climbed K2 from the north, it was the first great new climb on the Chinese side of the Karakoram. That was 1982. In August 1992 another one came into being: our route up the secretive East Face of Broad Peak.

Extreme difficulty in ice, and considerable avalanche danger could not frighten off my companions. I myself went once as far as Camp 2, but a breakdown in the weather foiled my attempt to reach the desired plateau at 7000 metres, so I returned to my explorations, leaving the youngsters to bring an old idea to an honourable conclusion. During the final risky dash – I can hardly call it anything else – I prayed for them. To God and to all the Spirits of the Air. Also to Julie. Because on these great mountains so much of the fate of people depends on circumstances beyond themselves.

Our four are back down again, safely!

*

Sometimes I find myself remembering an hour on the crest of a peak in the Shaksgam Dolomites, high above the glacier world. A butterfly dances around me in the warm light of the sun. It circles many times, alighting at last and opening its pale white wings to reveal strange eye-markings: large black circles around dark red.

What does it hope to find up here?

Perhaps it is wondering the same about me . . .

'I want to know . . .' it seems to say.

What brings me here?

Because I want to know something, too.

And I am not alone. We have met one another.

APPENDICES

Note on heights

Summit heights of Himalayan peaks vary on maps and in expedition literature. For example, Makalu appears variously as 8481, 8475 and 8463 metres, and Everest was for a long time given as 8848 metres; but a measurement in 1987 by the Global Positioning System apparatus (using Navstar satellite data) established 8872 metres as a new height, until in 1993 another GPS measurement came to 8846 metres. Not to worry, peaks will always be measured again!

CONVERSION TABLE – METRES TO FEET (from the *American Alpine Journal*)

metres	feet	metres	feet	metres	feet	metres	feet
3,300	10,827	4,700	15,420	6,100	20,013	7,500	24,607
3,400	11,155	4,800	15,748	6,200	20,342	7,600	24,935
3,500	11,483	4,900	16,076	6,300	20,670	7,700	25,263
3,600	11,811	5,000	16,404	6,400	20,998	7,800	25,591
3,700	12,139	5,100	16,733	6,500	21,326	7,900	25,919
3,800	12,467	5,200	17,061	6,600	21,654	8,000	26,247
3,900	12,795	5,300	17,389	6,700	21,982	8,100	26,575
4,000	13,124	5,400	17,717	6,800	22,310	8,200	26,903
4,100	13,452	5,500	18,045	6,900	22,638	8,300	27,231
4,200	13,780	5,600	18,373	7,000	22,966	8,400	27,560
4,300	14,108	5,700	18,701	7,100	23,294	8,500	27,888
4,400	14,436	5,800	19,029	7,200	23,622	8,600	28,216
4,500	14,764	5,900	19,357	7,300	23,951	8,700	28,544
4,600	15,092	6,000	19,685	7,400	24,279	8,800	28,872

A chronology of main climbs and expeditions

1948	Larmkogl (3014 m) in the Hohe Tauern, Austria, my first mountain climb, when I decided to go for

	the top instead of making a crystal hunt (alone), at the age of sixteen.
1952	Matterhorn, Breithorn, Monte Rosa, Bernina-Biancograt, Piz Roseg, with two companions, Erich Warta and Gundl Jabornik, travelling on my grandfather's robust 1909 model bicycle.
1953–54–55	Many difficult climbs in the Alps on rock and ice with my friend Wolfgang Stefan as a steady team of two.
1956	Matterhorn North Face (among others), first climb of the Königswand Direttissima. The Giant Meringue was the most difficult crux on snow and ice at the time in the Alps.
1957	My first Himalayan expedition to Broad Peak (8047 m) with Hermann Buhl, Markus Schmuck, Fritz Wintersteller; this was the first ascent of an eight-thousander in *Westalpenstil* (no high-altitude porters, no oxygen-aided climbing). The term, as well as the idea, was created by Hermann Buhl.
1958	Eiger Nordwand, Jorasses Nordwand (Walker Spur) and integral Peuterey Ridge of Mont Blanc, filming with Franz Lindner, still the only existing documentary of the five-day traverse of the greatest ridge in the Alps; first award at the International Trento Film Festival, 1962.
1960	First ascent of Dhaulagiri (8167 m) with an international Swiss expedition; climbed without oxygen apparatus. The assisting Pilatus-Porter aircraft crashed without loss of life.
1965–66–67–69	Expeditions to Africa (Mount Kenya and High Semyen mountains), to Greenland (three times), to the Hindu Kush (twice); in 1967 several two-man alpine-style enterprises, including the first ascent of Tirich West IV (7338 m) from the north; also Tirich Mir (7706 m) and five other peaks.
1974	First ascent of Shartse or Junction Peak (*c.*7500 m).
1978	Ascent of Makalu (8481 m) in the spring and of Everest (8848 m) in the autumn.
1979	Ascent of Gasherbrum II (8035 m).
1980	Another Everest expedition, filming as far as the

South Col. Because of my film work I missed out on the possible ascent of Lhotse. Since the first sync-sound filming from the top of Everest two years earlier, I had become the cameraman of the eight-thousanders.

1981 Film director of the American Everest Expedition to the unclimbed East Face. Received Emmy Award 1982–83.

1982 Exploration of K2 (8611 m) and the Gasherbrums from the Shaksgam, afterwards filming the French Nanga Parbat Expedition. This was the first film I made with Julie Tullis; its awards included the Grand Prix of the Diablerets Film Festival, 1983.

1983 Italian K2 Expedition from the Shaksgam side; Julie and I established ourselves as the highest film team in the world, climbing and working together up to 8000 metres; another exploration of the Gasherbrums from the north.

1984 Filming and climbing with Julie to 7350 metres on the Abruzzi Ridge of K2, making the film *K2, the Elusive Summit*, and climbing Broad Peak again with her.

1985 Filming and climbing with Julie on Everest North-East and North Ridge, and later on Nanga Parbat (8125 m) up to 7600 metres; filming Tashigang, a Tibetan village.

1986 Filming Tashigang again, then went to K2 with Julie, the third expedition together to our dream mountain. At the second attempt we reach the summit, but – for the loss of one day – we end up imprisoned by a terrible blizzard at 8000 metres. Julie and four other mountaineers die. Account in *K2, the Endless Knot: Mountain of Dreams and Destiny* (Grafton, 1991).

1987–88–89–90 Mainly scientific expeditions and exploration in the Himalaya and Karakoram. Filming the GPS-Measurement of K2 and Everest (to establish which is the highest mountain in the world) of Prof Ardito Desio's Everest-K2-CNR Expedition 1987 and returning to the Shaksgam and Nanga Parbat.

1991–92   Participating in two expeditions with Catalan mountaineers to the Shaksgam, first exploration and then first ascent of East Face of Broad Peak. I also explored for the future in this area.

1993   Filming with daughter Hildegard in winter on ethnological research in Tibet.

Note on terminology

Abseiling is the technique of descending through the air or down a steep face on a (usually double) rope.

Bivouac means passing a night or waiting out a storm in the open without the protection of a tent. A bivvi bag or a snowhole can be a valuable shelter. But using a tent (including a so-called bivvi tent) is not bivouacking, and a mobile lightweight camp should not be confused with a bivouac.

Blacklight: geologists and prospectors use this device when searching for certain minerals in the night, which in daylight would hardly be noticed because of their insignificant appearance (for instance Scheelite, a valuable Wolfram ore, which under the ultraviolet rays of the prospector's lamp gives an extraordinary reflected glare).

Nuts: are made of metal and, inserted into cracks, can be used to protect a leader against a fall.

Friends: are camming devices used for protecting rock-climbs in the same way as nuts, but more flexible.

'Penitentes': a Spanish term for penitent. Refers to peculiar pointed forms of ice on the glacier surface in the Andes, the Hindu Kush and other high places where, during the melting process of ice, a combination of temperature factors create hundreds of pin-sharp and often slightly bent figures, sometimes so close together that they become an almost impenetrable obstacle.

Prusik slings are loops of thin cord fixed by a special sliding knot on to the main rope (under weight, the knot tightens and you can stand in the sling; without weight it can be easily pushed upwards on the rope – thus using two Prusik loops you can ascend vertically through the air on the main rope).

Sérac is an ice tower or ice cliff.

Westalpenstil was a new way for climbing an 8000-metre peak without the help of high-altitude porters and without using oxygen apparatus which Hermann Buhl devised in 1957. Fixed camps and a limited number of fixed ropes were permissible. Broad Peak became the first 8000-metre peak to be climbed in this 'alpine-style', which was a true pioneering achievement and still remains the only first ascent of an eight-thousander by this new technique. Today what climbers call alpine-style implies also a refusal to use fixed camps and ropes. In fact, Buhl and Diemberger climbed Chogolisa in modern alpine-style, and Wintersteller and Schmuck climbed Skil Brum that way immediately after the first ascent of Broad Peak in 1957 without inventing a separate label for a method which they saw as simply a lightweight version of *Westalpenstil.*

A select bibliography

Benoît Chamoux, *Le vertige de l'infini*, Albin Michel, Paris 1988

Miles Clark, *High Endeavours* (life of Miles and Beryl Smeeton), Grafton Books, London 1991

George Cockerill, *Pioneer exploration in Hunza and Chitral* (in *The Himalayan Journal* 11), 1939

H. P. Cornelius, *Grundzüge der allgemeinen Geologie*, Vienna 1953

Adolf Diemberger, *The problem of Istor-o-Nal* (in *The Himalayan Journal* 29), 1970

Hildegard Diemberger, *Beyul Khenbalung – the Hidden Valley of the Artemisia*, Institut für Völkerkunde, University of Vienna 1991

Hildegard Diemberger in, *Von fremden Frauen* (proceedings of the *Arbeitsgruppe Ethnologie Wien*), Suhrkamp, Frankfurt 1989

Kurt Diemberger, *Summits and Secrets*, George Allen & Unwin, 1971; new edition Hodder & Stoughton, London 1991

Kurt Diemberger, *The Endless Knot – K2, Mountain of Dreams and Destiny*, Grafton Books, London 1991

Kurt Diemberger, *Some climbs from the Upper Tirich Glacier* (in *The Alpine Journal* 71), London 1966

Günter Oskar Dyhrenfurth, *Der Dritte Pol. Die Achttausender und ihre Trabanten*, Nymphenburger Verlagshandlung, Munich 1960

Peter Gillman, *Everest, the best writing and pictures of seventy years of human endeavour*, Little Brown, London 1993

Leroy and Jean Johnson, *Escape from Death Valley* (from accounts of William Lewis Manly and other 49ers), University of Nevada Press, Reno, Nevada 1987

Reinhold Messner, *All 14 Eight-thousanders*, Crowood Press, Marlborough 1988

Reinhold Messner, *The Challenge*, Kaye & Ward, London 1977

Pierre Mazeaud, *Everest 78*, Editions Denoël, Paris 1978

Arne Naess, *The Norwegian expedition to Tirich Mir* (in *The Alpine Journal* 58) 1951/52

Jill Neate, *High Asia – an illustrated history of the 7000-metre Peaks*, Unwin Hyman, London 1989

Josep Paytubi, *Tirich Mir*, *Quaderns d'alpinisme* Nr 5; Servei General d'Informacio de Muntanya, Sabadell 1994

Reginald Schomberg, *Derdi and Chapursan Valleys*: *Mountains of NW Chitral* (in *The Alpine Journal* 48), Nov. 1936

Doug Scott, *Himalayan Climber*, Diadem, London 1992

Eric Shipton, *Blank on the Map*, Hodder & Stoughton, London 1938, and in the collection *The Six Mountain Travel Books*, Diadem Books, Macclesfield 1985

Ernst Sorge, *With Plane, Boat & Camera in Greenland*, Hurst & Blackett, London 1935

Julie Tullis, *Clouds from Both Sides*, Grafton Books, London 1986, n/e 1987

R. Vogeltanz, M. A. Sironi-Diemberger, *Receptaculites neptuni DEFRANCE* from *Devon des Hindu Kusch* in Anz. Österr. Akad.d. Wiss., math,-naturwiss, Klasse.Jg. 1968, Nr.5

Hermann and Dietlinde Warth, *Makalu, Expedition in die Stille*, EOS Verlag, St Otilien 1979

Hermann Warth, *Tiefe überall*, Rosenheimer Verlaghaus, Rosenheim 1986

Else Wegener with Fritz Loewe (ed), *Greenland Journey*: *the story of Wegener's German Expedition to Greenland in 1930–31*, as told by members of the expedition and the leader's diary, Blackie, London 1939